Economic Rationalism

Dead end or way forward?

Economic Rationalism

Dead end or way forward?

Edited by Stephen King and Peter Lloyd

Allen & Unwin

First published in 1993 by
Allen & Unwin Pty Ltd
9 Atchison Street, St Leonards, NSW 2065 Australia

National Library of Australia
Cataloguing-in-Publication entry:

Economic rationalism.

Includes index.
ISBN 1 86373 537 2.

1. Australia—Economic policy—1990-   . 2. Australia—Economic
policy—1976-1990. 3. Australia—Economic conditions—1990-   .4.
Australia—Economic conditions—1976-1990. I.Lloyd, P.J. (Peter John).
II. King, Stephen P., 1962- .

338.994

Set in 10.5 point Garamond by text-art
Printed by Southwood Press Pty Ltd, Sydney
10 9 8 7 6 5 4 3 2 1

Contents

Part III A Politician's View

Stephen King and Peter Lloyd

Introduction

The debate on Australian microeconomic policy has recently centred on the term Economic Rationalism. This debate started in earnest with Michael Pusey's critique of the influence of 'economic rationalists' within the Commonwealth government bureaucracy (Pusey 1991). Subsequent publications on the subject include those edited by Carroll and Manne (1992), Horne (1992) and Rees, Rodley and Stilwell (1993).

The basis for these critiques is simple. The critics believe that economic theorists and their followers in the public sector have got it wrong. In their view, economists put too much emphasis on the objective of efficiency and have failed to understand the workings of the economy. The policy recommendations of these 'economic rationalists' have led to Australia's decline.

The one-sided nature of the debate on economic rationalism has at best led to some misconceptions about economics and economic policies. At its worst, the argument has degenerated into diatribe. The majority of these critics are non-economists: sociologists, political scientists, business-administration specialists, journalists, and others. Evaluation and dissent from the outside is healthy for any profession, and a profession such as economics that trumpets the virtues of competition and to its credit, does not restrict entry or limit the right to use the title of 'economist', must be receptive to criticism or rival doctrines. Throughout this debate, however, mainstream economists have remained remarkably silent.

To help redress this imbalance, a conference on 'Economic Rationalism: Economic Policies for the 90s' was held at the University of Melbourne on 15 and 16 February 1993. The conference provided a forum for mainstream economists to meet and debate their critics. Participants at the conference included both supporters and opponents of 'economic rationalism'. The papers include both criticism and defence of specific policies as well as wide-ranging discussions on the methodology and philosophy of economics. To paraphrase the current Prime Minister, this is a debate the country has to have.

This volume brings together the proceedings from the conference and in it, we have tried to capture the general tone of the debate and its application on specific policy issues. Part one begins with Geoffrey Brennan on what economics (and economists) can and cannot say. Michael Pusey then presents a critical view. This is followed by a series of essays by Richard Blandy, John Freebairn and Robert Manne. Anne Kreuger's chapter on the training of economists in the US addresses Pusey's claim that economists are narrowly trained technicians and would be better served by a broad-based education. Michael Keating rounds up the section with an essay that examines the advice given to governments by their economic advisers and shows that the influence of economists on federal government policy is not as great as is popularly construed.

Part two of the book deals with a variety of government policies. Each chapter presents a specific policy issue that is then followed by a comment. Where possible, discussants have been chosen to provide a balanced critique of the issues. Among the markets covered in this volume are the financial services, tradeable goods, labour and infrastructure services markets. Other chapters discuss the traditional grounds for government intervention to promote competition, protect the environment and stimulate growth. Two chapters deal with changes in income distribution over the issue of government failure.

Part three presents the views of Senator Peter Walsh, a former minister in the Hawke ministry who gave the after-dinner speech at the conference. He discussed how politicians choose policies and emphasised that many of those opposing microeconomic reform are protecting their own interests.

The debate in this volume is revealing. The term 'economic rationalism' is demonstrably not well-defined. The word 'rationalist' suggests disagreement with the models of economic man as a selfish, maximising agent, disagreement that is apparent in some of the papers. The debate is, however, primarily about the means of achieving government objectives. The tendency of critics has been to draw an equivalence between economic rationalism and neoclassical (micro)economics. But as Quiggin shows, this is a term that came into use in Australia only in the early 1970s and has, in its chequered history, encompassed a variety of different views.Economic rationalism does not so much describe a type of economic modelling as a microeconomic *agenda* that focuses on reducing government intervention in markets.

These interventions include industry protection through tariffs or subsidies and the regulation of financial, labour and other markets. The agenda favours the corporatisation and privatisation of government business enterprises and addresses environmental problems through market-based solutions. It centres on microeconomic reform and is based on the concept of efficiency.

The difference between what neoclassical economics actually says and what its critics think it says is enormous. Pusey, for example, equates neoclassical economics with 'a doctrine that says that markets and prices are the only reliable means of setting a value on anything and further, that markets and money can always, at least in principal, deliver better outcomes than states or bureaucracies'. This, however, is not how economic rationalists see neoclassical economics.

These critics of neoclassical economics have ignored many developments and the vast literature on public goods, externalities, economies of scale, imperfect competition, and information asymmetries. All of these factors can justify government intervention to enhance the efficiency of the national economy and are integral to microeconomics. Recent developments in strategic trade theory, modern industrial organisation and new growth theories are all based on models of imperfect markets. These theories developed rapidly in the 1970s and 1980s, and will influence policy decisions in the 1990s and beyond.

Despite popular conception, opinion among economists, even mainstream economists, is not homogeneous. Brennan and Pincus in their essays question the emphasis on efficiency. FitzGerald, Quiggin and Isaac all raise serious points of issue and disagreement in response to other economists. This internal dissent helps explain the surprise shown by many economists at the nature of the economic-rationalist debate. Serious criticisms have been levelled at neoclassical economics by economists themselves and critiques have been made of modelling procedures that assume perfect foresight or rational expectations. Theories such as the standard decision-making theory that assumes that an individual facing uncertainty is aware of all possible outcomes and game theory that assumes that all participants fully understand the game have shown that there *is* a vulnerable underside to economics.

The critics from outside the profession have, as Brennan notes, concentrated their attack not on the weakest, but the strongest points of neoclassical theory. They argue for more government intervention in the market place and claim the need for industry-specific assistance. Meanwhile, the interventionist regimes of Eastern Europe collapse and governments around the world try to dispose of the massive agricultural stockpiles created by just such assistance. The critics oppose the introduction of competition against government monopolies. Conversely, economists emphasise the benefits to consumers from the lower prices and better service that competition can provide.

The critics have launched their attack against a programme of reform which, as Harper and Leslie demonstrate, may be unavoidable. The policies they criticise as 'new right' have been introduced by a Labor government. It was the Hawke government following its election in 1983 that deregulated the financial sector, lowered tariff barriers and introduced other microeconomic reforms. The re-elected Keating government shows no sign of slowing down the reform process. Instead of being to the right, so-called 'economic-rationalist' policies are at the centre of the political spectrum.

Australia is not alone in pursuing its current reform agenda. Countries of the former Soviet bloc are adopting capitalist economies. The UK, Mexico, Japan and New Zealand, to name but a few, have adopted policies favouring the deregulation of markets and the privatisation of government-owned enterprises. The direction of these policies is broadly similar to that in Australia. Indeed, the American historian Francis Fukuyama (1992) has heralded this world-wide movement as 'the end of history'.

To a large degree, the Australian debate mirrors that in the US and the UK. The centenary symposium of the Royal Economic Society provides a sample of the English debate. Both the Report of the US Commission on Graduate Education in Economics and Krueger's essay in this volume show that many of the questions being asked of the economics profession in the US are the same as those in Australia.

What, then, is the alternative agenda proposed by the critics of economic rationalism? The papers and comments in this volume suggest that, where such an alternative exists, it is conservative. The critics of microeconomic reform hark back to a golden age of the 1950s and 1960s. Their alternative involves the re-regulation of financial markets and a return to fixed exchange rates. An activist industry policy that includes an import replacement programme is favoured. Labour market reforms should be suspended or reversed. The Industrial Relations Commission should be reinstated as the centre for wage determination. In short, there should be a return to the 'good old days' when markets were managed.

As this volume shows, economists can draw cold comfort from the 'economic-rationalist' debate. While the alternative offered by the non-economists appears both undesirable and unrealistic, this does not reduce the importance of their criticisms. That these criticisms often attack what the profession sees as the strongest elements of microeconomics suggests how poorly economists have presented their views. If outsiders perceive neoclassical economics as untenable, it is the economists who must wear the blame. The occurrence of a similar debate in other countries merely shows Australian economists that their failings are not unique.

Neoclassical economics does not suggest unambiguous government policies for individual markets. Too often subtle aspects of market failure have been lost in the rush to reform. The debate has centred on static measures of market efficiency, often ignoring the issue of long-run growth. Little attention has been paid to the timing and sequencing of reforms and adjustment costs have been underemphasised.

Theoretical developments during the 1980s have left economists with an embarrassing array of models to explain behaviour in imperfectly competitive markets. Understanding such markets and resolving these competing theories is critical for the design of economic and social policies. Empirical analysis of these markets, however, has lagged behind. Microeconomic reform is a centrepiece of government policies at both the state and federal level, but at the same time, public disaffection with both politicians and their economic advisors is high.

In macroeconomics, our failings are blindingly apparent. Economists have not designed policies that will simultaneously reduce unemployment, restrain inflation, increase the rate of factor productivity growth and prevent a deterioration of the balance of trade. As Manne notes, economists cannot even agree whether a balance-of-trade deficit is problematic. While the critics of neoclassical economics have avoided macroeconomic issues, the failure of economists in this area has not gone unnoticed. With one million Australians unemployed, the general public's scepticism of economists appears well-founded. High unemployment also raises the adjustment costs of microeconomic reform. The failure of economists at the macroeconomic level may cause public support for microeconomic reform to deteriorate.

Even as we write, the economic-rationalist debate continues unabated. The papers presented in this volume provide a wide range of views on economics and the 'economic-rationalist' agenda and demonstrate that the resolution of these issues is fundamental to Australia's future prosperity. This book, we hope, presents a step towards such a resolution.

Acknowledgements

We would like to thank the numerous people who worked tirelessly towards organising the conference and producing this book. Richard Blandy and Ian Harper provided invaluable help and expertise in planning the conference. The conference organisation was carried out by Bob Speechley and Anne Seuling of the Community Programmes Unit at the University of Melbourne. We owe them a great debt. Thanks also go to the Chancellor of the University of Melbourne, Sir Edward Woodward, for opening the conference, and to the speakers, discussants and active participants in the audience. We are grateful to the Department of Economics and the Faculty of Economics and Commerce at the University of Melbourne and to the corporate sponsors for providing financial support.

Neither editor was quite aware of the work required to turn a set of conference papers into a readable volume. If we have succeeded at this task, it has been due mainly to the support and assistance of Patrick Gallagher, Mark Davis and Foong Ling Kong.

We would also like to thank Sokola Jovanovski for her assistance throughout this project.

Part I
_____

The General Debate

Geoff Brennan

Economic Rationalism: What Does Economics Really Say?

My task here, I take it, is to kick the conference off. I should therefore warn you from the outset that I intend to kick if off in an oblique direction. In particular, I am *not* going to provide a review of the recent policy debate. I am not going to provide this, because to do so seems to me to concede too much; not least, that the debate over so-called 'economic rationalism' (henceforth ER) is, or ought to be seen as, a debate over alternative policy directions, rather than as a debate over economics as such.

There *is* a debate over the policy directions at stake. Much of the critique of ER contained in John Carroll and Robert Manne's *Shutdown* (1992) has a strong neo-mercantilist thrust. ER is identified as equivalent to free trade, and the critique of it is to the effect that all our current horrors could be much ameliorated if only we returned to the tried and true protectionist policies of Jack McEwen that served us so well during the halcyon days of the 1950s and 1960s. Alternatively, as Robert Manne asserts in his contribution to *Shutdown*: 'most critiques [of economic rationalism] begin with the question of foreign debt' (p. 51), and more particularly with the perceived 'complacency of . . . the economic rationalist intelligentsia in regard to it' (p. 52).

But there is more at stake here than disagreements about protectionism and/or appropriate responses to increased foreign debt. Just what 'more' is is not easy to discern, but it surely includes disagreements about *method* ('economic rationalists have wired themselves up to highly abstract mathematical models of a fantasy economy', says the back-cover blurb of *Shutdown*); about attitudes to the state and its proper role; about the role of expertise in democratic politics; about consequentialism as an ethical doctrine; and doubtless other things as well.

Truth be told, it's by no means easy to isolate what *is* at stake. One of the chief difficulties in responding to the critique of 'economic rationalism', to the extent we might want to respond, is a lack of clarity as to what is under attack. As Bill Maley (November 1992) observes in his *AJPS* review of Michael Pusey's *Economic Rationalism in Canberra*, nowhere in the book does Pusey actually *define* economic rationalism. Pusey, however, *does* define it in the *Sydney Morning Herald* (17 October 1991) as 'the dogma which says that markets and money can always do everything better than governments, bureaucracies and the law'. But noting the 'always' and the 'everything', ER, so defined, is such an extreme form of anarcho-capitalism that no-one I know (with the possible exception of David Friedman) would ever endorse it. No such position could, I think, be identified as either 'economic' or 'rational'.

John Carroll's definition (Carroll & Manne 1992, p. 7) is more broadranging: ER is simply '*laissez-faire* or neo-classical economics' (as if the two were coterminous) as defined by the works of Adam Smith or Friedrich Hayek (as if Smith and Hayek were indistinguishable). Peter Ventila and his colleagues in their *Markets, Morale and Manifestations* identify ER as defined by the Liberal Party's *Fightback!* package, and more particularly the moral and cultural dimensions of the *Fightback!* rhetoric — 'self-reliance', 'rugged individualism', the 'pursuit of excellence', the 'rejection of mediocrity' and so on. It is no easy business engaging in a debate with the terms so ill-defined, and it may be that one important service we can perform for our critics is to clarify what the terms of the debate might be.

A certain vagueness in definitions may be strategic. If one's ambitions are to mobilise mistrust and prejudice — and Pusey's attack on the economics profession has certainly had that *effect* — then a certain lack of clarity in definition, even a lack of clarity in argument, may be quite shrewd. I do not mean here to be insulting to the critics of ER: I do want to emphasise that the assault on economic rationalists has long since passed out of the academic seminar.

A friend of mine, something of a figure in the debt debate, recently confessed to me that he has given up admitting to people he meets socially at dinner parties or on the golf tee that he is an economist. He now tells them that he's a kind of statistician. To admit being an economist is to invite either decided coolness or, worse, an eruption of invective — as if he was responsible for the unemployment level or the latest slate of bankruptcies. The term 'economic rationalist' has entered popular vocabulary as a term of abuse; economic rationalists have been made scapegoats for the current economic distress and thereby become the objects of extreme prejudice. To admit to being an economist is to render oneself publicly accountable in ordinary forums that can, beyond some point, become tedious and extremely unpleasant. My point here is that the debate over ER has become a rhetorical, political, populist 'cause', and that it is silly to pretend that we economists are anywhere other than in the middle of it.

All the same, those of us here are academics and not street-fighters. Personally, I feel that we have a kind of moral obligation to debate the issues as intellectual matters. We ought to take the arguments and the intuitions of our critics seriously; and we ought to engage those critics at their best, seek to answer the *best* arguments they can muster.

Speaking as someone disposed to contractarianism, I want to declare myself a fan of *dis*agreement. The point about genuine disagreement is that it is only possible if there is much that is already *agreed*: anything else is merely talking at cross-purposes. I have no interest in talking at cross-purposes. It seems to me, therefore, that before we rush headlong into the contest, we should spend a little time clarifying what it is that we are arguing about. And since on many fronts there seems to be such confusion about what ER is — and more particularly what neoclassical economics actually *says* — I have seen it more profitable to concentrate on those questions than to try to summarise who has said what on current policy issues. My object here is to make genuine disagreement possible.

Because I don't know quite what ER *is*, it seems to me more useful to focus on conventional neoclassical economics, with which I *do* have some passing familiarity. To the extent that Carroll's broadest definition of ER carries some weight (and the Pusey identification of economists in the public service as responsible for the rise of ER thinking suggests it might), it may be useful to clarify just what neoclassical economics does say about a number of salient matters.

I shall set the discussion out in terms of a number of propositions. They are all propositions about neoclassical economics (NE) and what standard NE analysis implies, that I believe to be uncontroversial among economists. Perhaps if such professional agreement were established and widely declared, some of our critics would be reassured. If we cannot agree, then I shall be surprised; but I will certainly find the fact of our disagreement instructive.

Proposition

Strictly speaking, modern neoclassical economics makes no policy recommendations at all.

Discussion

Without denying that the positive/normative distinction is problematic, and that treating it as *un*problematic has often meant trouble for economists, it is clear that such distinction is an important part of our disciplinary orientation. And if the distinction can be maintained, (that is, assuming that they're not thinking rubbish) it is clear that economists think of their discipline primarily *as* positive analysis that cannot in itself offer any policy recommendations at all. Put another way, the term 'economic rationalism' has this much right—that economics appeals to a 'rationalist' method in the sense that it presupposes a distinction between ends and means, both at the level of analysis of individual actors and at the level of policy analysis, and that in the latter context it is concerned with the relation *between* means and ends rather than the appropriateness of those ends. On this reading, economics examines the consequences of alternative policies or alternative institutional arrangements in the light of policy *ends* that economics itself doesn't specify.

What, on this account, are we to make of those familiar (perhaps notorious) theorems in welfare economics that assert the 'efficiency' of competitive markets? On this reading, welfare conomics should not be seen as part of economics at all. Welfare economics is, strictly speaking, a branch of ethics since welfare economics holds up certain notions as ethical ideals (e.g., Pareto optimality or Pareto desirable changes and so on). Although these ideals may be abstract and general and make only weak demands on our ethical sensibilities, it is confusing to talk as if, say, efficiency or Pareto optimality is a value-neutral concept. And it is also confusing to think that all ethical considerations can be collapsed into questions of equity and efficiency without making quite strong claims of an ethical kind.

I should perhaps clarify my own position. I believe that economists ought to make policy recommendations. (And economists will do so whether I believe they ought to or not.) But we ought to recognise that doing so commits us to ethical judgments. And we ought to be prepared to argue for our ethical premises in open argument; and to recognise that by doing so, the ethics that lie on the economist's shelf are distinctive, and by no means self-evidently compelling.

Failure to recognise the ethical dimension to welfare economics often leads to confusion. The truth is that the claims of standard-welfare economics — the ethical underpinnings of standard economic policy recommendations — are subject to widespread misinterpretation both outside and within the profession. The rest of this piece of work focuses on trying to clarify what welfare economics does actually say on a number of relevant matters.

Proposition

There is nothing in welfare economics that suggests that having the highest growth rate in GNP in the international league tables is the only game in town (or indeed that it is a particularly worthy game).

Discussion

It is worth emphasising this proposition because so much of the current policy discussion seems to focus on relative growth rates, and because it seems to me quite clear that relative growth rates are very much a side-play in welfare-economics orthodoxy. There are many obvious points to be made in this connection: there is the simple arithmetic point that a high income nation can have a lower growth rate than a poorer one, even though the absolute differential is increasing; the point that GNP is a poor measure even of economic wellbeing; the index-number problems that bedevil both intertemporal and international comparisons; to say nothing of the general ethical question as to why the international distribution of national incomes should remain unchanged with Australia at the top; or why we should care if the Singaporeans or Taiwanese happen to catch us up, particularly if we all continued to grow. Much of the popular discussion of these things seems to presume a zero-sum world in which the improvement in any one country's lot must be at the expense of some other country's (and our own most notably). It hardly needs to be pointed out that no neoclassical economist thinks of the world in this way. A typical recent conversation with one of the science-policy set illustrates the point: his claim was that through the halcyon days of the 1950s and 1960s we could afford quality universities (such as the ANU) but in the more pressed days of the 1980s and 1990s, we simply *could* not, *cannot*, and cannot expect to be able to in the future. Current unemployment levels apart (and it's a major proviso to be sure), I don't think the evidence supports his claim. Real GDP growth per head has been positive throughout this period (1990-plus excepted) — we have, on average, higher real incomes now than we did in 1950. So where does the impression of national grinding poverty come from? Why is there the impression of widespread disaster looming — so disastrous that we had to have this recession to help us do something about it, and so disastrous that we seem destined to run around like headless chooks 'fighting back' in a war where it's entirely unclear that the enemy is worth fighting?

Proposition

There is no presumption in welfare economics in favour of a minimal state.

Discussion

This proposition *does* need some discussion. It is clear that for purely private goods (ordinary goods like oranges or socks or watchbands) there is no presumption against market provision, in the sense that the standard welfare-economics theorems about the relation between Pareto optimality and perfect competition are applicable. However, to turn that absence of presumption-against into a presumption-in-favour of markets itself requires a little public-choice theory (or 'welfare politics' as it is more generally known). It requires, specifically, the demonstration that political provision of private goods is unlikely to be Pareto optimal: market success, no less than market failure, must be judged against relevant feasible institutional alternatives. Any absence of presumption against markets is modified once one moves away from the extremely polarised private-goods case. Welfare economics, after the public-goods revolution, is as much a catalogue of possible market failures as of general market success. To argue that mainstream economics argues for a minimal state is in that sense simply a mistake. As we public-choice people keep insisting, welfare economics cannot settle for any answer to the question of how large the domain and extent of government economic activity should be without some reasonably extensive analysis of the efficiency and equity properties of political processes.

What welfare economics *can* provide is a kind of grammar of argument about what activities a government is likely to have a comparative advantage in. Welfare economics can offer a *ranked* list that indicates which activities governments ought to be involved in first. This list will reflect the 'degree of market failure', and in turn, reflect the extent to which goods exhibit 'non-appropriability', 'non-rivalness in consumption', decreasing costs and so on. This grammar of argument is by no means decisive, both because of the welfare-politics point already made, and because 'non-appropriability' and 'non-rivalness' are partly a matter of the nature of individuals' preferences, and partly because market failure cannot simply be equated with the technical properties of the goods in question (though the technical properties give us some useful clues in many cases).

This latter point is worth elaborating, because it is so frequently ignored. Consider a simple example. Suppose we are attempting to assess whether there is any case for subsidising higher education. We calculate the costs of providing the marginal place. We then estimate the extra income that graduates earn by virtue of their degrees, the probability of success in obtaining a degree (and thereby the wasted investment in failures), and the income forgone by students while at university. By this means, we calculate the present value of the expected return to the average student from attending university. Setting aside the obvious problem of comparing the return for the average student with the cost of the marginal one, we can conclude that if the benefit/cost ratio exceeds unity, then more student places should be made available (or obversely if the ratio is less than unity). All this calculation is beside the point. If welfare economics is to be taken seriously, these matters can be left for the individual students to decide. The crucial question in deciding optimal subsidies (and thereby the optimal number of places) revolves around the benefits that persons other than the graduate derive from an additional student. And that is the kind of information that cannot be read off from market values directly (and perhaps not from market values at all). The case, if any, for intervention in the higher-education market depends on market returns providing the *wrong* signals; calculations in terms of those (potentially erroneous) prices cannot inform us if prices are wrong, and if so, by how much. Obviously, whether (and to what extent) higher education is a 'public good' in the relevant technical sense is a matter of individual preferences, and depends also on dimensions of those preferences that *by definition* receive inadequate market expression. To those who believe that there are no relevant externalities in higher education, I ask, where is your evidence? And I address the same question to those who think that the case for government intervention is clear. The truth of the matter is, welfare economics itself provides negligible information on this issue. What welfare economics tells us is what the question is.

And it is on this basis that economists are likely to dispute any case for government intervention in the case of goods such as electrical tools, washing machines or tinned pears (examples that Carroll cites in *Shutdown*) based on the argument that Australia had, at some point, produced them. Economists will insist on some 'externality'-based reasoning; and will do so whatever their general views on market performance or the efficiency properties of electoral competition or (derivatively), on the appropriate size of the fisc.

Proposition
There is no presumption in welfare economics against 'redistribution'.

Discussion
This seems self-evident to me. Economists may not say much about the desirability of redistribution or how much there should be — but this is probably because they feel that they do not have much that is particularly distinctive to add. They may be mistaken in this. But when they do talk about such things, it is often with scepticism, either because incidence complications mean that what appears to benefit one group may benefit

other groups much more, or because the opportunity costs of policies undertaken (in terms of other policies forgone) are ignored.

Some economists do occasionally make arguments against redistribution — of the kind that economists *qua* economists have no business making (e.g., dependency arguments), or those that are while almost certainly true, not decisive (e.g., the argument that raising unemployment benefits tends to raise unemployment levels *ceteris paribus*). But it seems clear to me that nothing in welfare economics indicates that public-transfer activity is a bad thing, and much in welfare economics indicates that it is a good thing — though exactly how much we should have of it is a question economists tend to avoid.

So, is there a presumption in favour of income-related, as opposed to non-income-related, transfers? In my view, there is a well-grounded presumption in public finance in favour of economising on fiscal resources. Tax revenues are 'scarce' because they cost something at the margin to increase. In general, therefore, a transfer programme that achieves the same reduction in poverty at less fiscal cost is preferred. But there are special complications here. Sometimes it can be less 'distorting' to target transfers to groups who are on average poorer, such as the elderly or the unemployed or Aborigines (even though there may be many non-poor in these classes). And there are public-choice considerations as well: equilibrium transfers may be lower when they are restricted to, say, the poorest 10 per cent than if transfers are universal. Voters are more likely to support programmes from which they benefit and vote against programmes that involve them paying more in tax.

At this point I want to shift ground a little and talk not of what orthodox economics supports and does not support by way of policy conclusions, but rather, of the analytic methods — and, somewhat more abstractly, of the assumptions — that economics employs. I do this because I believe that critics of 'economic rationalism' may be concerned as much about these matters as about policy questions directly. Again, the propositional method has its expositional advantages, but here there is no presumption that the propositions are ones to which economists would consent.

Proposition
For economists, greed is a virtue.

Discussion
We are often accused of this belief, so we ought to address it head-on. It seems clear to me that it is just plain wrong — that it is a mistaken view of what we are really saying — egotism is abundant and that the

best institutions are those which, *ceteris paribus*, bend egoistic motivations to serve public interest. To treat greed as a fact rather than a scandal is to treat it somewhat philosophically; but there need be no sense in making a virtue out of necessity. As Madison puts it in the Federalist Papers, our best security lies in institutions that 'bend interest to the service of duty' — or, as Bolingbroke has it, will 'make good statesmen even of bad men'.

It is an advantage of idealised competitive markets that we do not depend on the producer's benevolence to attend to the customers' wants. But the role of interests here may be more to nurture and encourage the virtues of benevolence than to render those virtues irrelevant. Moreover, there are many contexts where greed does have harmful consequences. What economists seek are environments where most of those harmful consequences are borne by the greedy — which is truer in the market place than is commonly supposed.

I think there is a set of propositions related to the last proposition that economists are guilty of:

- we tend to assume that greed is more abundant than it is — that no reliance can be placed on public interest at all
- we tend to argue as if all relations were instrumentally grounded
- we tend to argue as if all relations were arms-length ones, mediated solely or predominantly by price
- we tend to focus exclusively on 'invisible-hand' mechanisms for social control and ignore other social mechanisms that are, in many contexts, much more significant (ones, for example, that depend on prestige or shame — and the good regard of others more generally)

These are large topics. And in critiques of 'the economic way of thinking' elsewhere in the literature (say, Amitai Etzioni's *The Moral Dimension* or Amartya Sen's *Ethics and Economics* or Don McCloskey's *The Rhetoric of Economics*) they are rather more in play. In the Australian context, however, the attack on 'economic rationalism' seems to map onto a rather simple-minded assault on economists' arguments against protectionism. The assault seems to be in support of the neo-mercantilist doctrine that Australia's current and/or long-term economic ills would best be attacked with more protection (i.e., higher tariffs) and more aggressive policies of supporting domestic industries through public subsidy.

The proposition at stake seems to be that more protection implies higher rates of GDP growth. There is, no doubt, an argument that can be mounted along these lines; an argument that does a bit more than look back nostalgically to the Korean War and its aftermath when

Australia was one of the most highly protected economies in the OECD group. But I would prefer not to engage that argument here. Rather, I will note that this is an argument propounded mostly by sociologists (Pusey, Carroll), political scientists (Manne, Sawer), and science-policy people (Ventila), arguments that offer little that professional economists can take seriously. This comes as a surprise to me; I would have thought that other disciplines might have wanted to take economists to task over a range of other issues such as the (possible) inadequacies of consequentialist ethics, the arguably excessive claims of agent rationality, the presumed exogeneity of preferences, the almost exclusive focus on 'invisible-hand' mechanisms for social control and so on. Instead, our critics seem to want to accept us at our weakest and take us on at our strongest. I confess that I find this puzzling. Puzzling and disappointing, because I believe there is an engagement between economics and other social sciences that is likely to be profitable. I don't think engagement on the current terms is.

Michael Pusey

Reclaiming the Middle Ground . . . From New Right 'Economic Rationalism'

> The intellectual and moral basis of Australian society is being corrupted
> . . . [and] the driving force behind this . . . [is a] view of the economy as
> a machine independent of social purposes. (Coombs 1992)

'**N**ugget' Coombs, Australia's most distinguished public servant and a former Governor of the Reserve Bank said this some time ago. But then, are we not all in agreement with Joan Robinson, a Cambridge economist, that 'Economics . . . has always been partly a vehicle for the ruling ideology of each period as well as partly a method of scientific investigation' (Alford 1992, pp. 766-84)? There is, then, nothing especially new in my claim that economics is intertwined with ideology. 'In modern life no clear line separates economics from political interest', says Harvard economist John Galbraith (1991, pp. 41-7). 'To cope with these problems the master [sic] economist must possess a rare combination of gifts . . . He [or she] must . . . reach a high standard in several different directions and combine talents not often found together . . . and . . . must be a mathematician, historian, statesman, [and] philosopher — in some degree' — that's John Maynard Keynes (1933, p. 170).

Please allow me now a rather longer quotation from the eminent French economist Malinvaud. In proffering the view that in the next fifty years economics will be a less isolated science he says:

> During the past decades economic logic was put to work on phenomena that belong to the realms of other social sciences: demography, politics, sociology. . . . [The] time is now coming when reverse flows are going to be found interesting for economics. More and more people among us will recognise *the limits of the dominant concepts of economic rationality* and *economic equilibrium*; without abjuring their faith in the value of these concepts, they will realise that exclusive reliance on them is not always warranted. Psychologists, sociologists, political scientists will offer us a rich body of evidence on when and how economic behaviour and economic interactions

systematically deviate from the patterns implied in our paradigms. . . . Interdisciplinary collaboration will thus have to become much more frequent; we see it already at work for instance in the management of the environment or *in the study of public issues* by national academies. That is just the beginning. [*emphasis added*] (Malinvaud 1991, pp. 64-9)

In that same paragraph Malinvaud says that, *'Eventually* the profession will find these contributions useful and palatable'. In this respect I am enormously encouraged by the reception of my book *Economic Rationalism in Canberra* (1991) among many very senior Australian economists. With Malinvaud they see the limits of economic rationality. So too do the 203 academics from Economics, Commerce, Management and other social-science departments who, in December 1991,[1] supported me in a petition sent to the then Prime Minister and Treasurer to warn of the costs of adopting any more policies cast in the 'new right' 'economic rationalism'.

Confirmation that people of a rather different kind are allowed to speak for the economics profession in Australia was not slow in coming from other quarters. A few quotations will illustrate what I mean. Dave Clark, an academic economist, chose to rest his *Financial Review* article (1991) on an introduction depicting me as an 'irrational, sandal wearing, Volvo-driving associate professor of sociology'. In another outburst, John Stone, the former Head of Treasury writing in *Quadrant* (1992, pp. 61-4) and later in the *Canberra Times* (1992a) described my research as a waste of taxpayers' money and the book as, 'sludge', 'unpleasant', 'nasty, brutish and long', as an error of judgement on the part of the publisher, as the sort of offering one would expect from 'someone in . . . his late twenties' who should therefore 'grow up'. He goes on, 'Having in mind that Dr Pusey is now aged 52 the book can only be seen as the product of a kind of retarded development'. In his *Australian Quarterly* review Richard Blandy (1992, pp. 101-6) misrepresents the data and then refers to the work as 'rubbish', 'speaking in tongues (sociologese)', 'hare-brained', a 'farrago of fact and fantasy', 'amazing nonsense', 'multiple schizophrenia' and 'silly marxism'. And so it continues: but only from 'new right' economic 'rationalists'.[2] I am of no special importance in all of this, yet, do we detect some nervousness? And does the economics profession in Australia need an ethics committee?

Reclaiming the middle ground . . . from ideological economics

Like 'Nugget' Coombs I am a middle-of-the-road Western-European social democrat and it is from this position that my book has challenged the phenomenon called 'economic rationalism'. The term has a history in academic discourse. However, since I am generally blamed or praised (according to taste) for giving broader public currency to this term I accept some responsibility for defining, again, the grounds and the object of my criticism of 'economic rationalism'.

'Economic rationalism' is a doctrine that says that markets and prices are the *only reliable* means of setting a value on anything, and, further, that markets and money can *always*, at least in principle, deliver better outcomes than states and bureaucracies. A great many neoclassical economists accept this definition of their own position and equate neoclassical economics with what they call 'mainstream economics' and equate both with economic rationalism *tout court*.[3] But others would not since this is quite obviously a definition that excludes Keynesians, institutionalists, most economic historians, many of the 'hands-on' industry economists, and all the other moderates and eclectics who have been squeezed to the margins of the discipline as it has redefined itself over the last twenty-five years in surrender to what Peter Groenwegen and Bruce McFarlane (1990, pp. 232-5) call the 'fatal embrace of American economics'.

The definition points beyond itself to the heart of the problem with economic rationalism, that is, the absence of limitations. In this uncertain intellectual world, one of the few things that remains given now and in every possible future is that the final limits of economies and economics are social, or, if you prefer, 'socially constructed'. That is why everyone, except our economic rationalists, have understood the danger evoked in the images of the 'tail that is the economy wagging the dog that is Society' and of a society defined by our economic 'reformers' as some kind of 'stubbornly resisting sludge' through which they must somehow drive 'the economy' (Pusey 1991; 1990). The final a priori of economic reason must always be that its own limits are socially given. Economic rationalists have, in various ways and with different motivations, set themselves in reaction to this limitation. This explains the ideological aggression and the intellectual helplessness of economic rationalists in the face of the challenges that have been set upon them by moderates from every quarter. On what criteria should we question the limits of economic policy? On what social and non-economic criteria should we evaluate economic ideas and policies? Economic rationalists cannot cope with these questions.

My purpose in the remaining pages should now be clear. My shots are aimed not at philosophically intelligent economists but rather at the ideological cuckoos who have occupied the nests and endangered the species. The piecemeal comments — there is space for nothing else — should all be taken as tokens and surrogates of the longer arguments for limitations that will be necessary for the eventual rehabilitation of economics to its rightful place among others as a great academic discipline and, one hopes again some day, as one of the 'moral sciences'. There are five such comments that are preceded now by the briefest outline of the evaluative framework from which they proceed.

A first assumption of social democrats everywhere is that nation societies (and federations such as the emerging Europe) have not one coordinating structure but two. On the one side they have states, bureaucracies and the law and on the other, economies, markets and money. It is with these structures that we collectively coordinate our relations with the rest of the world, our work, social interactions, and most other aspects of life that we understand as 'civil society' and normatively define with notions of citizenship, democracy, and human rights. Social democrats reject ideological Utopias and know, with a second assumption, that coordination exacts its own costs on civil society: economies, and markets cause some unemployment just as states and bureaucracies carry the sting of authority and some repression. And moderates everywhere insist, thirdly (and, for the most part, 'counter-factually'), that the capacity of a democratic society to reproduce and maintain itself over time depends on something more than the rituals of voting. It depends on the quality of its institutions and most especially on a mediating public sphere through which public culture sets limits and directions on coordination through the political system. Limits that are set and discerned, ultimately, in the conditions for the reproduction and maintenance of society itself.

And so, broadly speaking, the criteria for what can and cannot count as rationality and reason in the policy arena are given in the very constitution of democratic societies. Specialised knowledge of government, administration, and the law is rational in its application only to the degree that it accepts as well its external limitations. The same is true of specialist economic knowledge of money, prices, and markets. Its claim to rationality can only be realised in its construction as policy and through a process of limitation and accommodation with other differently grounded priorities and imperatives (Berlin 1990). All policy is synthetic and the rationality and reason of the synthesis depends now, as before, on the quality of the institutions through which it is negotiated. All of this used to be held safe in what we once called a liberal education. At its best it produced statesmen/stateswomen who, in Keynes's words, 'combined talents not other-

Michael Pusey

wise often found together' and were, only then, equipped to redeem in part the limitations of technical knowledge and to reconcile incommensurate value ends with defensible compromises.

These criteria for what can and cannot count as rationality are amply demonstrated in the devastation and instability that we see around us in the contemporary world. Again, broadly speaking, it seems clear enough that the old Soviet empire collapsed because one coordinating structure — the state — blocked economic coordination, became a law unto itself, and inflicted tremendous damage on civil society. The conditions for social reproduction were violated and the 'system' could no longer reproduce itself. The other extreme is prefigured in what is now routinely seen by mainstream policy leaders in Europe and Japan as the failure of the American and British experiment with new-right economic rationalism. Even senior blue-blooded Republicans such as George Cabot Lodge (teaching at the Harvard Business School) and some of the former cold-war warriors such as Edward Luttwak now agree that we are at 'the end of the American Century'[4] in as much as aggressive individualism and free-market Reaganomics have destroyed so much of both the economy and the social fabric of the nation. The ideologues who articulated and applied the new-right 'attack politics' of Reaganomics are the direct counterparts of the Soviet party ideologues. In both cases the logic of coordination is totalitarian because its claims are intellectually conceived and then applied with the assumptions of an 'unbounded' rationality that assumes its own self-sufficiency and sets itself against the very limitations that could ever make it rational, socially constructive, and, in short, intelligent.

The lesson for us is that the principal threats to the integrity and longer-term survival of modern nations such as Australia could not be clearer. We are not threatened by war and famine. Nations such as ours fail when they make mistakes and lose their way, and destroy the structural foundations for their own development. Policy institutions and cabinets are the only means we have for making collective decisions about our future. This brings me to my first point, that

Our Canberra policy apparatus is no longer 'intelligent'. It is cut off from the nation and its history. It is cut off from the middle ground. The earlier 'Coombs' generation of top policy advisers brought with them a broad life-experience of big wide Australia before Canberra as we know it today was built. Canberra's geographical isolation was not yet a problem because they all came from somewhere else. Nor were they intellectually isolated. On the contrary, as Hugh Stretton

(1987, p. 202) puts it, the economics they learned at university was taught as a practical tool for nation-building and acquired within a liberal-arts curriculum that gave generous attention to both the means and the ends of reform. Economics was still in both 'theory and practice' one of 'the moral sciences' and firmly grounded within an 'intelligent' context of philosophical, historical, and social understanding.

In the passage from one generation to the next the top Canberra policy apparatus has failed in a double isolation of both geography and training. The new generation of top public servants have a narrow life and work experience. In 1985 the Senior Executive Service of the coordinating departments of Treasury, Finance and Prime Minister and Cabinet, consisted of predominantly Anglo-Saxon males with a median age of 41 who, depending on departmental location, were up to nine or ten times more likely than the rest of us to have passed through one of Australia's élite fee-paying private schools. 71 per cent of them are economists narrowly trained in what then became, from the 1950s, Australia's overspecialised, technically oriented economics departments in which economics shrank to a lower form of applied mathematics[5] and notions of equity and humanity were displaced by American free-market economics (Butlin 1987, pp.170-3).

As the central coordinating departments have been captured by this single line of 'new right' 'free-market' economic rationalism the real problem-solvers in the public service, the 'hands-on' economists in the industry departments, the educationalists, the engineers and the scientists, the other professionals in the industry and programme departments upon which we depend for useful services have been demoralised or driven out. Real power in the federal public service is now inversely proportional with one's knowledge of real tasks, or indeed of reality. In France, Germany, and other West-European nations where the policy apparatus is still safely in the hands of 'committed centrists'[6] there is a clear understanding that the task of the policy apparatus is to help the banks, the unions, and the industrial corporations to work together in the long-term interests of the national population. Here, in Australia, incredible as it may seem, our economic rationalists are doing just the reverse: setting the market 'free' by undermining the government's always limited margin of intervention, shutting down as much of the public sector as possible, and abetting an assault on the trade unions and the industrial-relations system that has been the cornerstone of our history for a century.

Economic rationalism has so reduced the deliberative capacity of our Canberra policy apparatus that it can no longer think intelligently about the larger mid- and long-term conditions for national development or take what the older generation called 'a broader view'. The few remaining moderates in our two major political parties can already see that until something is done, no government of either side can get independent, rational, reasonable, and adequate policy advice from our top public service, a point I have raised also in my book. In most departments, the quality of technical advice is probably very high, but it remains technical and lacks any redeeming balance and contextualisation because the public intellectuals, the statesmen and the stateswomen have, for the most part, gone. Last July the Public Service Commission, replacing a Public Service Board that was once the official guardian of independent policy culture, responded without too much embarrassment to a question from a Parliamentary Committee about the dangers of economic rationalism with the comment that this was 'the sort of thing that one could debate quite well over a glass or two of red wine'.[7]

The economics on which we have mortgaged our future is in crisis. In the US the American Economics Association appointed its own Commission on Graduate Education in Economics (COGEE) 'to take stock of what is being done in [graduate] economics education' in that country. This Commission, set up from within the profession itself, mentions what many economists call the empty formalism of their own discipline and goes on to state its disquiet at the declining demand for academic economists among non-academic employers in the private and public sectors and links these causes of its 'disquiet' with its 'central concerns' that included 'the reported disaffection of top undergraduate students with graduate school economics; with the underemphasis on "'linkages" between tools, both theory and econometric, and real world problems'. The Commission was told by faculty members in top liberal-arts colleges such as Harvard and Yale that

> some of their best students have decided against going to graduate school in economics, or have dropped out in their first year, because of the abstract technical nature of the core curriculum. It is not economics as they know it. (1991, pp. 1035-53)

In Australia, the best liberal-arts students have already rejected a core curriculum that has for the most part imploded into formula mongering and artificial mind games that have little or no relevance to anything in the real world. The others use economics in just the way that the new right has redefined it: as an ideological shield against intelligent introspection and civic responsibility and as a guilt-free entry passport for yuppies to 'real' jobs in finance, marketing, and (tragically) the public sector. In Britain, the one-hundredth anniversary issue of the *Journal of the Royal Economic Society* canvassing the views of twenty-one of the world's best-known economists on the state of the discipline begins with a fine editorial deploring the blindness of the dominating number crunchers, the inability of the profession to think beyond the short run, the lack of attention to economic history, and the lack of eclecticism in the economics discipline. Most of the contributors seem to concur in one way or another and, indeed, Nobel laureate James Buchanan (1991, pp. 15-21) (who is even further to the right than Hayek was) is able to recognise both the endemic positivism and what he calls the prevailing 'antiseptic aridity' of his own discipline. John Pencavel (1991, p. 81) refers to what he calls 'professional tyranny' and thus alludes to the de facto censorship of the top economic journals that only publish articles conforming to the one ideological line. In Australia, a similar inquiry into COGEE (AVCC 1992) charged with a review of the honours curriculum in Australian universities chose not to pursue an earlier observation by one of its authors that 'none of the universities visited had a unit on the distribution of income in its honours course'.[8] The inquiry did echo many of COOGEE's concerns and it does recommend that 'at least one semester unit should be given to institutional historical analysis'. But there are no other major recommendations for change.

With Malcolm Anderson, Richard Blandy has surveyed eighty-one economics professors and showed that Australia's economics departments remain in the grip of his own one-line school of 'new right', free-market, economic 'rationalism'. There is no hope of any moderating pluralism or of any saving reintegration of economics with the liberal-arts disciplines.

Economic rationalism creates poverty and dependence. Economic rationalists insist that potential value is destroyed by tariffs, price floors or ceilings, and prohibitions on entry or exit from the market: markets are assumed to be efficient in the measure that they are 'free'. Although no historian worth his or her salt would suffer such nonsense for an instant, some even want to insist that free markets are coterminous with equity. All the evidence points in the opposite direction. After a spate of deregulation, commercialisation, privatisation, and 'marketisation' we saw a sharp upward redistribution of income under Thatcher, Reagan, and Hawke. In the US between 1977 and 1988, family income declined in every decile except the top decile where it increased by 19.5 per cent. According to Robert Heilbronner (1992), 'At least 60 per cent and as much as 70 per cent of the increase in national wealth during the Reagan years went to the richest one percent of families'. Bob Gregory's and F. Vella's (1992) comparisons of Australia and US figures point to a dispersion of middle incomes in both countries. In Australia, IBIS Business Information has used census data to show that over a period of only fifteen years from (1976 to 1992) 'the proportion of Australian households with an income of more than $72 000 (based on constant 1991/92 values) rose from 15 to 30 per cent . . . [while] at the same time, the proportion of households with an income of less than $22 000 rose from 20 per cent to 30 per cent' (Mackay 1993, p.137). This is what 'free' markets do. Markets are not 'value-neutral' or equitable! The market is an 'up escalator' that moves income and 'life chances' upwards from the 'have nots', and 'the have-a-bits', to the 'have-heaps' and economic rationalism provides the theory and the 'technology' to make just this happen.

For economic rationalists and 'mainstream economists' (not just welfare economists) 'economic efficiency' still means 'Pareto optimality'. This notion remains absolutely indifferent to inequalities. In the words of Amartya Sen (1988, p. 32), one of the world's most distinguished economists, it comes 'like Caesar's breath hot from hell' because it requires that one person's gain shall be another's loss. The model for what economic rationalists call 'reform' is a closed system of zero-sum power relations that delivers the mass of increasingly powerless individuals — perforce the 'price takers' — into dependence upon an ever smaller and more powerful minority of people with increasing leverage over markets — the 'price makers'. Economic efficiency is measured by the dependency and helplessness of national populations upon markets over which they have less and less control. Dependency is redefined as 'freedom' and the model of personality follows the same nihilistic logic. The ideal person shrinks to a socially autistic 'choice-receiver' that responds only with yes/no decisions that are externally coordinated by prices and free markets!

New right 'free' market economics is a virus that destroys its host society. Or, as Visiting Professor at the Harvard Business School Amitai Etzioni (1988) puts it: '*The more people accept the neo-classical paradigm as a guide for their behaviour, the more the ability to sustain a market economy is undermined*' (p. 250). Most economic decisions are made not by isolated and maximally self-interested individuals but corporately in organisations both public and private. Every Japanese and European business leader knows that the effectiveness and viability of those organisations depend on pre-contractual social norms of trust, co-

operation, and honesty and so on the civic, familial, and educa
institutions through which they are internalised and reproduced—in
society and with the sustenance of good government. Ultimately, these
are the resources that matter most *both* for economic production *and*
social integration and national integrity. But with 'public-choice' theorists,
'rational-choice' theorists, and other anachronistic extremes of American
libertarianism, economic rationalists have set themselves in reaction to
such limitations. The consequences are visible on at least three fronts.

Although 'mainstream economics' is the 'natural' integrative discipline for management it has in fact failed the business world by
retreating into various forms of model mongering and artifice. As John
Kay (1991, pp. 57-63) sees it, the models are based on a false science
of spaceless, timeless, and rationally maximising individual agents
that have *little or no relevance* to the behaviour of institutions and
business organisations in the real world. The real scholars and the
business economists know this. Not so the new right! Economic
rationalists understand no limitation and have instead keenly abetted
the 'casual amorality of the business world, [and its] retreat from civic
consciousness and responsibility' (Steinfels 1979, p. 212). A scan of
the financial press will show how Skase, Bond, Elliot, Connell,
Spalvins and others were touted as model entrepreneurs by economic
rationalists who have learned nothing from what the demise of the
'entrepreneurs' says about 'the model'. An ironically appropriate
judgement on all this was delivered by an eminent American
conservative with the reluctant observation that economically rationalist 'culture does indeed succeed in breeding aggression out of the
privileged classes and after a period in which this enriches [!!] the
culture, it begins to deplete it'.[9]

Economic rationalists have made war on the institutions of democratic
government in Australia. In 1984/85 as the Hawke government loosened
controls on foreign investment the National Social Science Survey showed
that only 16 per cent of the population disagreed with *tighter* control over
the activities of multinational companies. The national survey showed,
similarly, that three-quarters of the Australian population favoured
Arbitration Commission regulation of the labour market when a similar
proportion of economists in my Senior Executive Service (SES) sample
wanted to deregulate the labour market. 70 per cent of the national
sample supported 'redistributing income and wealth in favour of ordinary
working people' while 45 per cent of the economists in the SES said
outright that the distribution of income was biased to wage and salary
earners (with another 29 per cent of them saying that it was 'balanced').
The same picture emerges in relation to consumer protection laws. Even

ers we find that 88 per cent of the national sample
er laws against fraudulent selling and misleading
t only 4 per cent of them disagreed with stronger
the environment against pollution. Only 36 per cent
e were opposed to *increased* taxes for the rich that
under pressure from a militant unanimity of voices
..ew right' economic rationalists.[10] All this may be taken as evidence
of the prejudice of economic rationalists against democratically constituted government that is viewed, for the most part, as an unwarranted
limitation on rationally maximising agents in a free market. On this,
Etzioni delivers the appropriate judgement, 'If those whose duty it is to
set and to enforce the rules of the game are out to maximise their own
profits, *à la* Public Choice, there is no hope for the system' (p. 250).

On a more fundamental level and well before the LA riots the
effects of the virus on American society were clearly visible for all to
see, in 'highly visible pathologies: the three million homeless, the
violent drug-filled ghettos, the failing schools, the explosive racial
climate . . . and the rotting infrastructure' (Heilbronner 1991). In the
four years to 1992 the number of families with no health insurance
increased by 15 per cent; the number of Americans unemployed for
six months or longer increased by 133 per cent; the number of families
receiving Aid to Families with Dependent Children increased by 25
per cent; the number of children living in poverty increased by 4 per
cent; the number of violent crimes increased by 21 per cent; and the
number of Americans in prison increased by 28 per cent (Davids
1992, p.13). Heilbronner continues, 'the country is visibly decaying.
I do not know of anyone who sees a bright future for it'.

*From the failure of Thatcherism and Reaganomics to the 'fatal
embrace' of Hewsonomics?*[11] In the light of the British, American, and
New Zealand experience the political thrust of new right economic
rationalism could not be clearer. In Australia it will be seen by
historians as a radical attack upon the two remaining potential
restraints on the upward redistribution of power and income in
Australia. These two restraints are our unique award and industrial-
relations system and our public sector.

In its various forms the award and wage-setting system has been the
anchor of social and economic democracy in Australia since Federation.
In this century it has been the key structural component in a political
economy that gave us the highest per capita incomes and one of the most
equal distribution of (male) incomes in the 'developed' world. It may very
well stand out as the most resilient and effective solution to the problem

of distribution in the history of modern capitalism. In our own time, and even from the narrower perspective of economic performance, the OECD makes the broad judgement, that in terms of labour-market flexibility Australia has been, on average, among the more flexible of OECD countries. The Report goes on:

> Despite arguments that centralised bargaining systems lead to a lack of movement of relative wages, Australia's performance does not appear to have been significantly different from other countries. Further, Australia's labour force has been extremely mobile by international standards, both between industries and regions.[12]

After more recent rapid structural changes no-one doubts that the labour market is still more flexible today than it was when the report was written five years ago. The 'reasons' for its destruction are ideological: new right economic rationalism will not suffer limitations on the 'free' market, on economic efficiency, and on the upward redistribution of 'life chances'.

The other protecting bulwark of middle Australians has been the Australian public sector that is marked for draconian cuts and routinely touted by the leaders of the Liberal Party as our 'bloated public sector'. Here, international comparisons show that even before the Hawke government's cuts to the public sector began in earnest in 1985, we already had, relative to twenty OECD nations, a *small* public sector and very *low* levels of taxation. In 1989 the public sector accounted for only 15.7 per cent of total employment — half that of Norway, Sweden and Denmark! On another measure, our general outlays to government were, in the same year, the second *lowest* in the OECD and the *proportion of those outlays that is redistributed to the needy* is also at the bottom end of the OECD table.[13] In the absence of all redemptive intelligence the Hewson cuts would be made as the new Clinton administration approaches the hopeless task of repairing the damage caused by similar policies in the US — policies that were unsuccessfully opposed in a petition to the US Congress by 327 American economists including six Nobel laureates.

Once these structural restraints on the upward redistribution of income have been broken the last step is to pull up the ladders and cover the tracks. Since the strategies are simple adaptations of Thatcherism and Republican 'attack politics' the third predictable prong of the strategy will be an assault on the quality press, public broadcasting, the remains of the liberal university, and on other constituents of critical debate in a 'public sphere'. Funding will be withdrawn from public advocacy organisations so that the market will not have to suffer limitations from 'vested interests' and an informed citizenry. Nor is there much doubt about the ferocity with which the 'reforms' would be delivered. As John Hewson told the New Zealand Chamber of Commerce, 'You cannot tinker. You have to make dramatic change. . . . You cannot have too much change and you cannot do it quickly enough' (Woods 1992).

When historians try to make sense of the wave of destruction that swept through the great English-speaking nations in the 1980s they will, as always, have a hard task in dealing with the complex questions of cause, agency, and mediation. In every country, the productive apparatus has been crippled and social integration endangered or even destroyed. In each nation, interests and ideology are differently intertwined and driven or mediated by many different groupings. It is not often that one group of actors turns out to have been decisive in throwing the points and switches of history. In making a similar point Galbraith comments on a meeting at which Murray Wiedenbaum, the Chairman of the US Council of Economic Advisers, was asked directly what weight of influence, on a scale of one to ten, economists had enjoyed in drafting the original tax programme of the Reagan administration. Wiedenbaum answered, 'Zero'.[14] In reviewing the devastation of the Lucky Country the historian will take an equally unambiguous answer from the other end of the scale — ten! Responsibility will be apportioned accordingly!

Like it or not, we are a nation society in a continental territory. We do not belong to a transnational federation like the EEC. It is our fate to defend our own sovereignty. We have only *our* history and no alternative but to restore our connections with it — if for no other reason, then so that we do not summarily betray what has been bequeathed to us. We desperately need economists who are once again, like the 'Nugget' Coombs generation, liberally educated nationalists and nation-builders. To achieve this we must reconstruct public culture and the liberal university from the ashes of the Dawkins reforms. And we must create new institutions that can once again connect the Canberra policy apparatus with the nation and redeem what is now the double isolation of geography and scientism. We must reconstruct a consensually negotiated middle ground in which the finance sector, Australian corporations, and the unions, together and in partnership, lead economic development for the greater mid- and long-term benefit of the nation.

Some encouragement comes, with a touch of bleak irony, from the clarity of the historical moment. In the wake of the LA riots and especially in developed nations where most of our social resources — institutions, local communities, churches, families, etc. — have been burned up as fuel for economic development, blind Freddie of either gender can see that social integration will be the central problem that will stand over politics in this decade just as surely as 'efficiency' had done in the last.

Notes

1 The petition was organised by Associate Professor Frank Stilwell, Department of Economics, University of Sydney.

2 Like P. P. McGuiness before him, and without any sign of having read the book, Alan Wood, the Economics editor of the *Australian* uses Blandy's misrepresented data in a feature-length article attacking the research. See 'The Economists Who Ate Canberra', *Australian*, 20-1 February 1992.

3 This was the assumption of the organisers of this conference that was originally billed as 'Economic Rationalism: Mainstream Economics Strikes Back'.

4 'The Rise and Fall of the American Century' is a chapter title in R. Bellah et al., *The Good Society*, Knopf, New York, 1991. 'The End of the American Century?' is the title of an excellent editorial essay by R. Manne in *Quadrant*, vol. 36, no. 11, 1992 which gives a list of the new critics.

5 Mathematicians say over and over that economists too often use distorted mathematics with 'too many free parameters'; reality is doctored in the construction of the mathematical models to produce ideologically predetermined results. Even Milton Friedman admits as much in criticising many of his contemporaries — on methodological grounds that seem to have come straight from a father of modern sociology, Max Weber! See Friedman, 'The Methodology of Positive Economics', *Essays in Positive Economics*, University of Chicago Press, 1953.

6 A central finding of the seven-nation comparative studies of *Bureaucrats and Politicians in Western Democracies*, eds Joel Abarbach et. al., Harvard University Press, 1981 is that senior public servants in the seven nations were, on the whole, 'committed centrists'. See my discussion of this in *Economic Rationalism in Canberra*.

7 Hansard transcript of evidence given to the Joint Committee of Public Accounts by the Public Service Commission on 21 July 1992.

8 That observation was made by of one of the authors, Professor John Nevile, while the inquiry was still in progress. No-one imagines that it has been contradicted. See John Nevile's Sir Robert Madgwick Lecture, 'Economics and Ideals: Has the Age of Chivalry Gone?', given at the University of New England in May 1990, p. 9.

9 The words of Daniel Moynihan speaking to the Harvard alumni in 1976 and quoted by Michael Walzer, *Radical Principles: Refections Of An Unreconstructed Democrat*, Basic Books, New York, 1980, p. 104. Moynihan says 'liberal' culture but I have said 'economically rationalist' here to reflect the meaning set in the context — i.e., economic liberalism. The exclamation marks are mine.

10 For the results and discussion of the National Social Science Survey see John Braithwaite's chapter 'Economic Policy: What the Electorate Thinks', *Australian Attitudes*, eds Jonathan Kelley and Clive Bean, Allen & Unwin, Sydney, 1988, pp. 26-35.

11 Since I am non-partisan but still perceived to have been a strong critic of the Hawke government's economic rationalism I feel bound to speak out against a more extreme form of the same phenomenon.

12 OECD Economic Surveys, *Australia*, 1987/88, OECD, Paris, p. 70. Critics from the left will appreciate the cruel irony that the system is judged, quite explicitly, to be 'flexible' in the measure that it follows 'the trend decline in real wages'.

13 See Peter Saunders, 'Recent Trends in the Size and Growth of Government in OECD Countries', Public Sector Research Centre, Discussion Paper no. 20, 1991 and his internationally celebrated study, *The Role of the Public Sector: Causes and Consequences of the Growth of Government*, OECD Economic Studies, OECD, Paris, no. 4, Spring, 1985.

14 James K. Galbraith, 'The Grammar of Political Economy', *The Consequences of Economic Rhetoric*, ed. Arjo Klamer, Donald McCloskey and Robert Solow, Cambridge, 1988, p. 224. No, according to the preface, this is not John Kenneth Galbraith but a professor at the University of Texas and a former Executive Director of the US Joint Economic Committee.

References

Alford, Katrina 1992, 'Econotalk: the Case of Financial Deregulation', *Meanjin*, vol. 51, no. 4, pp. 766-84

Berlin, Isaiah 1990, *The Crooked Timber of Humanity: Chapters in the History of Ideas*, ed. Henry Hardy, Knopf, New York

Blandy, Richard 1992, 'Multiple Schizophrenia: Economic Rationalism and its Critics', *Australian Quarterly*, vol. 64, no. 1, pp. 101-6

Buchanan, James 1991, 'Economics in the Post-Socialist Century', *Economic Journal, Journal of the Royal Economic Society*, vol. 64, no. 1, pp. 15-21

Butlin, N. G. 1987, 'Human or Inhuman Capital? The Economics Profession 1916-87', Department of Economic History, RSSS, ANU, Working Paper no. 91

Clark, Dave 1991, *Financial Review*, 25 November

Coombs, H. C. 1992, 'Coombs: Australian Society Being Corrupted', *ANU Reporter*, 9 December

Davids, Jeffrey et al. 1992, 'Out Front', *Mother Jones*, San Francisco, September-October, p. 13

Etzioni, Amitai 1988, *The Moral Dimension: Towards a New Economics*, Free Press, New York

Freedman, Craig 1992, 'Why Economists Can't Read', mimeo, School of Economics, University of New South Wales

Galbraith, John K. 1991, 'Economics in the Century Ahead', *Economic Journal, Journal of the Royal Society*, vol. 101, no. 404, Basil Blackwell, pp. 41-7

Gregory, R. G. and Vella, F. 1992, 'Real Wages, Employment and Wage Dispersion in US and Australian Labour Markets', mimeo, Australian National University, Research School of Social Sciences

Groenewegen, Peter and McFarlane, Bruce 1990, *A History of Australian Economic Thought*, Routledge, London, pp. 232-5

Heilbronner, Robert 1991, 'Lifting the Silent Depression', *New York Review*, 24 October

Heilbronner, Robert 1992, 'The Deficit: A Way Out', *New York Review*, 19 November

Kay, John A. 1991, 'Economics and Business', *Economic Journal, Journal of the Royal Society*, vol. 101, no. 404, pp. 57-63

Keynes, John Maynard 1933, *Essays in Biography*, Macmillan, London

Mackay, Hugh 1993, *Reinventing Australia*, p. 137

Malinvaud, E. 1991, 'The Next Fifty Years', *Economic Journal, Journal of the Royal Society*, vol. 101, no. 404, pp. 64-9

Pencavel, John 1991, 'Prospects for Economics', *Economic Journal, Journal of the Royal Society*, vol. 101, no. 404, p. 81

Pusey, M. 1991, *Economic Rationalism in Canberra: A Nation-Building State Changes its Mind*, Cambridge

— 1990, 'The Impact of Economic Ideas on Public Policy in Canberra', *Economic Papers*, vol. 9, no. 4, pp. 80-90

Report of the Academic Standards Panel (Economics) to the Australian Vice-Chancellors' Committee 1992, AVCC

Report of the Commission on Graduate Education in Economics 1991, *Journal of Economic Literature*, vol. 29, pp. 1035-53

Sen, Amartya 1988, *On Ethics and Economics*, Basil Blackwell, Oxford

Steinfels, Peter 1979, *The Neo Conservatives: The Men Who Are Changing America's Politics*, Simon and Schuster, New York

Stone, John 1992, 'Book a Highly Distorted View', *Canberra Times*, 20 July

Stone, John 1992a, 'Michael Pusey's Economic Rationalism in Canberra', *Quadrant*, July-August, pp. 61-4

Stretton, Hugh 1987, *Political Essays*, Georgian House, Melbourne

Woods, Alan 1992, *Australian*, 13 October

R. Blandy, R. Manne & J. Freebairn

A Panel of Views: Economic Rationalists and Anti-Economic Rationalists

Richard Blandy

Economic Rationalism and Prosperity

I t is clear that the anti-rationalist critics are essentially opposed to the microeconomic reform agenda pursued by the Australian government (supported by the Opposition at least in general) approximately over the 1980s. Since this reform agenda derives from mainstream economics, they are opposed to that as well. Therefore, it is not surprising that there are hardly any academic economists to be found in the critics' ranks.

The critics rely for support for their position on:

- a harking back to the golden Australian eras and the policy prescriptions associated with those times
- an association between the present recession and the beginnings of implementation of microeconomic reform
- an assessment of the reasons behind the development successes of Japan and the 'tiger' Asian economies

From these bodies of evidence, the anti-rationalists conclude that government intervention in Australian economic affairs should be restored and even increased in some areas (such as industry policy). They believe that the present microeconomic reform agenda should be junked, and the policy clock wound back.

The recession

The recession is something Australia shares with all the economically developed countries, although it may be more severe here than elsewhere. It is insufficiently understood by Australian economic commentators, and perhaps Australian economists, that in the long sweep of economic events, Australia is part of the world economy and, with some timing differences and some local departures, tends to mirror global economic trends (and policies). Global inflation rates have fallen significantly in the 1980s and despite a lag, Australia's has followed. A global boom in asset prices occurred in the 1980s, perhaps spurred by a greater degree of integration of global capital markets following global financial deregulation and freer exchange-rate mechanisms. This boom has been followed by a global 'bust' of asset prices, particularly in property. Australia has shared in these global events.

The main cause of the global recession, mirrored again in Australia, appears to have been inadequate world macroeconomic management. The microeconomic reform agenda seems to have had little to do with the recession, a view supported by a number of economic analyses including one from the Reserve Bank of Australia.

On the contrary, a good case can be made that in an 'internationalising world' the scope for local demand management is severely circumscribed. As a small part of the global economy, Australia is a macrodemand 'policy taker' to an increasing degree. Effective macroeconomic management requires a greater focus on getting the supply side right so that Australia becomes a more competitive location for economic activity in a world context. This seems to have been a major ingredient in the long boom enjoyed by Japan and the Asian 'tigers': persistent and rapid growth in production (and, therefore, in employment and incomes) from gaining an increasing share of world trade and production based on maintaining low-cost positions through productivity gains and efficient infrastructure.

Japan and the tigers

The most comprehensive Australian analysis on the success of these countries has been that undertaken by the Industry Commission (1990). This section reproduces parts of that study.

According to the IC, the sources of Japan and the tigers' strong economic performances have been

- strong and effective government able to ensure the necessary legal, social and institutional frameworks to support free exchange and maintain public security so as to underpin the effective operation of markets in their economies
- a degree of 'autonomy' of these governments, enabling them to resist the pleas of special-interest groups, especially of trade

unions. Effective control over labour has been sustainable because the development strategy has produced a relatively even income distribution and rapidly rising income standards

- a 'catch-up' factor — a basic capability to exploit a large pool of technological and market opportunities already available from economically more advanced countries
- an outward orientation in economic strategy. This has meant that the economies have been faced with competitive pressure in world markets and continual efforts to improve their overall competitiveness were required. In Japan, intense domestic competition has been used to develop an ability to enter and compete successfully in world markets
- a winding back of import protection and export subsidies at an early stage in their growth strategy in favour of a policy of general liberalisation and allowing prices to be broadly market-driven. This policy permitted easy access to the imported inputs essential to their export industries and helped facilitate the remarkable growth in both exports and imports that are behind their rapidly growing incomes
- highly flexible, competitive and hard-working labour forces, with low absenteeism and turnover and low industrial unrest. (There may have been some deterioration in the labour markets of some of these countries in recent times.)
- high national savings
- excellent infrastructure provision, high private R&D spending, and international marketing assistance

The anti-economic rationalists (see, for example, Carroll and Manne 1992) focus almost exclusively on industry policy ('picking and supporting winners') as the reason behind the success of these countries. But once other factors are allowed for, it is not clear that there is much left for industry policy to explain in these countries' growth performance. As some assisted industries became international successes, so too have others failed. Some industries succeeded without government intervention, and countries such as Hong Kong, for example, were successful without any targetting of assistance.

The evidence amassed by the Industry Commission (1990) on the whole points to strategic interventions being unimportant in explaining success compared with a number of other factors such as

- social commitment to achieving economic success
- effective government in supporting the basics of markets and in resisting special pleading by organised interests
- technological 'catch-up'

- vigorous domestic competition in products and services
- highly flexible and competitive labour forces

When assistance was used, most measures were significantly reduced or withdrawn *within a decade*. By contrast, in Australia, the motor vehicle and TCF industries have received significant and sustained assistance over many decades. In the dynamic Asian economies, protection would have been greatly reduced a long time ago.

Whatever the merits of start-up assistance in countries that are willing to remove such assistance after a short space of time may be, those merits evaporate in countries such as Australia that find it extraordinarily difficult politically to cut assistance once it starts giving it. It is fortunate for Australia that industry policy ('picking winners') has not played a major role in the successful strategies pursued by the dynamic Asian economies.

On the contrary, it is our present, bipartisan reform programme that has the agenda right, with its emphasis on increased competition, outward orientation, more flexible labour markets, and resistance to special interests that ensures free-market basics, improves the efficiency of the operation of infrastructure, encourages skill formation and research and development. The beginnings of success are now starting to show through in Australia. Exports of elaborately transformed manufactures are growing strongly and their share of total exports is increasing. These exports are coming from small- to medium-sized firms that are growing in significance world-wide. The top priority for government action is more microeconomic reform. Tariff reductions, the recession and increased competition are major reasons why these firms began exporting (McKinsey & Co. 1992).

The golden past

The conservative critics of economic rationalism hark back to Menzies and McEwen — the post-war golden era of low unemployment and inflation and rising living standards. The socialist critics hark back to Whitlam or possibly to the Federation era.

These periods have two thing in common — protectionism and a rising tide of government interventionism. That the Whitlam era should be seen as 'golden' is particularly ironic. Gregory (1992), for example, has shown that a structural worsening of labour-market outcomes occurred under Whitlam that Australia has not yet been able to reverse. The massive real-wage breakout during 1974 (and again, to a lesser extent in 1981/82) has been closely associated with a massive deterioration in our labour-market performance relative to the US. The Whitlam era saw a 4.5 percentage point worsening of our unemployment rate relative to the US's. The cost of Whitlamism to Australia has been huge and is ongoing.

The present trend of labour-market reform towards an enterprise focus and away from occupational 'awards' is a belated recognition of the employment disaster that the Australian industrial-relations system inflicted on us under Whitlam, of the failure of a centralised Accord to deliver rapid productivity growth, and recognition that an 'internationalising' Australian economy cannot successfully face heightened international (and internal) competitive pressures with a tightly regulated labour market unfocused on enterprise productivity and performance.

The Heylen survey (1992) of the New Zealand labour market under the New Zealand Employment Contracts Act showed that 74 per cent of employees were satisfied with their contract outcomes, 42 per cent have had an increase in take-home pay, 40 per cent registered no change, and 18 per cent, a reduction. In addition, strikes have fallen by 90 per cent. Women's pay has improved relative to men's. Productivity has increased due to a reduction in work demarcation.

The Menzies era coasted on the back of the global post-war reconstruction boom while steadily setting in place protectionist measures that gradually muted participation in the boom in international trade on Australia's part. The Menzies era was one where the direction of much policy came from the opposition benches, and an international trend towards 'bigger government'. 'Protection all round' became even more an Australian ambition. Menzies sowed seeds of uncompetitiveness and complacency that were to be harshly exposed as the world economy continued to change.

Out of protectionism came further government intervention to assist those disadvantaged by earlier protectionism. Protectionism made possible arbitrary wage-fixing by squaring the circle in order to raise prices to accommodate the increased costs of labour. Those unable to square this circle — those competing on export markets — were squeezed out. The share of exports in GDP fell despite the subsidies given to farmers 'in compensation'. Our engagement with the global economy and the great growth engine — world trade — declined.

Out of government intervention emerged a lobbying approach to economic salvation. Governments came under increasing pressure to order particular groups' living standards through government spending patterns, monopoly GBEs, monopolies or cartels supported by legislation, subsidies, financial regulations and preferential access to resources granted to favoured groups.

It is not too far-fetched to suggest that the failure of many state governments in the 1980s and the corruption of the political process have their seeds in our tolerance for government intervention in response to pressure from special interests. The easy way to the good life lies in good relations with the government and not in the arduous task of endlessly sharpening a competitive edge.

This 'golden past' laid the framework for our miserable present. A return to its policies would condemn our descendants to confront an even more difficult adjustment problem. History is littered with cases of countries that went into rapid decline relative to their neighbours because they were unwilling or incapable of adapting to the ever-changing demands of international evolution.

The economic-rationalist agenda

Mainstream economics is not *laissez-faire*. Government has an essential economic role in setting in place laws and institutions that define and protect property rights; support competition; protect the environment; and provide efficient growth-promoting infrastructure, a social safety net and a spread in living standards that is acceptable to all Australians.

This sort of government involvement is different to what the anti-rationalist critics have in mind. In particular, laws and processes should be of general applicability and benefit and not tailor-made to suit the special pleading of various groups. If there is a case for a law to be changed, it should be a general case with general applicability.

Protection policy is a case in point where 'tailor-making' became an art form until the Industry Commission (and the Industries Assistance Commission before) and the present Labor government began a serious assault on the privileges being handed out. A favourite argument of protectionists is that if domestic prices fall as protection is removed firms will close and unemployment will rise. At a general level, this cannot be true. For example, if there are 500 000 cars in the car market and consumers spent $4000 less per car, there will be $2 billion worth of extra spending on items other than cars in the economy. This extra $2 billion in spending on, and production of, other items will employ about an extra 70 000 on average earnings — which is about the same as those employed in the whole car industry. But, more than that, the reduction in transport costs feeds through to lower costs in the rest of the economy. This would increase the economy's capacity to export and compete against imports. In the end, more people would have been employed as a result of the higher real incomes (and expenditures) that have been created.

But why will the car industry close down? Some firms may withdraw. (The Button car plan was supposed to bring about a reduction to two to three assemblers anyway.) But will *all* firms close with a 500 000-strong domestic car market at stake and a world market for components and specialised cars? Already, world-class components are being sourced out of Australia for assembly into cars elsewhere. Transplant production is an increasing feature of Japanese manufacturing. World trends are towards global sourcing of bits and pieces, and parts of product lines.

It is true that there are likely to be displaced individuals who encounter employment difficulties because of their skills or location. These difficulties have also to be dealt with by training, relocation and safety-net provisions. But on the whole, more jobs and higher living standards will be created by freer trade than by protectionism. It should be remembered that annual labour turnover in cars and TCF is usually very high. In general, these people have moved on to other jobs.

The interests that *will* suffer from freer trade are the present capital interests in the highly protected sectors, that is, the value of capital that includes a premium for the monopoly 'rent' that protection has accorded them. Once these 'rents' have been removed, some new entrants will emerge at the new, lower-entry prices. They will be able to make normal returns on much reduced outlays for the assets of those who have passed out of business, employing people in the process.

The Fashion Industries Association gave evidence in the Industries Assistance Commission's TCF Inquiry (1985, p. 36) that 'even if the fashion industries received a subsidy equivalent to 100 per cent of direct labour costs, they would still face an average cost disability of 66 per cent against Asian suppliers'. In other words, with the world's cheapest labour — cost zero — the industry still could not compete against Asia on an open market. Clearly, it is not labour that is the problem here, but the capitalisation of the monopoly rents created by protection in the first place.

Competition policy under the Trade Practices Act and similar legislation is also an area where governments needs to maintain vigilance so that private and public producers are constrained by competitive forces from monopoly or cartel behaviour. In this way, producers' interest in efficiency and productivity is sharpened, and more employment at higher incomes is generated in the economy.

Labour-market reform is necessary to permit more effective response to the challenge of more competitive product markets. Enterprise-enhancing arrangements, such as those that focus on collective (or individual) agreements are more likely to incorporate productivity, make jobs more secure and enable higher wages than do uniform arrangements that have been locked into place by law under multi-employer awards.

Financial-market deregulation also means that creditworthy borrowers can always borrow at the market price rather than be rationed out of cross-subsidised funds (allocated to privileged classes of borrowers) into high-priced alternatives for the non-privileged. The financial institutions that failed to take sufficient prudential care during the 1980s are now paying a high price (world-wide, and not just in Australia). It is unlikely that this lesson will be quickly forgotten. Small lenders now get a competitive rate of return on their funds rather than artificially restricted rates. Bank margins have been competed down and banks have had to become more efficient.

Privatisation and corporatisation (within a created framework of competition for these former GBEs) focuses decision-making on costs, efficiency and productivity within these organisations. Privatisation offers an additional advantage over corporatisation by offering competition for management of the assets of these enterprises. The reduction of monopoly rents and the impetus to productivity gains within these key infrastructure enterprises offer large benefits to the economy by increasing its competitiveness as a location for global production.

Environmental policy can be made more effective and less costly through price mechanisms: effluent charges rather than regulations; congestion charges for city traffic at particular times; transferable fish quotas; park administration handed over to environmental groups subject to performance agreements; and so on. Ways of accommodating conflicting interests within a regime of environmental protection are likely to be discovered and put in place more readily under such arrangements.

The economic-rationalist (i.e., microeconomic reform) agenda is necessary in the circumstances in which Australia finds itself in the modern world. It represents a considered, coherent response to the problem of achieving the goals that most Australians have for their society and themselves. These goals have not changed over time but the circumstances confronting Australia have, and experience with some past solutions has found them wanting.

References

Carroll, J. and Manne, R. 1992, *Shutdown: The Failure of Economic Rationalism and How to Rescue Australia*, Text Publishing Co., Melbourne

Gregory, R. G. 1992, *Aspects of Australian Labour Force Living Standards: The Disappointing Decades 1970-1990*, The Copland Oration, Conference of Economists, University of Melbourne, July

Heylen Research Centre 1992, *A Survey of Labour Market Adjustment under the Employment Contracts Act 1991*, prepared for New Zealand Department of Labour Industrial Relations Service, October.

Industries Assistance Commission 1985, *Draft Report on the Textile, Clothing and Footwear Industries*, AGPS, Canberra

Industry Commission 1990, *Strategic Trade Theory: The East Asian Experience*, AGPS, Canberra

McKinsey & Co. 1992, *The Challenge of Leadership: Australia's Emerging High Value-Added Manufacturing Exporters*, presentation to the Australian Manufacturing Council, 15 December

Robert Manne

'Economic Rationalism'

I n the pre-battle manoeuvres to this conference Richard Blandy and Ian Harper — the former in the *Age*, the latter in the *Australian* — fired some opening shots across the bows of the critics of economic rationalism. I do not think I do either an injustice in suggesting that their line of argument was far from complex. Both suggested the following: there exists such a thing as solid, mainstream economic knowledge. The possessors of this knowledge are the current economics professors at Australian universities. This knowledge can be satisfactorily reduced (for purposes of survey) to a series of propositions no more complex than the idea, for example, that free trade is good, protection bad; financial deregulation good, financial regulation bad; and so on. According to Blandy and Harper, the doctrine that Australians have come, rather sourly, to call economic rationalism is nothing other than a compendium of the knowledge currently in the possession of Australian professors of economics. Anyone who might express uncertainty or disagreement with one or another of these pieces of certain knowledge or the policies that are supposedly derived from them is a dispenser of what is inevitably, if not originally, labelled snake oil. To put the matter simply, the defences of economic rationalism, as expressed recently by Professors Blandy and Harper are undisguisedly arguments from authority — no more, no less. We are experts, *ergo* we know. If indeed matters were as simple as Professors Blandy and Harper think they are it is difficult to see what purpose — other than the restoration of morale — could be served by this conference. I would like to suggest that they are not. I shall try to do this by two guerilla incursions concerning issues raised in the newspaper articles of Professors Blandy and Harper.

It seems to me that for the Blandy-Harper view to be accepted one would have to, first of all, accept that economics can genuinely be regarded as a science (if their articles do not imply this let them dissent) — and as science not only in the relatively weak sense (of my discipline, for example, history) of a more or less organised body of knowledge wherein a hundred flowers bloom or wither, but in the strong, positive sense — that is to say of a tight and coherent body of knowledge in which there have been uncovered certain general laws (of the Hempelian kind), governing the phenomena under study and from which, therefore, reliable predictions concerning these phenomena can be made.

This has certainly been the dream of many economists. Here, for example, is the young Milton Friedman in his famous methodological essay of 1953:

> The task [of economics] is to provide a system of generalisations that can be used to make correct predictions about the consequences of any change in circumstances. Its performance is to be judged by the precision, scope, and conformity with experience of the predictions it yields. In short, positive economics is, or can be, an 'objective' science, in precisely the same sense as any of the physical sciences.

Some wiser heads, however, have always known this dream to be unfulfillable, seeing in the peculiar combination of intellectual problems and demands confronting the economist the reason why the discipline remains forever closed to the kind of certainty open to the physical sciences. No-one has put this more eloquently than Keynes:

> Good, or even competent, economists are the rarest of birds. An easy subject, at which very few excel! The paradox finds its explanation, perhaps, in that the master economist must possess a rare *combination* of gifts. He must reach a high standard in several different directions and must combine talents not often found together. He must be a mathematician, historian, statesman, philosopher — in some degree. He must understand symbols and speak in words. He must contemplate the particular in terms of the general, and touch abstract and concrete in the same flight of thought. He must study the present in the light of the past for the purposes of the future. No part of man's nature or his institutions must lie entirely outside his regard. He must be purposeful and disinterested in a simultaneous mood.

Beyond this fundamental recognition of economics as a practice rather than a science, there are also peculiar epistemological difficulties that undermine the positivistic scientific pretensions of economics. One difficulty is the consequence of the assumption that is made in so much economic theorising — the assumption of *ceteris paribus*, roughly speaking, 'this then that, all other things being equal'. But all other things are never equal. In a world where everything is related to everything else causal laws or regularities discoverable in physical sciences remain stubbornly undiscoverable. Or again, as is well known, there is a particular difficulty in the 'scientific' study of human behaviour in the fact that one of the forces influencing human behaviour is scientific self-consciousness, that is, the knowledge in the human actor of the supposed laws affecting his or her behaviour.

These are, in fact, ancient problems that stand stubbornly in the path of the genuinely scientific study of economics. As many here will know far better than I, many eminent economists, beginning with

Wassily Leontief, regard the recent mathematicisation of economics as introducing into the discipline not rigour so much as pseudo-precision. Let me quote him:

> Year after year economic theorists continue to produce scores of mathematical models and explore in great detail their formal properties; and the econometricians fit algebraic function of all possible shapes to essentially the same sets of data without being able to advance, in any perceptible way, a systematic understanding of the structure and operations of a real economic system. How long will researchers working in adjoining fields . . . abstain from expressing serious concern about the state of stable, stationary equilibrium and the splendid isolation in which academic economics now finds itself.

For many who stand outside economics, its practitioners seem either unaware of, or at least unwilling to make clear to their public, the limits of their knowledge. In an essay entitled 'Rationalism in Economics' (a title echoing Michael Oakeshott's 'Rationalism in Politics') the American neo-conservative sceptic, Irving Kristol, captured this dimension rather well:

> There can be little doubt that economics is on its way to becoming a much more modest science and will experience the loss of its grandiose scientific pretensions. . . . Those pretensions accumulated under the influence of a spirit of rationalism — a belief that a comprehensive understanding of all human affairs (i.e. of ourselves) can be achieved through the same methods, and with the same degree of success, as our understanding of physical processes in nature. . . . If one wishes to be theological about it, one might say that rationalism in the social sciences is a case of *hubris* or *superbia*, of affliction with the sin of pride.

Indeed how little certainty there is in the economics profession — except in its pronouncements to the lay public — is symbolised for me in the fact that members of the contemporary Australian economics mandarinate are presently quite deeply divided over so essential and critical a problem as whether the current level of Australia's public and private foreign debt is or is not a matter of national alarm.

Let me move one step down the ladder of generality to comment on Blandy's second preliminary contribution to this debate, in the *Age* of 3 February. This article attempted to demonstrate that the recent economic successes of the Asian tigers represented a triumphant vindication of the doctrines of economic rationalism. Blandy based his entire analysis here on what he called 'the most comprehensive Australian analysis' of this success. As it turns out this comprehensive study is one conducted in 1990 by the Industry Commission. Blandy does not explain why he chose as authority only one study. There is, after all, vast and excellent scholarship on the question of industry policy in the rise of East-Asian economies — Chalmers Johnson and Daniel Okimoto on Japan; Robert Wade and Alice Amsden on Taiwan; Richard Luedde-Neurath on South Korea; Gary Rodan on Singapore — which arrives at very different conclusions from those presented, quite uncritically, by Blandy to the *Age* readership. Nor does Blandy explain why he chooses as his one authoritative source a study produced by the Industry Commission, a bureaucratic office that even its keenest defenders would acknowledge as militantly rationalist in persuasion. It is not, to put it mildly, likely that the Industry Commission would use a study of the Asian tigers to test rather than to confirm its pre-existing prejudices.

Research and ye shall find! According to Blandy, the Industry Commission's study concluded *inter alia* that the success of the Asian tigers was based on 'a winding back in import protection and export subsidy measures early on in their growth strategy in favour of a policy of general liberalisation'. As it happened, an article by Paul Kennedy, a Yale history professor, appeared in the *New York Review of Books* the same week Blandy's article appeared in the *Age*. Kennedy reached a somewhat different balance on the question of the East-Asian miracle: 'While entrepreneurship and private property are encouraged, the 'tigers' never followed a *laissez-faire* model. Industries targeted for growth were given a variety of supports — export subsidies, training grants, tariff protection from foreign competition' and so on. For those who know the literature, this is a far less idiosyncratic description than the one favoured by Blandy.

Moreover, those who are familiar with the arguments will not be surprised that Blandy drew from his one-sided account of the rise of the tigers a conventional economic rationalist moral: industry policy does not work. They may, however, be surprised to discover that Blandy supports his characterisation of all industry-policy advocacy as snake oilery by appealing to the authority of the scholar he calls the originator of strategic trade theory, Paul Krugman. Presumably Blandy is unaware that Krugman has recently announced his conversion to the position of what he calls a 'cautious activist' in industry policy — or, to be precise, of $10 billion worth of subsidies for selected industries. This, I believe, is what the rationalists disparage as 'picking winners'. This example may help explain why some of us are resistant to the idea of deferring to the collective opinions of Australian professors of economics.

Let me summarise. I see no evidence that economics as a discipline has yet attained, or indeed can ever attain, even that degree of certainty available to the physical or biological sciences. As Keynes understood, economics is an extraordinarily difficult practice requiring from its practitioners a variety of talents only rarely combined in a single individual. I see no evidence, moreover, that economists as a professional caste are less prone to being influenced by swings in fashion or the pressure to conform than other university disciplines. On the other hand, as Irving Kristol's comment implies, of all the social sciences, economics seems the last to abandon the nineteenth-century dream of being able to arrive at something like the coherence and certainty of the physical sciences. Indeed, in one crucial respect, contemporary economists are more ambitious than scientists. A nuclear physicist or engineer may feel able to advise on how to build a nuclear power plant but will not generally believe that only nuclear physicists are able to debate usefully on whether or not the plant should be built. Economists, however, go further. To judge, at least, by the articles appearing recently in the press, Australian professors of economics and their colleagues in the press, bureaucracy and the think-tanks claim to belong to the only group that can participate legitimately in the debate about the economic future of the country. If economists generally know as much as they claim to, the effective removal of the citizens from the debate about the future of their country would merely be an awkward paradox of contemporary democracy. If, however, they know less than they claim to know, the bid to exercise an effective monopoly over economic debate — and to characterise all the religious leaders or business people or the dreaded 'sociologists' or concerned citizens, who bring different perspectives to the discussion, as dispensers of snake oil — looks to me suspiciously like an abuse of position.

John Freebairn

Economic Rationalism?: Economic Policies for the 1990s

My focus will be on the subtitle of this conference, 'Economic Policies for the 1990s'. What are the main causes of the economic malaise of the 1990s, and what policies and strategies should be adopted to restore full employment, higher living standards, reasonable distributions of opportunities and outcomes and so forth? Clearly, the economics profession and others have many intriguing questions in need of articulate answers.

Over the last two years a number of writers, generally from disciplines other than economics, have attacked economic orthodoxy under the strange title of 'economic rationalism' as the cause of our current malaise. These include Pusey (1991), Carroll and Manne (1992) and Ventila, Phillimore and Newman (1992). Reviews of these studies by economists such as Argy (1992), Blandy (1992), Valentine (1992) and Snape (1993) have been critical. What do the critics mean by 'economic rationalism', have they convincingly deciphered the prime causes of Australia's recent poor economic performance, and do their assertions constructively contribute to improving future policies?

Economic performance

After a promising recovery from the 1982/83 recession, the late 1980s and the 1990s have witnessed a dismal economic performance in Australia. Some of the adverse indicators include:
- high unemployment, especially long-term unemployment and youth unemployment
- high levels of bankruptcy and business closures
- continuing large current-account deficits and build-up of overseas debt, although not all economists regard this as a major problem *per se*
- apparent redistribution away from the middle class to the rich, while at the same time better support for the bottom 20 per cent as a result of higher pension and benefit rates

Australia has not been alone in experiencing bad economic outcomes in the 1990s, although we did start earlier and in general have fallen more spectacularly than any other mixed economy. All the Anglo-Saxon countries have encountered increased unemployment, business failures, shortfalls in saving, and less equal distributions of wealth and income. But these patterns also appeared for Japan and most of Continental Europe, including Germany and Scandinavia. By contrast, the Asian tigers and some Latin-American countries have prospered during the last five years or so. Among the centrally planned economies, the collapse of the former USSR and East-European economies might be pitted against the economic advances of mainland China, especially the Special Economic Zones. For the main part, economic performance in the Himalayan subcontinent and Africa has been poor.

It is difficult to draw strong conclusions about the relative merits of policy options from these cross-country comparisons because of the large number of different factors affecting economic performance.

The critics

Pusey, Manne and others have asserted that economic rationalism is the cause of Australia's current economic difficulties. They have gone on to say that a return to the centralised Australian institutions of the 1950s and 1960s is the road to salvation for the 1990s.

Dimensions of the debate

The first point I want to make is that the term 'economic rationalism' is a nonsense term which is unhelpful and ought to be deleted from the debate. Nowhere is a coherent definition or description of the term given. The closest we have to a definition is Carroll and Manne's (1992, p. 1) 'radical free-market economics'. Presumably Pusey, Manne and colleagues should be labelled 'economic irrationalists'.

Economists attempt to describe what goes on in economies and develop policies through models that are directed at improving performance. Such models are simplified abstractions of a very complex reality, and of an evolving reality. They are based on assumptions and logic. The relevant debate, and a debate that has been ongoing in the profession over the decades and centuries, should be about the appropriateness or otherwise of the models used. In my view, that is where the current debate, and this conference, should be pitched. No economist I know honestly believes he or she has the 'right' model and all the answers. If we were to focus our energies into critical evaluation of the assumptions, analytical methods and the results generated by models as descriptions of reality, then we could move to a better understanding of what has gone wrong, what the options and opportunities to improve matters are, and how to improve economic performance.

I have struggled to comprehend what Pusey, Manne and friends are about, on one level they seem to be especially critical of the institutional mechanisms or processes that have been favoured by Australian political parties over the 1980s and early 1990s. Let me canvass some of these issues.

Reliance on markets

Generally the irrationalists are critical of the use of markets, especially market prices, in the allocation of national resources. At the same time they argue for greater reliance on centralised institutions that directly determine quantities. They are against financial deregulation, the use of interest rates in monetary policy and a free-floating currency; and are in favour of fixed interest rates, exchange rates, and a centralised allocation of funds for particular investments. They are also in favour of the highly centralised Accord arrangement for labour markets but against decentralised enterprise bargaining; they are in favour of an active interventionist industry policy; and against the opening-up of health and education to market forces, preferring government direction via quantities.

The irrationalists have built a number of straw-man arguments here. First, economists have a diverse set of views on these same topics. For example, there is a wide range of views about the relative merits of the Accord in influencing labour-market outcomes. In the context of the education of economists, this diversity of views is found within particular units taught at university, and certainly across units taught to students in any particular degree programme. Secondly, economists have always argued for quite extensive roles for government if economies are to perform effectively. Much of conventional textbook material is devoted to government roles in defining and monitoring property rights, to overcoming market failures associated with public goods, externalities, natural monopoly, and non-competitive behaviour, to redistribution, and to achieving greater macroeconomic stability. Thirdly, and a point skated over by the irrationalists, economists have been concerned with political failure. The purpose of the policy debate is to find a balance between the realistic options of market failure and political failure.

Recent experience has highlighted some areas of market outcomes that economists are only beginning to grapple with. These include the long-standing problem of policy advice in a second-best world of existing distortions, the issue of speculative behaviour, including speculative bubbles in asset and currency markets, the implications of asymmetries of information between buyers and sellers, and how to incorporate and model expectations in intertemporal decision situations. The critics have not honed in on these challenges, yet many economists have done so.

Industry policy

Most in the irrationalist school are highly critical of reductions in tariffs and other forms of industry assistance. Further, they prefer quotas and other quantitative restrictions to tariffs and price supports. Many look fondly on corporatist industry schemes, often uncritically suggesting that Japan's MITI was both the key to Japan's success and the magic potion for Australia's future. For some, there is a manufacturing industry fundamentalist streak reminiscent of discredited agricultural fundamentalism.

I find a lack of analysis and supporting evidence in Pusey, Manne and others against current industry policy. They simply assert that current industry policy has caused unemployment and current-account deficits. There is almost complete disregard of second-round effects on other industries and prices. For example, lower tariffs mean cheaper prices for inputs used by other industries and in turn, a stimulus to their profitability, output and employment. This translates into lower prices for household purchases and an increase in hosehold's real expenditure. Also, the first-round increase in imports induces a currency depreciation which in turn stimulates exports and import-competing industries. A large body of economic analysis shows that the second-round effects of reductions in tariffs and other forms of assistance to specific industries approximately offset the first-round effects on aggregate employment, the current account and the capital account. Cross-country comparisons and comparisons over time provide mixed results, with many contradicting the assertions in Pusey, and in Carroll and Manne.

This is not to say that the economic models are beyond criticism. No doubt, some may think that the neoclassical models assume too much flexibility and ease of substitution, costs of change are higher than modelled, and so on. But, at the same time, the implicit assumption of zero flexibility in the irrationalists' first-round effects model is also unrealistic.

The level playing-field argument is misused by the irrationalists. Economists agree that high levels of protection in northern-hemisphere markets against Australian primary products (and some manufactured and services exports) is detrimental to Australia, and that we would gain much from a successful outcome of the Uruguay Round. Further, many see government spending on back-up research and lobbying to reduce overseas protection against our exports as a good national investment. But if our trading partners persist with their distortionary industry policies in the long term, world prices reflect the real costs and benefits facing Australian exporters and importers. In the context of a long-run full-employment situation it is in Australia's own selfish interests to operate an internal level playing-field (subject to second-best considerations). That is, if the world price of butter and aeroplanes is zero, then Australia increases its wellbeing by accepting the free butter and planes as gifts and by shifting its resources to other activities. That clearly is not fun for the dairy and aerospace industries, but the reallocated labour, capital and other resources would add more value for Australia producing, say, education and widgets valued at $1 or more. The policy challenge is to facilitate the movement of people, capital and other resources from less to more productive activities.

Redistribution

Pusey sets up a straw-man argument about economists' lack of concern about distribution, an absence of a certain morality, and a lack of feeling or appreciation for history. While economics as a discipline is limited in what it can contribute to articulating social views about a 'fair' distribution, economic models do reveal the effects of different policy options on distribution, and much analysis is directed to distributional assessments.

Where the irrationalists and most economists differ is in their arguments about the preferred choice of instruments used to achieve a prespecified redistribution. In particular, economists consider behavioural responses to changes in incentives associated with redistribution, whereas irrationalists such as Pusey and Manne implicitly ignore such second-round effects.

Pusey and colleagues are attracted to government regulation of factor markets and product markets to achieve redistribution. For example, Accord-type labour markets are required to enforce minimum wages with little concern that such action would increase unemployment of the unskilled. Interest-rate ceilings are favoured to keep housing and other investment costs down with no consideration for the costs of queuing and other forms of non-price rationing; government ownership of transport, electricity, communications, and so on is favoured to enforce community service obligations via cross-subsidies and/or direct government subsidies with no consideration of the economic costs of the associated misallocation of scarce resources.

Many economists, but not all economists, would argue for more direct income support to meet redistributional goals via the social-security and income-tax systems. Such redistribution also has some allocative effects with associated dead-weight efficiency costs. The challenge for the future is not so much for one extreme or the other, but for a reasoned analysis of the relative efficiency, distributional and other properties of the different instruments for achieving the social goal of an equitable distribution. A subtle point, but nevertheless an important one, made by Parish (1992), among others, is that the redistributional effects of existing regulations are already capitalised into asset prices. Proposals for policy change should recognise this starting position when assessing redistributional effects, rather than use the free-market outcome as the starting point.

Macroeconomic policy

Generally speaking, the irrationalists are more attracted to simplistic fiscal pump-priming, and also to fine-tuning macroeconomic policy to restore full employment than are most economists. This is not to say that economists see no merit in some fiscal stimulus in the context of the present recession as indicated in Anderson and Blandy's (1992) recent survey of economics professors.

An important distinction between economists and Pusey and Manne is that the former see greater second-round effects than the latter with stimulatory macroeconomic policies. At the extreme, Ricardian equivalence would see 100 per cent crowding out, although the model has failed most econometric testing. An important challenge for the current policy debate is to gain a greater understanding of the interrelationships between fiscal expansion, and of different forms of fiscal expansion, on private investment, net exports, consumption and ultimately, on employment.

We need a greater understanding of the medium- and longer-term linkages between fiscal expansion and Australia's perceived problem of a net savings deficit. The contemporary twin-deficits link was argued to hold only partially at an ANU conference held in 1991. What about a longer-term perspective? While Pusey and colleagues have not raised these types of modelling issues, it seems to me that this is another example of the type of rethinking the profession should follow.

As has been the case in the past, economists do not have all the answers, we have our disagreements, and we are looking to improve our game. In my biased view, Pusey, Manne and other irrationalists have done little to help the debate. Progress will be made not by

ideology and sloganeering, but by critical assessment of models and
thorough analysis. The general failure of the critics to incorporate
second-round effects in their arguments has left them more with
assertions than logical criticism that can lay the foundations for
revamping the Australian economy and appropriate assessments of
how it can recover from the mess.

References

Anderson, M. and Blandy, R. 1992, 'What Australian Economics Professions
    Think', *Australian Economic Review*, vol. 4, pp. 41-50
Argy, F. 1992, 'Review of Pusey', *Economic Papers*, vol. 11, no. 1, pp. 83-90
Blandy, R. 1992, 'Multiple Schizophrenia: Economic Rationalism and Its
    Critics', *Australian Quarterly*, vol. 64, no. 1, pp. 101-6
Carroll, J. and Manne, R. 1992, *Shutdown: The Failure of Economic Ration-
    alism and How to Rescue Australia*, Text Publishing Co., Melbourne
Parish, R. 1992, 'Economic Rationalism', mimeo, Monash University
Pusey, M. 1991, *Economic Rationalism in Canberra*, Cambridge University
    Press, Sydney
Snape, R. 1993, 'Don't Debate: Shout', policy, forthcoming
Valentine, T. 1992, 'Reply — Pusey on Economic Policy', *Economic Papers*,
    vol. 16, no. 4, pp. 87-90
Ventila, P., Phillimore, J. and Newman, P. 1992, *Markets, Morale and
    Manifestations*, Institute for Science and Technology Policy, Murdoch
    University

Anne O. Krueger

The Training of Economists

When it comes to analysis for policy purposes, economists are a lot like doctors: there is a fair amount that they know (or know how to find out), but there are also many questions that remain the subject of further research. Moreover, economists — again like doctors — are better equipped to identify serious mistakes than to formulate precise optimal policies. Carrying the analogy still further, it is often difficult to convince non-specialists that there is evidence that informs issues and that the 'obvious' may in fact be wrong.

This last point is worth illustrating. In the early 1970s the American Congress legislated stricter standards for auto emissions on new cars in order to improve air quality. The initial result, however, was the opposite as the increase in car prices induced people to maintain their older cars for longer periods and actually increased the average age of the cars in the US stock. The net effect of even older cars more than offset the reduced emissions from newer cars.

Examples such as this are frequently used in economics and are called the general equilibrium effects of policies. Despite being powerful, their effects are often ignored. This is the case with protection; everyone can see the industries they believe will be hurt if it is removed but few can see the many large potential beneficiaries, including new factories and jobs that would appear (in the absence of protection). It is often difficult to find evidence to convince non-economists of these powerful, but indirect effects. The same has been true in medicine; for example, it was well over a quarter century after European doctors had accepted evidence that washing hands before touching patients would cut mortality before that evidence became accepted in America.

What graduate training in economics has to offer is a way of approaching and analysing problems; marshalling evidence in the context of a general equilibrium framework. In policy analysis, a starting point must be to analyse why people behave as they do (that is, what incentives, economic or otherwise, they are responding to). Most policy analysis then proceeds to analyse how various changes in the incentive structure would alter peoples' responses. For many problems, the question involves the alternative uses for resources, and cost-benefit analysis must be applied to alternatives.

These fairly powerful tools do not provide perfect answers, but they do help in avoiding big mistakes. Graduate training, most policy economists believe, should both provide young economists with the tools of analysis for these, and other, problems, and equip them with the capability for applying the tools appropriately.

In part because well-applied economic analysis can be so useful, some observers in the early 1980s became increasingly uneasy as the training of graduate economics students in the US seemed to shift its emphasis more and more towards training in tools, without appearing to provide students with the necessary base for knowing when and how to apply them. The National Science Foundation held a two-day conference on the training of economists, and several American foundations joined the National Science Foundation to finance an evaluation of graduate training in economics. In response, the American Economic Association appointed a Commission to consider graduate economic training and present a report (which was in no way to represent the views of the American Economic Association) with respect to that training.

This report has been published in the *Journal of Economic Literature* [1] and need not be repeated here. During the course of discussions among Commission members, I think it is fair to say that all of us learned and changed our perspectives a good deal. Here I want to focus on some of the ways in which my perceptions changed.

My starting point for the analysis of graduate training is that good economics, and good economic analysis, can inform policy discussions in ways that can permit outcomes that are preferred by all relative to what can happen in the absence of such analysis. The auctioning of taxis or import licenses is, for example, in almost all circumstances preferable to bureaucratic allocation. Anticipation of what can go wrong with bureaucratic allocation should be something that any well-trained economist can provide. The tools of statistics and econometrics can be used to provide better estimates of the revenue effects of alternative taxes, of behavioral responses to various government policies, and a host of other issues. Well-trained economists should know how to analyse the incentives arising from any government action, and to identify the sorts of evidence that will shed light on the consequences of such actions.

The sort of good economics I am describing can best be regarded as problem-solving. Graduate training should consist, at least in part, of providing economists with an adequate understanding of responses to incentives, the macroeconomic framework, and tools of analysis. By adequate I mean a knowledge of 'what is out there' that may be useful, as well as enough in-depth experience, so that Ph.D. economists can, within their chosen area of concentration, be confronted with a problem and know enough to look up what they need to know and use the appropriate tools for analysis.

This definition leaves some ambiguities. First, there is a question as to 'how much' needs to be learned by way of tools, as opposed to what can be looked up. Secondly, there is a question as to the role of advanced training in specialities such as mathematical economics, and whether those who will contribute significantly to advancing knowledge in such fields should also receive the same training. Thirdly, there is a serious question as to what the 'common core' of economics that all Ph.D. economists should have access to. Almost all would agree that a thorough understanding of markets and microeconomic theory is important, and that basic tools of statistical analysis (econometrics) should be taught at a sufficiently advanced level so that economists can evaluate the appropriateness of statistical evidence. Beyond that, there is a question of how much institutional knowledge should be imparted at the graduate-school level, how much advanced theory should be taught, and the balance between breadth and depth in teaching. There is, however, little doubt that the common core in economics is substantial and powerful.

One or two members of the Commission might disagree somewhat with what I have just said. They would argue that the Ph.D. is a research degree, and that training of the sort I have just described is more appropriate for applied masters programmes or even undergraduate economics. However, in the course of the Commission's deliberations, some interesting insights emerged.

Before discussing ways in which the Commission felt graduate education should be improved, it should be emphasised that Commission members generally agreed that economics was not in terrible shape. While it was recognised that there was room for improvement, that scope was from a good base. Interestingly, we did not find any historical precedents in any other disciplines for the type of 'professional self-examination' that we undertook.

Turning, then, to the view of the Commission members, first, and importantly, after only brief discussions the Commission unanimously concluded that the problem (or problems) lie not in the teaching of the tools of economics, but rather with teaching the relevance of those tools to real-world economic problems. In terms of this conference, that conclusion is important for two reasons. On the one hand, economists better trained in using their tools can improve policy analysis, by itself an important goal. But on the other hand, economists better trained in applying their tools to real-world problems can contribute more effectively to public discussion of economic problems, and as such influence ideas. Since ideas are so important in public discussions of policy issues, an improved contribution by economists in conveying their insights will help improve policy formulation and execution for the good of all. Perhaps some of the Australian debate over economic policy would be more focused in the areas where there can be legitimate disagreements if economists were more successful in linking their research to the policy issues!

When the Commission began its deliberations, many thought the critical question was whether there was 'too much' or 'too little' mathematics required for economists in the graduate programme. We quickly realised, however, that it was the wrong question. The real question was whether the mathematics used was linked to real-world issues such that those acquiring the 'high-tech' tools of economics understand where the tools apply and how they may be used to shed light on important issues. The difference between good and not-so-good papers in economics more often lies in the relevance of the analysis to the problem addressed than it does in the technical accuracy of the tools.

Related to this is the problem that understanding the linkages is not easy, and there is no simple 'formula' for teaching it. For students to see markets in operation is something that comes with practice and not from reading a few pages. In that regard, the Commission members felt that there was little they could recommend other than that educators spent more time problem-solving with the tools they are teaching.

Another contributing factor to the emphasis on tools concerns the 'signalling' that economists do to graduate students in their admissions policies to graduate school. As members of the Commission deliberated, they began to focus on ways in which we signal that tools are important and downgraded institutional knowledge on application. We convinced ourselves of this by recognising that in most American graduate schools, if there were two top undergraduate students applying, one with honours in economics but little mathematics training, the other in mathematics with no economics training, the treatment would be highly asymmetric. The potential graduate student with no economics would almost certainly be admitted to graduate school with no remedial requirements. By contrast, the student with the economics background is likely to be informed that remedial work in mathematics be undertaken before commencing graduate school.

Most of us would agree with the need for remedial mathematics. But in graduate school, the teaching of institutions and economic history is largely omitted on the grounds that it is taught at undergraduate level. And while the best students may learn the requisite institutional background through their own initiative, the asymmetric admissions policy surely runs the risk that some graduates are deficient in understanding the linkages of tools to real-world problems because they are blissfully ignorant of all that happens in the real world.

Before turning to Commission suggestions for improvement, one additional facet of the apparent problem requires comment. That is, slightly more than half of all new economics Ph.D.s in the US start out in academia; the remainder take jobs in industry, government, non-profit organisations, and elsewhere. Many of those taking academic jobs are placed at undergraduate institutions.

For those not going to major research universities, the need is for economists who are skilled at applications. Yet economists receive the same training, regardless of whether they are talented and motivated to undertake frontier state-of-the-art research at major universities, whether they will teach bright undergraduates, or whether they will become economists in industry or government. There was some speculation and sentiment on the part of Commission members that such problems did not greatly pertain to those who would continue at research universities, but was much more important for those destined for undergraduate teaching and non-academic posts. There was also speculation that what may be happening is that weaker graduate students in core theory courses take jobs at lesser-ranked institutions, where they then teach from their lecture notes that are inappropriate in their new environment and do not address the needs of bright undergraduates. Again, the issue of linkages is critical: what is needed for good undergraduate education for those not planning to become research economists is an understanding of economists' ways of analysing real-world issues; if this is a weakness in teaching at major graduate schools, the real losers may be the undergraduates who then learn (or don't learn) economics from people whose ability to handle linkages is weak.

The Commission had no real answers to the problem of 'economic literacy', but did make a number of suggestions.[2] It was thought that the combination of these possible changes might, in total, make a significant difference. A first recommendation was that entering graduate students without undergraduate economics be assigned remedial courses in parallel with remedial mathematics requirements. It was also urged that there be more attention to applications of theory in the core theory courses in the first year of graduate work. While it was recognised that core courses must teach theory, it was urged that departments view core courses as 'public goods', and include economists from applied fields (such as labour economics, industrial organisation, or international trade) in the group overseeing the first-year theory courses, rather than leaving those courses entirely in the hands of theorists. This would help ensure that students would be able to apply the theory they had mastered.

In this regard, there was recognition that educators teaching core courses would have to make decisions as to the right trade-off between teaching a few tools, or theories, in depth and covering the broader range of topics in the field. However, it was felt that educators should consider themselves under some obligation to inform students as to 'what is out there' so that young economists would know where to look and what materials to consult when they were confronted with applied problems.

There were some members of the Commission who felt strongly that additional graduate work in economic history might be useful in furthering students' abilities to link the theory they were learning with real-world issues. The Commission stopped short of recommending that economic history be a requirement, though it did warrant some consideration.

In general, it was felt that more applications, not only in core courses but also in applied fields, would be helpful in improving the ability of graduate economists to carry out applied work. This would include assigning term papers to students, especially to those in applied courses.

Another major concern that arose from examining the evidence collected from individual degree-granting departments was the time lapses between completion of coursework — typically the first part of the Ph.D. programme — and the development of a workable thesis topic, usually the second half of the Ph.D. programme. In part, there was a suspicion that the failure to teach linkages might account for the very long lags — apparently often more than a year — that elapsed in this crucial transition. The lack of term papers was also thought responsible for these delays.

Commissioners believed that the increased emphasis on application in course work might help reduce the painful transition from course work to dissertation. In addition, they urged more focus on thesis-writing workshops, and student presentations at early stages in those workshops. A variety of innovations that were thought successful in various graduate departments were listed, although no specific ones were recommended.

These were the major areas where the Commission felt it could recommend improvements. There were, however, a number of interesting questions that could not readily be answered. The available evidence was simply inadequate to provide insights into those important questions. For example, an effort was made to obtain data on those beginning work for the Ph.D. but dropping out, but little information was available. An effort was also made to ascertain faculty, and current and past graduate students' satisfaction with the Ph.D. programme in economics. Interestingly, both faculty and past and present graduate students generally indicated strong satisfaction with the programme. Although many thought changes could usefully be made, it was not clear that those suggesting changes would all have made them in the same direction, and there was surprisingly little difference between faculty and graduate student attitudes.

There were also questions raised about the emergence of public-policy programmes, programmes in agricultural economics departments, business schools, and elsewhere that 'compete' with economics teaching. To some degree, this is healthy competition, and not a source of concern. Indeed, there may even be an increased demand for Ph.D. economists to staff these programmes. However, some programmes (such as business schools) are increasingly training their own Ph.D. graduates to teach economics. This leads to concern that teaching of economics in other parts of universities may be so applied that students are not given adequate understanding of how markets function; the emphasis could become too institutional and descriptive.

One final phenomenon which was noted and analysed, but about which the Commission had little to recommend, concerned the very large fraction of foreign students from non-English speaking countries in Ph.D. programmes. Almost half the places in American graduate programmes in economics now are taken by these foreign students who have prevented overall enrollments in Ph.D. economics programmes in the US from dropping as much as in many other fields. This seemed to indicate a 'comparative advantage' for American universities in training economists, although questions were raised as to the institutional background of foreign students, and also of the extent to which their discomfort with English might discourage professors from assigning term papers.

Overall, the Commission results suggested considerable satisfaction with graduate education in economics, combined with recognition that there was scope for improvement. For me, one of the most interesting results of the Commission exercise was to discover how little we understand about the ways in which knowledge is imparted, and how the next generation of economists is 'acculturated'. Since that generation is important for advancing the frontiers of knowledge, providing economic analysis for policy choices, and for improving public understanding, it raises a large number of questions for which additional research is needed.

Notes

1 Krueger et al. (1991). See also Hansen et al. (1991) and Kasper et al. (1991). The Hansen article provides a great deal of background data on graduate education, collected by the Commission staff. The Kasper article focuses on perceptions of graduate education by a group of college professors at top undergraduate programmes in the US.
2 The Commission quite properly could do nothing other than write a report. Neither it nor the American Economic Association has any authority over the content of the graduate curriculum in individual economics departments. Each department is responsible for its own graduate programme, although one of the interesting questions that arose from Commission deliberations was why there was not more product differentiation between departments.

References

Hansen, W. Lee et al. 1991, 'The Education and Training of Economics Doctorates', *Journal of Economic Literature*, vol. 29, no. 3, September, pp. 1054-87
Kasper, Hirschel et al. 1991, 'The Education of Economists', *Journal of Economic Literature*, vol. 29, no. 3, September, pp. 1088-109
Krueger, Anne O. et al. 1991, 'Report of the Commission on Graduate Education in Economics', *Journal of Economic Literature*, vol. 29, no. 3, September, pp. 1035-953

Michael Keating

The Influence of Economists

Practical men, who believe themselves to be quite exempt from any intellectual influences, are usually the slaves of some defunct economist. (Keynes 1936)

I t makes little sense to consider the influence of economists separately from an assessment of economics and its strengths and weaknesses. For this reason, the first part of this essay summarises economic advisers' understanding of the analytical foundations of economics, and consequently its potential for advancing policy. In the second part, there is some assessment of the nature of the advice given and its influence on policy, focusing particularly on the role of official advisers.

What is economics?

The textbook definition of economics typically describes it as the study of the allocation of scarce means among alternative ends. As such, economics relates to an aspect of human behaviour and does not purport to cover all aspects. If, however, the essence of government is to choose, then, (following Keynes) economics does provide an apparatus of mind or a technique of thinking that is especially useful to government.

This is not to say that all policy decisions have a price tag. But many do, and even those that do not can often be improved by the economist's natural insistence on examining the most fundamental contribution economics has to make to policy advising, being relevant to many day-to-day situations.

Most of the above would, I hope, be generally accepted by both economists and non-economists; especially the need to consider the opportunity cost when assessing most policy issues. Where I think economists and their critics tend to part company is when we turn to consider means; in particular the importance that economists attach to markets as the means for allocating scarce resources among alternative ends. Economists differ regarding the efficiency of particular markets and the appropriate response to inefficiency, including the desirability of government intervention. But the non-economist's concerns about 'market-based' (market-imposed?) solutions is frequently more fundamental. It goes to the very heart of what economics has to contribute to public policy and as such deserves major consideration in its own right.

What can economics contribute to policy?

The significance of economic behaviour

At least since Adam Smith, a great deal of economics has rested on a number of postulates that attempt to describe the characteristics of 'economic man'. As Blaug has pointed out, these postulates were derived from

> introspection or the casual observation of one's neighbours and in that sense constituted a priori truths, known, so to speak, in advance of experience; a purely deductive process led from premises to implications, but implications were true a posteriori only in the absence of disturbing causes. (1980, p. 55)

As such, 'economic man' is essentially an abstraction where it is assumed that for the questions under consideration, the possibility of other relevant factors (or 'disturbing causes') can safely be ignored. Moreover, these a priori truths defy validation. Modern economists have preferred not to put these truths to the test directly. Rather, they test their applications by making predictions. The usefulness of their assumptions is determined by the supporting theories of economic behaviour, and the ability of those theories in making predictions. The soundness of those predictions (or otherwise) justifies the simplification involved in ignoring other possible 'disturbing' (economic and non-economic) factors.

At the same time, 'in economics, as in the other sciences, theories are overthrown by better theories, not simply by contradictory facts' (Blaug 1985, p. 703). Certainly, prediction without theory is generally not considered to be a sufficient guide to policy, and in most situations governments would be unwilling to determine policy without some logical explanation for the predicted outcome.

While the foundations of economic analysis depend upon an abstraction regarding the nature of 'economic man', this is not in itself a criticism of the application of economics to public policy. Other major areas of public policy, such as the nature and desirability of freedom, justice and equality similarly proceed from a logical base founded upon introspection and observation regarding the nature of one's fellow human. Unlike economics, however, no-one suggests that discussion of these important policy issues is flawed because of the impossibility of scientifically validating the underlying assumptions about human nature.

What is different about economics as a source of policy advice is not so much the nature of the underlying assumptions but the fact that economists are prepared to test the theories based on those assumptions by their ability to predict. The principal assumptions of economics: that 'economic man' seeks to maximise satisfaction and orders his preferences while receiving diminishing marginal utility from additional consumption of any particular good; that a firm faces diminishing returns at a given state of technology and an infinitely elastic labour supply at a given wage rate; and so on, are used to derive the demand and supply curves that underpin so much economic analysis. These curves are sometimes referred to as the 'laws' of supply and demand, reflecting their very high statistical corroboration and the extent to which the supporting theory allows the curves to be considered as 'causal laws' (Blaug 1980, p. 162).

However, because of the possibility of disturbing causes, all economic predictions are in principal probabilistic and not definitive. As Blaug has commented, 'If economics could conclusively test the implications of its theorems, no more would be heard about the lack of realism of its assumptions' (1985, p. 703). On the other hand, and unlike discussions of other public-policy issues including freedom, justice and equality, theories of economic behaviour and their underpinning assumptions do not imply any particular moral values, or that people have no other values. Rather, the usefulness of economic behaviour depends upon their previous experience as robust predictors of an important aspect of human behaviour.

Thus, for many microeconomic issues including industry policy, the pricing of a variety of publicly provided services (water, airports, etc.), and the analysis of labour markets, partial-equilibrium analysis allows us to predict with considerable confidence the general tendency of the response to a proposed policy change. Furthermore, the analytical foundations of this type of analysis are typically not very controversial, and to a significant extent are accepted by non-economists as well as economists. For example, the typical industry lobby firmly expects that an increase in assistance will reduce the price and increase demand for the product, just as it sometimes acknowledges the possibility of a supply response. Similarly welfare groups, while sometimes denying that the high level of minimum wages is responsible for unemployment among the affected groups, will nevertheless argue for wage subsidies that achieve their intended effect by reducing the relative price of employing the targeted groups.

Partial-equilibrium analysis has greater difficulty in assisting policy when it goes beyond predictions of a tendency and attempts to quantify the extent of the policy response. Take the recent case of the wool market; without precise knowledge of the elasticities of supply and demand and the influence of the stockpile, economists were not able to predict with any confidence at what level the market-clearing price would finally settle. Indeed, it is the very uncertainty surrounding such an exercise that leads many economists to reject the attempt and choose an auction system to the alternative of governments and their advisers 'second guessing' the market.

But perhaps the most important criticism of this type of partial-equilibrium analysis, mostly by economists rather than non-economists, is the assumption of *ceteris paribus*. It is economists, particularly those in the Industry Commission and its forerunners, who have pointed out that assistance to one industry will invariably increase the costs to other industries. Consequently partial equilibrium analysis does not allow the determination of the eventual impact on aggregate employment from industry-assistance programmes.

Macroeconomics and the significance of economic identities

Confidence in economic predictions declines as we move from microeconomic analysis of individual markets to macroeconomic analysis. Such analysis depends not only upon summing the behaviour of all individuals to establish a number of aggregate behavioural relationships, but reliance on *ceteris paribus* becomes much less appropriate and interrelationships, much more important.[1] The problems with macroanalysis are widely recognised, but less attention seems to have been paid to the significance of the identities that perform the valuable role of stabilising the key interrelationships by closing the macroeconomic system.

At the outset, it is important to recognise that a relationship that essentially rests upon an identity or tautology has both strengths and weaknesses as a basis for policy advice. On the one hand, if two factors or variables are by definition equal, then logically any attempt to vary one will inevitably have consequences for the other. Clearly this is both a simple and convincing way to derive and present a policy conclusion. On the other hand, an identity does not of itself establish the direction of causality between the variables concerned; something that has been too superficially treated in much economic policy advice.

In this context it is instructive to consider the role of monetarism and its influence on policy advice. Monetarism took as its starting point the identity $MV \equiv PT$, and provides perhaps the best known example of the use of an identity to underpin policy advice. From the outset, it was recognised that there was a need to establish specifically the direction of causality and the transmission mechanism. Other problems were the stability of the velocity of circulation (V) and consequently the stability of the demand curve for money, and what determined the split between P and T resulting from any monetary stimulus. In response to these problems, Friedman tended on occasion to argue that the theory's ability to predict was more important than its explanatory power. This was, however, unlikely ever to satisfy policy decision-makers and their advisers.

In the 1980s further problems have been experienced in defining, measuring and controlling the money supply. As a consequence, Keynesian economics has tended to absorb monetarism rather than vice versa. Probably the most important legacy from monetarism is, first, it contributed to a renewed interest in the importance of the supply side of the economy that the earlier Keynesian model tended to ignore. Secondly, there is a much greater interest in the speed of adjustment of prices and quantities to restore equilibrium. The second identity worth noting for its influence on the policy debate is that commonly described as linking the 'twin deficits' of the budget and the current account.

Simplification is an important attribute of good policy advice, not least because of the difficulty of engendering support for a policy prescription that cannot be readily presented or understood. Perhaps for this reason, many commentators who are concerned about the current-account deficit have argued that there is a direct link with the fiscal deficit. In Australia the considerable tightening of fiscal policy in the second half of the 1980s was not matched by a commensurate reduction in the current-account deficit. One explanation of the failure of the outcome to live up to the policy prediction is that the other variables in that particular identity — private domestic saving and investment — did not remain unchanged. In other words, *ceteris paribus* was an invalid assumption.

Equally important, especially in terms of its ongoing implications for policy, has been the failure of economists to resolve the underlying issues of causality and the transmission mechanism involved. The ongoing policy issue of concern to many Australians is the spectre of excessive foreign borrowing and the sale of Australian assets to foreigners. There is little or no comprehension as to why this occurs. According to some commentators, the (implied) causality would seem to run from excessive foreign borrowing to increased consumption (private and public). This would lower savings, and some would claim poor quality investment as an additional factor.

In contrast, the more probable view held by many officials is that inadequate domestic saving relative to investment is the cause of the reliance on foreign borrowing and domestic asset sales. This reliance on foreigners is the only way to equilibrate the imbalance between domestic saving and investment. Furthermore, this logic suggests that in order to reduce the current-account deficit, and the consequent reliance on foreign borrowing and asset sales, the domestic saving and investment imbalance must also be reduced. This in turn means that attempts to improve competitiveness, either by exchange-rate depreciation or by increased productivity, will not in themselves improve the current account unless they also in some way affect the imbalance between savings and investment. Why this imbalance should respond to changes in competitiveness is uncertain.

To the extent that improved competitiveness favoured the production of more tradeable goods and services, it could be the key to reducing the imbalance between production and expenditure — the counterpart of the saving-investment imbalance. This would seem to be a much stronger possibility if there is spare capacity or scope to increase capacity via productivity improvement. In either case the higher output and incomes could be expected to lead to higher savings and possibly a higher rate of savings. But whether savings would increase relative to investment is more problematic, and unless this occurs the original improvement in competitiveness is unlikely to be sustained. Indeed, consistent with this logic, the real exchange rate is the price relativity which, over time, allows the saving-investment imbalance to be equilibrated through the current-account deficit. Unless the imbalance is corrected, it is difficult to see how or why there would be a sustained change in the real exchange rate.

These views are still gaining currency. They do not seem to have influenced the demands for various forms of industry assistance that purport to be justified in terms of Australia's need to compete but would very likely lead to a reduction in national savings. Until there is wider acceptance of the significance of the saving-investment imbalance, its impact on policy will necessarily be limited.

Dynamic adjustment process

A major consideration in economic advising is uncertainty. One can often be fairly confident about the nature of individual economic relationships, but there can be difficulty in establishing their quantitative significance. Such difficulties become much greater when trying to allow for the interaction of various variables and the lags involved. On the other hand, while comparative statics is useful for much policy analysis, its greatest shortcoming is its failure to address the dynamic adjustment process.

Uncertainties regarding adjustment processes have underpinned some of the main controversies in economics since Keynes. For example, Keynesians initially concluded from Keynes' apparent indifference to the overall level of nominal wages and his manifest concern about effective demand that the price of labour was not the cause of unemployment. Indeed, attempts to lower the average wage were resisted on the grounds that any favourable impact on the relative price of labour and capital would be offset by a likely reduction in consumer demand.

The long debate that preceded the current degree of policy synthesis established that if nominal wages and prices are sufficiently flexible, then full-employment equilibrium can be re-established. This led many economists to conclude that the critical assumption in Keynes' theory is that nominal wages are rigid downwards. The apparent downward stickiness of wages relative to prices pointed to a close association between increases in real wages (for those who are employed) and an increase in unemployment in a recession. This conclusion is readily compatible with neoclassical analysis, and its widespread acceptability has underpinned the approach taken through the Accord to restore full employment while relying on wage restraint.

But Keynes' General Theory can equally be viewed as a description of how markets adjust to an initial disturbance. The best known element in this process was his concept of the multiplier that raised the possibility that the process of adjustment could amplify deviations from equilibrium. This contrasts with classical analysis where there should be only deviation-counteracting forces at work following any disturbance. Subsequent research has, however, established the stability of consumption relative to fluctuations in wages, meaning that Keynes overestimated the significance of the multiplier and its role in magnifying any initial disturbance.

Pursuing a somewhat different approach, Leijonhufvud (1967; 1969) has suggested that Keynes' main contribution was to address a case of market failure resulting from the lack of complete information to participants. In the classical system prices are automatically set at their market-clearing level. By contrast, in the Keynesian system, market participants largely base their expectations about future prices on previous experiences and that they adjusted slowly. It is not necessary in Keynesian analysis 'to deny the existence of a vector of nonnegative prices and interest rates consistent with the full utilization of resources. To be a Keynesian, one need only realise the difficulties of finding the market clearing vector' (Leijonhufvud 1967, p. 404).

This difference in the nature and speed of market adjustments not only affects the views regarding stabilisation policy, it also affects policy directed towards economic growth. A Keynesian-type growth model that assigns a key role to autonomous investment makes perfectly good sense if less than full employment is the norm. On the other hand, if prices (including the price of labour) are sufficiently flexible that full employment is the norm, then neoclassical models where growth depends critically on savings rather than investment, would be more appropriate.

How inexorable are economic forces?

One of the features of economic advice that I suspect most concerns non-economists and some economists is the tendency to present economic forces as having their own inexorable logic. This raises the question of how powerful 'economic imperatives' and how binding 'economic realities' are.

Certainly an exchange-rate crisis can have its own imperative logic. But apart from such crises, views regarding 'economic realities' to some extent reflects confidence in the types of behavioural responses and the nature of the identities discussed above. In addition, the notion of an inexorable economic force can also be relevant to policy when there is some long-run and ongoing change that reflects changing behaviour or the impact of changing technology or institutions.

An example of the influence of such changes on behaviour was the breakdown of the earlier system of financial regulation as borrowers and lenders sought to evade the existing regulations; not least because many of the regulations created their own incentives for evasion. With a commodity as fungible as money, there was little the authorities could do to reinforce the regulations. While not denying the importance of government decisions, particularly for the design of the new system, in the end the old system broke down under the weight of its own distortions, inefficiencies and inequities as much as by way of any pressure from economists. In effect, even the very influential Campbell Report largely reflected ideas whose time had come.

Similarly, the huge volume of speculative capital funds along with major improvements in communications technology have led to the globalisation of capital markets. As a result it is very difficult for any government to control its exchange rate. Critics object that the large oscillations in exchange rates are not conducive to trade and growth, and they can plausibly point to how differences in adjustment speeds across markets can lead to exchange rates 'overshooting'. But as Chris Higgins has responded, 'Although these observations may command a deal of support, unfortunately they do not give rise to clear policy implications for improving the functioning of foreign exchange markets' (1984, p. 10). Rather, the immediate policy implication of the internationalisation of capital markets is that countries do not have the reserves to manage their exchange rate in opposition to market forces, and the only other alternative put enormous pressure on monetary policy and risked self-defeating pressures on demand. At the time there was no practical alternative to the decision to float the Australian dollar. Any attempt to hold the exchange rate would have been overwhelmed by capital flows or would have undermined the government's overall economic strategy.

The globalisation of markets through improved technology (particularly communications technology) has also removed or reduced natural barriers of protection. In order to survive in this 'new world', Australian industry has had to become more competitive, with implications for both wages and industry policy.

The role of economic advisers has been to draw attention to these implications. It has been the government's decision that the best way was not to try and build a protective wall against the incoming tide of greater international competition, but to take the lead in promoting the internationalisation of the Australian economy and fostering the necessary adjustments to make Australia competitive.

While governments can influence the business environment in this way, it is also important to recognise that they do not, and cannot control everything. The Accord itself was founded upon the recognition that governments cannot deliver full employment unless they can achieve a better resolution of competing claims by different market participants for improved incomes.

Government policy has sought to blend policies to make markets work better with a bargained consensus that results in a more satisfactory resolution of income claims. This consensus included a recognition by the parties that profits needed to rise and that it was counterproductive for the government to pursue higher taxes if the other parties responded with higher income claims.[2]

Where has economics been least helpful?
This essay has identified a number of strengths and weaknesses in the capacity of economists to contribute to the formulation of policy. Single relationships predicting a general tendency are at one end of the spectrum and the uncertainty of more complex dynamic adjustment processes are at the other. The emphasis has been on where an understanding of economics can assist policy, notwithstanding the limits of that understanding. It is appropriate, however, to recognise specifically the limits to the contribution economics has made, or can make to two important areas of policy; namely an explanation of the sources of economic growth and the role of stabilisation policy.

Interest in the supply side has risen in recent years and this has been reflected in the drive for microeconomic reform. While one can be reasonably confident that these reforms will enhance the supply potential of the economy, economists have had remarkably little to say about the sources of economic growth. There is only a limited understanding of the factors influencing the long-run supply of labour and capital, and in most growth studies, after allowing for the contributions of labour and capital, there is still a very large residual. This is commonly attributed to technological progress but in fact remains largely unexplained. Furthermore, the apparent tendency in the 1980s for the contribution to economic growth from this residual to decline in a number of countries also remains unexplained.

Romer (1986; 1990) and Lucas (1988) have built on earlier work by Arrow who had sought to render technological progress endogenous in growth models by incorporating the concept of 'learning by doing'. In Romer's model, knowledge is added as a separate factor of production that admits the possibility of increasing returns to capital as new investment spurs knowledge. Both the theoretical and policy implications of Romer's work are important, but significant questions still arise. At this stage, a 'new growth theory' is still at the symposium stage and has not yet influenced the typical policy adviser's thinking.[3]

In the case of stabilisation policy, the importance of uncertainty and the difficulty of quantifying key relationships has already been emphasised. Beyond that there is a larger question of what can reasonably be expected from stabilisation policy. The apparent successes of the 1950s and 1960s may have created unreal expectations. What stands out in retrospect, first, is the relative absence of shocks during that period. Secondly, 'money illusion' has disappeared as inflationary expectations adjusted and most prices were indexed, so that achieving the shift in relative prices necessary to sustain full employment in response to economic disturbances has become much more difficult.

It is partly because of this experience that economists emphasise reforms that improve the flexibility of markets (and thus their response to disturbances), and give greater weight to the medium term and to be cautious about fine-tuning. The majority of economists would still see a role for stabilisation policy in response to a strong disturbance, but realistically expect the mixed economy to experience some fluctuations. Continuous full employment cannot be guaranteed although economic advice can play a useful role in seeking to minimise unemployment.

Is economics value-free?

The other area where economics has traditionally seen itself as having less to contribute is in the consideration of public-policy issues that involves transfers of incomes, particularly where those transfers affect the distribution of income. At least since the 1935 publication of Robbins' *An Essay on the Nature and Significance of Economic Science* there has been a widespread belief that interpersonal comparisons of utility represent value judgments that have no place in 'scientific' or 'positive' economics. At the same time, many issues of public policy do involve some change in income distribution. Indeed, the principal purpose of many programmes is to improve horizontal or vertical equity.

Advisers have typically resolved this dilemma by relying on the presumption that in a democratic society it is the role of the people's elected representatives to determine questions of equity and the desirable distribution of income. Official advice is important in clarifying the nature of any trade-offs involved, including the nature and extent of possible 'winners' and 'losers', and in analysing the incidence of expenditure, tax proposals and tariffs. Once a programme's objectives are established by government, advisers can then determine how efficiently and effectively they might be achieved. The ability to provide such advice is not confined to economists, although the right attitude to programme evaluation comes readily to those with economic training.

Beyond the questions of equity and income distribution, there has recently been some debate about whether economic advice can ever, or should, be value-free. There is a tendency among some economists to slide from describing 'what is' to defining 'what should be'; a move from positive to normative economics.

Economists are typically biased in favour of competitive markets. By contrast, many of those critical of the application of economic analysis to public policy have argued that the assumptions of perfect competition are rarely fulfilled in the real world. Harcourt (1992), for example, in a thoughtful critique of 'economic rationalism' has reminded us that for market outcomes to be socially desirable the 'actual prices of products should be a true measure both of social costs of the resources used to create them and of the satisfaction which their use is expected to bring to their purchasers' (p. 5). This in turn requires that competition is such that producers are price-takers rather than price-makers, and that price signals are not so diffused by stocks dominating flows that it leads to destabilising speculation.

One inference that can be drawn from Harcourt's critique is an acknowledgement that where markets work well this does lead to desirable outcomes. This is reflected in much policy that is directed towards improving the efficiency of markets, particularly by encouraging competition, but also through policies that make the polluter pay in response to externalities. Where Harcourt is more controversial is in determining what the response to the impact of stocks and associated price speculation should be. One answer is that policy should seek to avoid an 'excessive' build-up in stocks (e.g., government and foreign debt, wool stocks, etc.), but it also needs to be recognised that stocks do play a valuable role in cushioning adjustment, and how an 'excessive level' is determined and how government intervention will help.

In short, official advisers are properly cautious about advising on the broad objectives of public policy that should reflect the political preference function of the elected government of the day. This does not mean that official advisers are unconcerned about objectives, and there can be a degree of fuzziness in separating ends from means in policy advising. Official advisers can play an important role in helping governments to define their objectives and by advising on how any tensions between them might be alleviated by varying the policy mix (or means). This may require them to second-guess a government's real objectives; but it is not the same as determining the government's objectives, and the uncertainty regarding means is often such that the decision proper is made by the government.

Similarly, there can often be debate regarding the significance of externalities (such as the natural beauty of a wilderness area or the value of preserving an endangered species) because economics provides only limited guidance on how to make such valuations, although it does insist that externalities should be assessed. For these reasons the Resource Assessment Commission, for example, considers that where externalities loom large, a multidisciplinary approach to their valuation is likely to be most productive, but while 'analytical techniques can throw light on the issues, final decisions must be made by governments' (1992, p. 46).

What contributions have economic advisers made?

The role of advisers

Before turning to consider what contribution economic advisers have actually made to Australian policy in the last decade, it is appropriate to consider more specifically their role and their relation with the ministers concerned. Economic advice is not the only type of advice available to ministers and the influence of official advice, at least, generally depends upon convincing ministers; in the end it is the role of ministers to decide. Advisers can, however, assist ministers and influence their eventual decisions. In addition, the implementation of policy by officials can influence the eventual policy outcome, although in this respect the amount of delegation to officials is generally less for purely economic policy than in other policy areas.[4]

Advisers have most influence when they work constructively with ministers. To paraphrase Paul Keating (1989), ideas are important, and it is the responsibility of public institutions like the Treasury and the Reserve Bank to be continually generating ideas. John Stone (1992) believes that when ministers and their departments work well together, 'there tends to develop a sort of symbiosis between the advice that comes forward and what the advisers believe, on the basis of past experience, the Minister will be prepared at least to listen to (if not necessarily agree with)' (p. 15).

Good economic advice therefore begins with an appreciation of the government's objectives.[5] It clarifies the facts and the arguments, and separates the more probable from the less probable. It necessarily involves some simplification based on careful consideration of likely relevance. It should appreciate what economists don't know as well as what they do. It is frank about the uncertainties involved and identifies the key risks.[6] Most importantly, a good adviser has the moral courage to draw attention to the possibly unpalatable implications of government policy. The adviser should not be overwhelmed by practical constraints, although they should be recognised.

As Keating (1989) has stated, 'public policy does not have to be run by the lowest common denominator of what is acceptable . . . There is a role for vision and determination'. In fact, practical constraints are rarely immutable. They change over time in response to the pressures from changing economic circumstances, and real political leadership can play a vital role in seizing and creating opportunities to change what is possible. Advisers should complement political leadership by questioning and probing the apparent constraints to better policy, but once assured that the government is properly informed, advisers must recognise that the final decision rests with the government. For what it is worth, my assessment is that economic advisers have generally observed these principles.[7] This also seems to be the opinion of ministers of the day from both sides of the political spectrum.

Economists' advice

The foregoing discussion of economics has summarised the common threads of agreement among economists as well as the main sources of uncertainty. In broad terms, economists have been more confident and unanimous when advising on microeconomic issues, and this is in fact how most official economic advisers are employed. By contrast, the relatively few advisers involved in macroeconomic analysis have to contend with more complex interrelationships, with much greater uncertainty about the dynamic adjustment processes, and the changes in international developments that typically impact on their policy predictions.

The reforms of the last decade have mainly been microeconomic reforms, the area of economics where there is considerable consensus among economists. However, it is probably fair to say that during the 1980s the degree of consensus among macroeconomists also strengthened. This followed a period of divergent views sparked by the monetarist critique and the experience of stagflation following the first oil shock in 1973. Today the remaining areas of disagreement and the reasons for disagreement, have been clarified and are better understood.[8] Against this background, it is possibly useful to identify a number of propositions closely associated with economics that I believe have influenced policy; not always because of the persuasiveness of advisers, but sometimes in response to experience and the pressure of economic forces.

The first proposition is a predisposition in favour of competitive markets. Advisers do not assume that these always exist, but they share a presumption in favour of trying to establish them. In a world where change is the norm, and the ability to adapt readily to change is critical, competitive markets are viewed as being most likely to promote the necessary flexibility. In addition, competitive markets can spur efficiency and competitiveness, particularly dynamic efficiency, and maximise consumer choice. These views have particularly influenced industry policy, including government business enterprises, and have generally been more persuasive than the view that there are significant economics of scale.

There are some markets where advisers have tended to be sceptical as to how far the preconditions for full competition can be met. Health is a significant example. Consumer sovereignty cannot be assumed, and reasonable equality of access is a precondition of most countries' health policies. In those circumstances, supply tends to create its own demand and the most effective countervailing force has been the government.

Many would argue that the labour market is also different because of people's attachment to their relative incomes, the implicit contracts that are involved, the divergent interests of outsiders and insiders, the difficulty in establishing an appropriate balance of power when fixed costs are high relative to variable costs, and so on. Moreover, despite significant differences among countries in their institutional arrangements for wage determination, the outcomes are broadly similar in terms of wage flexibility. Under these circumstances and within a highly mobile labour force, quantity adjustment may be more efficient than price adjustment, provided it is not pushed too far. However, most advisers believe that there is scope to move from the old centralised system of wage determination that encouraged adversarial attitudes and discouraged responsibility and accountability. The debate has, therefore, not been so much about the desirability of change and its direction, but rather how best to achieve it and what that means for the speed of change.

The second proposition favoured by many official advisers is that government policy and programmes should focus on assisting consumers and beneficiaries rather than suppliers. One of the important benefits of programme budgeting is that it has encouraged the identification of, and focus on, programme objectives along with more attention to client outcomes and improved equity. Similarly, the introduction of user-charging and the commercialisation of service providers (such as the FAC and the CAA) has radically increased their client focus. Programmes and services have too often in the past been captured by supplier interests under the guise that what was good for service providers was equally good for the clients.

Thirdly, official advisers generally recognise the possibility of government failure as well as market failure. For example, the uncertainty associated with economic forecasting, in particular the uncertainty about the length of lags before policy begins to bite, has made most advisers more cautious about fine-tuning. Even when there is a clear case for government intervention in response to market failure, the risk of government failure increases according to the extent of detailed intervention. There has been a preference for more generic forms of assistance. While the government has relied to some extent on various industry plans there is a wariness of 'picking winners'.[9] More market-oriented forms of government intervention and service provision have also been favoured, such as the creation of internal markets, shadow pricing, the encouragement of benchmark competition, and the use of tax and other price incentives rather than quantitative restrictions.

The experience in all developed countries has led to a greater scepticism that government programmes will necessarily achieve their intended results. This is partly reflected in the public's resistance to 'big government' and higher taxes. The response to these concerns has caused a shift towards more effective and equitable outcomes in governmental financial management and budgeting reforms.[10]

Fourthly, through the 1980s there was an increasing consensus among advisers about the long-run damage from inflation. The expectation of continuing inflation affected the quantum of savings and investment decisions and their quality. In addition, with increasing *de jure* or de facto indexation, changing relative prices became more difficult and the effectiveness of stabilisation policy was consequently undermined.

In response, economic advisers have paid increasing attention to the formation of expectations. For many, this meant enhancing the credibility of policy to minimise the long-run pain of adjusting to low inflation. For others, it meant a direct attempt through the Accord to influence trade unions' expectations. This included a shift in bargaining away from the immediate-past experience of inflation to forecasts of inflation. These two approaches were not mutually incompatible and have been used in tandem.

Finally, official advisers tend to reflect the economists' general preference for transparency of information and decision-making. The underlying presumption is that better and more transparent information will improve both the quality of decision-making, and public accountability. This has been reflected in such decisions as to publish the government's economic forecasts, the forward estimates of budget outlays, the cost of meeting the community-service obligations of public enterprises, programme performance information, and in a much sharper analysis of public investment proposals.

Criticisms of economists' influence

Having outlined the nature of economic advice and its foundations, it is now appropriate to consider the criticisms of economists' influence. The first is that economists have too much influence, especially in the sense that they allegedly ignore other values. The critics object that people are motivated by other than self-interest and that economists only tend to value those goods and services that can be individually consumed and priced. At least as regards the official family of economic advisers, this criticism is not really apposite. As already described, official advice is presented on the assumption that it is the role of politicians in government to determine policy, having regard to the full range of community values. Moreover, useful policy advice does reflect an appreciation of other 'non-monetary' values, a recognition of various practical constraints, and the need to identify second-best as well as the best options. At the risk of emphasising the obvious, politicians are never short of advice and economists face plenty of competition in giving it.

A second criticism of economists' influence is that too often today's economists offer the wrong kind of advice. This reflects more the ideological objection by the criticised rather than a serious criticism of the economist's prescription of a market-based solution.

A related criticism is that today's economists do not have the vision of their predecessors, and their training is too narrow. Such comparisons are always difficult to make (especially for those directly concerned), not least because official advisers have largely observed a traditional anonymity, and one can never be sure how far their views were actually reflected in the policies of the day. The overwhelming sense, however, is more of a continuity in the mainstream of official economic advice.[11] What has changed is that others have joined that mainstream and that may have increased the influence of economists' advice.[12] Within that mainstream there is perhaps better recognition of the importance of the supply side and the resistance to higher taxation. Possibly for these reasons, governments may now be more inclined to insist on proper cost-benefit studies before they commit scarce public funds and spend taxpayers' money on untested projects such as the Ord River Scheme and other such improbable 'visions' of Australia's future.

A third strand of criticism of economists' influence has been to seize on the allegedly poor results achieved as a consequence of opening up the economy through deregulation and structural adjustment. These can be summarised as:

- the present level of unemployment which, in turn, reflects structural change imposed by economists, and the failure of investment and its quality following financial deregulation

- the loss of ownership of Australian assets and excessive borrowing in response to financial deregulation; and
- an increase in inequality, attributed to the Accord, the restructuring of the economy, and the restricted role of government

In the case of unemployment, the possibility of mistakes in forecasting and the limits of what can be expected from stabilisation policy have been acknowledged. It is, however, more difficult to establish the impact of structural change on employment. Instances of job losses are readily identified, but the role of structural change in reducing costs and encouraging the creation of new jobs elsewhere is much more difficult to pinpoint. What can be noted is that even in the recession, the net job loss is small relative to the gross flows of jobs created. This and other evidence suggests that the main reason for the present unsatisfactory level of unemployment is the recession rather than structural change.[13] Furthermore, because of the likely constraints from the balance of payments, inflation and living standards, it would be difficult without further structural change to sustain a high enough growth rate in the longer-run to absorb the present unemployment.

A more serious criticism of official advice is that it has overestimated the speed with which markets can adapt to structural change.[14] Whatever the validity of this criticism, there has been a considerable 'learning experience' in Australia among businesses and trade-union leaders in the last decade, and economists have played a leading role in raising public understanding and changing the culture so that Australia can more effectively hold its place in the world.

As regards the pace of financial deregulation, it may be that necessary improvements in prudential supervision and corporate law tended to lag behind. There is, however, a legitimate question as to how much can be expected from prudential supervision and the law, and particularly how far investors should be protected from the cost of their own mistakes. An innovative society does depend upon some investors being prepared to take risks and being rewarded and penalised accordingly. In the present context, the boom and subsequent bust in asset values does not so much reflect the quality of regulation and its supervision as adjustment to changing expectations regarding inflation. As people adjust to the expectation of continuing inflation they hedge by investing in assets and realised the tax advantages in borrowing to do so. What they failed to appreciate were the risks they were running when, contrary to their expectations, inflation spiralled. And it was these changes in incentives to hold assets that affected their prices, not the changes in financial regulation.

Turning to the alleged increase in inequality, it is first of all difficult to establish the facts. Most studies focus only on cash incomes and even they have difficulty in handling the impact of broadening the tax base to include fringe benefits and capital gains. More importantly, most studies of living standards and income distribution ignore access to government services and the ownership of assets such as a house and car. They do not really allow for key elements of the government's social policy, such as improved access to health services through Medicare and the proactive employment strategy to help people to help themselves, involving very big increases in expenditure on childcare and training programmes.

Even if we focus only on cash incomes, the available research suggests that government intervention did succeed in reducing 'poverty'. Looking just at market incomes (from wages and salary and investment income) Harding and Mitchell (1992) have found that 'pre-government action poverty' increased from 22 per cent of the population in 1981/82 to 23.4 per cent in 1989/90. However, after taking account of cash transfers and income taxes, the poverty rate fell from 11 per cent to 9.5 per cent over the same period, suggesting that government policies were doing a better job of looking after the poor by the end of the 1980s than at the beginning (pp. 283-4). This is corroborated by the big increases in transfer payments for the most needy. Families with children, those who rent, and the long-term unemployed in particular have experienced substantial increases in their real incomes, partly financed by tighter targeting, including thorough means testing that produced modest reductions in the real incomes of some part pensioners and beneficiaries (Harding & Landt, 1992).

For the population as a whole, the available data on the distribution of cash incomes suggest a small increase in the degree of inequality over the 1980s (Saunders, 1992).[15] It is important to note, however, that this change is not the direct effect of government policy. Rather, it reflects changes in the labour market and their impact on wages, the primary source of income for most people. In this context, it is important also to note the choice of starting date because the 1980s opened with a wage explosion and subsequently there was widespread agreement (e.g., at the 1983 Economic Summit) that real wages needed to fall relative to profits.

Probably the most important influence on income distribution through the 1980s, however, has been what Bob Gregory (1992) has described as 'the disappearing middle': the loss of one in four jobs in the middle 60 per cent of the earnings distribution (p. 17). This loss, however, began in the mid-1970s and seems to have affected a number of developed countries, with Australia so far suffering less than the US, UK and Canada. There is no obvious explanation why these jobs have disappeared, but it seems unlikely that it reflects industry restructuring. First, there is the pervasiveness internationally of the changes, and their timing. Secondly, all industries seem to be affected, including the public sector, and the job loss seems to reflect the reduced need for particular skills and occupations, rather than the fortunes of individual industries. Gregory's tentative explanation is that 'it seems as though technology and product demand patterns are changing the way in which work is organised and creating more low pay jobs' (p. 3).

The clear implication is that government policy (and by inference, economists' influence) cannot be held responsible for any increase in inequality in Australia over the last decade. Indeed, the direct impact of government policies has reduced any increase in inequality. However, while the government is not directly responsible for these labour market developments, they can still be of concern. The difficulty is our lack of understanding regarding them and therefore how amenable or otherwise they are likely to be to government policy.

Reviews of other countries' experience have concluded that the influence of economists has declined since the high point of the 1960's (Pechman 1989). Then, economists promised, and largely delivered satisfactory results. With rapid economic growth, distribution issues that were less contentious, and in the absence of shocks, forecasting was arguably easier. The world-wide deterioration in economic performance since then means that economists now promise less, and with slower growth, necessary adjustments are more likely to be resisted because of their distributional implications. Economic planning has also become more complicated as international economic forces assume greater significance.

As might be expected, this international experience is to some extent also recognisable in Australia. Furthermore, with Australia only slowly emerging from recession, there is a natural tendency by some to blame the advisers. The recent track record of public and private economic forecasters is poor. Policy advice also underestimates the relationship between changing asset values and inflationary expectations, and their significance for spending decisions. More recently, the interaction between expansionary policies and business and consumer confidence has proved elusive. But this is more a warning about the inherent uncertainty attached to all such advice, rather than evidence that the quality of economic advice in general has deteriorated.

I do not quite share in the trend that is emerging in overseas studies that the influence of economists is closely tied to economic performance. The prestige of economists may have suffered, but in retrospect the strong performance of OECD economies in the 1950s and 1960s had deeper underlying causes than the quality and influence of economists' advice.

For my part, I remain somewhat reassured by the Australian experience of the last decade or so. There has been a major opening-up and restructuring of the Australian economy largely along the lines advocated by economists. In particular, economists with the government have led the way in focusing attention on the supply side and the need for microeconomic reform, along with a recognition of the opportunities for a competitive and outwardly oriented Australia, particularly towards Asia. Many economists were also at the forefront in warning against the dangers of inflation. Officials have played a key role in developing and implementing reforms of the public sector and the government's major expenditure and revenue initiatives that have generally led to a more efficient and equitable fiscal system.

Admittedly, unemployment is still a major problem, but otherwise, the underlying structure of the Australian economy is more sound than it was at the beginning of the 1980s. Debt is a problem, but inflation is down, profit margins are more satisfactory than before, and the economy is more competitive. Most importantly, a major cultural change is occurring. Australia is experiencing a shift to a more outward and less protectionist orientation. There is a growing realisation that Australia must and can compete. Better relationships are being established in the workplace based on a more co-operative and productive set of values. These changes are being accomplished while preserving many of the good features of the Australian way of life such as environmental awareness and an improvement in welfare services and the pension benefits system.

It is difficult to assess the relative contribution of economists to these changes. To an important extent, the major challenges facing Australia are economic and it would be surprising if economists did not enjoy some influence. Some may consider that Australia's problems have forced or imposed their own solutions. For example, arguably a combination of balance-of-payments pressures and tax-payer resistance was almost bound to constrain budget outlays and force a re-evaluation of programmes. But even in that case, it is equally arguable that officials contributed significantly to the nature of the government's response with its emphasis on improving effective assistance to the most needy.

My sense is that in important instances, economic advice has been sufficiently prescient to make a positive contribution. At a minimum it has influenced Australian public opinion and helped to facilitate the changes that have been occurring and the adaptation to these changes. At its best, economic advice has been proactive, helping to initiate change that will stand to the long-run benefit of Australia.

Notes

I wish to acknowledge valuable comments by Geoff Dixon, Helen Williams, Rod Sims, Ric Simes and Alan Henderson. I also wish to thank Tom Ioannou for research assistance. The views expressed are my own and not necessarily shared by those mentioned or my employer.

1 This contrast between micro and macroeconomic advice is developed by Blinder (1987).

2 Keating and Dixon (1989) discuss this approach to policy-making in more detail.

3 Former chairman of the Council of Economic Advisers, Herbert Stein, reflecting on over 50-years' experience in Washington concluded that 'Ideas in economics deserve confidence only after they have been chewed over for a long time and been exposed to whatever tests may be available. For an economic adviser to rely on the latest, still-undigested ideas from the journals would be as irresponsible as for a medical doctor to try on his patients the latest ideas from the medical journals before they have even been tried on mice' (1991, p. 8).

4 This is consistent with the experience of many other countries, from which Nelson has concluded that 'the exercise of economic policy remained ultimately a political act, not a set of decisions that any society would entrust to economic experts alone' (1989, p. 11).

5 As Austin Holmes commented, 'the adviser who takes no account of political and bureaucratic factors will soon be excluded from decision-making processes' (1984, p. 10).

6 Regular reports from the Joint Economic Forecasting Group always contain a separate section assessing the key risks to the forecasts.

7 This is supported by the views of other senior economic advisers (Holmes 1981; Fraser 1984) and Whitwell's (1990) independent assessment of the Treasury.

8 Note the 'strength and degree of consensus' found by Anderson and Blandy (1992) in their recent survey of Australia's economics professors.

9 The critics who favour further moves in this direction might like to note that, apart from their dubious economic merits, there has been no consideration of what this would imply for business-government relations and public accountability. The Australian requirements in this respect are much more demanding than in many of the countries cited as examples of successful government involvement with business, and have been further reinforced by the Report of the Royal Commission following the experience of WA Inc.

10 See Keating (1989; 1990), Keating & Holmes (1990) and Codd (1991) for a detailed assessment of these reforms.

11 It is well-known, for example, that throughout the post-war period the Reserve Bank and the Treasury were pushing for the opening-up of the economy and the removal of import controls.

12 According to Whitwell, 'What is different now is that there is a much broader acceptance outside of the Treasury of the broad principles which Stone was advocating and which continue to make up the Treasury line' (Whitwell 1990, p. 137). See also Keating and Dixon (1989).
13 See Industry Commission (1992) and Reserve Bank (1992).
14 See Walsh (1992, p. 36) and Whitwell (1990).
15 Saunders reports an increase in the Gini coefficient from 0.31 in 1981-82 to 0.34 in 1989/90 (1992, pp. 20-4).

References

Anderson, M., & Blandy, R. 1992, 'What Australian Economics Professors Think', *Australian Economic Review*, no.100, October-December, pp. 17-40
Argy, F. 1992, 'Michael Pusey's Economic Rationalism in Canberra', *Economic Papers*, vol. 11, no. 1, pp. 83-90; reprinted in *Canberra Bulletin of Public Administration*, no. 68, pp. 152 6
Blandy, R. 1985, 'Soft Science', *Economic Record*, vol. 61, December, pp. 693 706
— 1992, 'Multiple Schizophrenia: Economic Rationalism and its Critics', *Australian Quarterly*, vol. 64, no. 1, pp. 101—6
Blaug, M. 1980, *The Methodology of Economics, or How Economists Explain*, Cambridge University Press, Cambridge
— 1985, *Economic Theory in Retrospect*, Cambridge University Press, Cambridge
Blinder, A. S. 1987, *Hard Heads, Soft Hearts: Tough-Minded Economics for a Just Society*, Addison-Wesley Publishing Co., Reading, Mass.
Codd, M. 1991, *Federal Public Sector Management Reform: Recent History and Current Priorities*, PSC SES Staffing Unit Occasional Paper no.11, February, AGPS, Canberra
The Economist 1990, 'Keynes Rides Again', 17 November, pp. 101-2
— 1992-93, 'The Search for Keynes: Was He a Keynesian?' 26 December-8 January, pp. 102-4
Fraser, B. W. 1984, 'The Treasury — Tendering Economic Advice', address to RIPAA seminar on Inside Government, 9 October; reprinted in *Canberra Bulletin of Public Administration*, vol. 11, no. 4, pp. 230-3
Friedman, M. 1970, 'A Theoretical Framework for Monetary Analysis', *Journal of Political Economy*, vol. 78, pp. 193-238
Gregory, R. G. 1992, 'Aspects of Australian Labour Force Living Standards: The Disappointing Decades 1970-1990', The Copland Oration, 21st Conference of Economists, University of Melbourne, July
Harcourt, G. C. 1992, 'Markets, Madness and a Middle Way', *Australian Quarterly*, vol. 64, no. 1, pp. 1-17
Harding, A. & Mitchell, D. 1992, 'The Efficiency and Effectiveness of the Tax-Transfer System in the 1980s', *Australian Tax Forum*, vol. 9, no. 3, pp. 277-303
Harding, A. & Landt, J. 1992, 'Policy and Poverty: Trends in Disposable Incomes March 1983 to September 1991', *Australian Quarterly*, vol. 64, no. 1, pp. 19-48
Higgins, C. I. 1984, 'Coming of Age in the 1970s: Reflections of a Practical Macroeconomist', paper prepared for symposium on Lessons from Recent European and Australian Macroeconomic Experience, Ottawa, 8-9 June

Holmes, A. S. 1981, 'The Good Fight', *Economic Record*, vol. 57, pp. 1-11

Industry Commission 1992, Annual Report 1991-92, Canberra, AGPS

Keating, M. 1989, '*Quo Vadis?* Challenges of Public Administration', *Australian Journal of Public Administration*, vol. 48, no. 2, pp. 123 31

—1990, 'Managing for Results in the Public Interest', *Australian Journal of Public Administration*, vol. 49, no. 4, pp. 387-98

Keating, M. & Dixon, G. 1989, *Making Economic Policy in Australia: 1983—1988*, Longman Cheshire, Melbourne

Keating, M. & Holmes, M. 1990, 'Australia's Budgetary and Financial Management Reforms', *Governance*, vol. 3, no. 2, pp. 168-85

Keating, M. & Mackie, K. 1991, 'The Tax-Transfer System in Australia', *Australian Quarterly*, vol. 63, no. 3, pp. 294-311

Keating, P. J. 1989, 'Farewell to Bob Johnston', statement by the Treasurer, 12 September

—1991, 'The Challenge of Public Policy in Australia', inaugural Higgins Memorial Lecture to the Economic Society of Australia, Canberra, 15 May; reprinted in *Canberra Bulletin of Public Administration*, no. 65, pp. 16-20

Keynes, J. M. 1936, *The General Theory of Employment, Interest and Money*, Macmillan, London

Leijonhufvud, A. 1967, 'Keynes and the Keynesians: A Suggested Interpretation', *American Economic Review*, vol. 57, pp. 401-10

—1969, *Keynes and the Classics*, Institute of Economic Affairs, London

Lucas, R. E. 1988, 'On the Mechanics of Economic Development', *Journal of Monetary Economics*, vol. 22, pp. 3-42

Nelson, R. H. 1989, 'Introduction and Summary', *The Role of the Economist in Government: An International Perspective*, ed. J. A. Pechman, Harvester Wheatsheaf, New York

Niehans, J. 1981, 'Economics, History, Doctrine, Science, Art', *Kyklos*, vol. 34, pp. 165-77

OECD 1988, *Why Economic Policies Change Course: Eleven Case Studies*, OECD, Paris

—1992, *Economic Outlook*, December, OECD, Paris

Pechman, J. A., ed., 1989, *The Role of the Economist in Government: An International Perspective*, Harvester Wheatsheaf, New York

Reserve Bank of Australia, 1992, *Bulletin*, November

Resource Assessment Commission, 1992, *Methods for Analysing Development and Conservation Issues: The Resource Assessment Commission's Experience*, Research Paper no.7, RAC, Canberra

Robbins, L. 1935, *An Essay on the Nature and Significance of Economic Science*, 2nd edn, Macmillan, London

Romer, P. M. 1986, 'Increasing Returns and Long-run Growth', *Journal of Political Economy*, vol. 94, pp. 1002-37

—1990, 'Endogenous Technological Chang', *Journal of Political Economy*, vol. 98, pp. 71-102

Saunders, P. 1992, 'Longer Run Trends in the Distribution of Income In Australia', paper presented at the 21st Conference of Economists, University of Melbourne, 8-10 July

—1992a, *Poverty, Inequality and Recession*, Study of Social and Economic Inequality Working Paper no. 5, October, Centre for Applied Economic Research, University of New South Wales

Schedvin, C.B. 1992, *In Reserve: Central Banking in Australia, 1945—75*, Allen & Unwin, Sydney
—1992a, 'Central Banking and Liberal Democracy: The Australian Experience', *Economic Papers*, vol. 11, no. 4, December, pp. 2-11
Stein, H. 1991, 'What Economic Advisers Do', *The American Enterprise*, March/April, pp. 7-12
Stone, J. 1992, 'Yes, Minister?'. *Quadrant*, vol. 36, no. 290, October, pp. 14-19
Walsh, P. 1991, 'Rationalists Winning Some, Losing Some', Cassandra column, *Australian Financial Review*, no. 19, November, p. 13
Whitwell, G. 1990, 'The Triumph of Economic Rationalism: The Treasury and the Market Economy', *Australian Journal of Public Administration*, vol. 49, no. 2, June, pp. 124-43

Part II

Case Studies

Ian R. Harper and Phillip J. Leslie

The Case of Financial Deregulation: 'Economic Rationalism' on Trial

For both critics and defenders of 'economic rationalism', the history of financial deregulation in Australia is instructive. Support for the deregulation of Australia's financial markets dates from the mid to late 1970s, but the process did not gain momentum until the election of the first Hawke Labor government in March 1983. Financial deregulation formed part of a political agenda to enhance the efficiency of the Australian economy through the systematic application of orthodox neoclassical microeconomic policy ('economic rationalism'), a process that continues to the present day.

Financial deregulation is an early instance of the use of 'rationalist' economic policy, and as such, a substantial run of historical data exists.[1] It is also the case (with the possible exception of tariff reform) that has been subject to the most comprehensive public scrutiny, both at the outset when the blueprint for deregulation was mapped out clearly by the Campbell Committee (AFSI 1981), and subsequently through the various public inquiries, most notably the recent Martin Inquiry (House of Representatives Standing Committee on Finance and Public Administration 1991), that reviewed the outcome of financial deregulation

Economic rationalism has come in for trenchant criticism in recent times. Numerous newspaper articles, radio interviews and several books point to the 'dogma' or 'ideology' that has supposedly bewitched policy advisers in Canberra, and set them on a path of destruction of the nation's economic fabric.[2] The phrase 'economic rationalism' has become a term of abuse and is used by critics of the economic policies of the present Federal Government (and significantly, of those proposed by the Opposition) to denigrate recent and proposed economic reforms including privatisation, tariff reductions, labour-market reform and financial-market deregulation. These are all seen as deriving from the same 'rationalist' view of the world and therefore as fundamentally wrong-headed.

However, economic rationalism is neither more nor less than an attempt to inject rational (reasoned, logical) economic principles into the formulation of public policy with the ultimate aim of improving living standards for all Australians. As such, it draws heavily on the body of orthodox economic knowledge that has accumulated over the past two centuries and can be found in the formal literature of the discipline. Would the critics of economic rationalism have us do less than apply rational principles to the formulation of economic policy in Australia, or would they have us ignore the body of economic scholarship and rely instead on uninformed opinion?

Of the various objections lodged by the opponents of economic rationalism, perhaps the most serious is the claim that rationalist policy prescriptions are based not on objective analyses of the evidence but on mere prejudice, devoid even of the pretence of addressing the 'facts'. Economic rationalism is characterised as a set of principles that have little or no basis in objectivity but merely reflect the dogma or blind faith of those who hold onto them. In the words of one critic, economic rationalism amounts to no more than 'a theory-driven series of assertions which emanate from the basic assumptions that market-based capitalism is optimally efficient (only Governments mar its performance) and that efficiency is synonymous with equity' (Alford 1993, p. 12).[3]

The aim of this essay is to defend economic rationalism, at least as it has been applied to financial markets, against the claim that it is mere dogma and ideology; that it is inspired and executed by a group of free-market zealots whose sole ambition is to abolish all forms of government intervention and grant free rein to market forces, regardless of the consequences. Three separate lines of argument are developed.

First, it is argued that the application of economic rationalism to the Australian financial system (in the form of financial deregulation) was a deliberative process, open to public scrutiny and debate and motivated not by a slavish devotion to market forces, but by a genuine concern to improve the performance of Australia's financial markets. To portray the Campbell Committee that constructed the rationalist blueprint for financial reform in Australia, or any of the subsequent committees of inquiry set up to review the results of financial deregulation, as anti-government and blindly pro-market is to paint a ludicrous caricature of the truth.

The second line of defence is to point out that financial deregulation was not unique to Australia. Indeed, countries with a wide variety of predispositions towards and against free-market economics all experienced a measure of financial liberalisation during the 1980s. Moreover, in our case as in others, the decision to liberalise financial markets was taken by governments largely in an effort to maintain control over their financial systems, not abandon it. While the net result of these events is that financial markets are now encumbered by fewer regulations than before, new regulations have been introduced as old ones are repealed. Financial liberalisation is not a one-way street.

Thirdly, the results of financial deregulation have been *broadly* in accord with the stated expectations of the rationalists. The word 'broadly' is emphasised because there have been some disappointing outcomes — some directly attributable to financial deregulation, others less so — and because insufficient time has elapsed for the full impact of financial-market reform to be reliably assessed. Had the architects of deregulation merely sought, as the critics suggest, to remove government as far as possible from the operation of financial markets, their efforts could be pronounced an abject failure. On the other hand, the positive results of the rationalist reforms, measured in terms of the improved performance of the financial system, lend credence to the view that their stated motives were genuine from the outset and not a smoke screen designed to gull an unwitting public into accepting deregulation for its own sake.

The Campbell Report — rationalist dogma?

The Campbell Report is perhaps the classic statement of economic rationalism in the Australian context. It states clearly and prominently that its 'main concern [is] to promote a financial system that is *efficient, competitive* and *stable'*(AFSI 1981, p. xxvii; emphasis in original) — in other words, to reduce waste, and to enhance the ability of the financial system to create wealth. It eschews judgements about the distribution of wealth and concentrates solely on the creation of wealth. The setting of distributional objectives is considered to be a prerogative of Parliament and the limits of the Committee's competence are seen to lie with technical questions of wealth creation. This encompasses analysis of the most efficient *means* of achieving particular distributional ends and the Committee offers its views on the relative merits of alternative distributional mechanisms.[4.]

The Campbell Report is shot through with 'economic rationalism'. It is a reasoned, logical attempt to weigh the advantages and disadvantages of particular means of achieving stated ends. The ends are strictly economic in character, that is, they concern the material welfare of individuals and families. There is nothing in the Campbell Report, or any other rationalist document for that matter, that has anything to say about the spiritual dimension of people's lives. The focus is strictly limited to the material.

Whatever parody of economic rationalism the critics may care to compose and whatever may have occurred in other contexts, it is clear to any impartial reader that the Campbell Report is not driven by dogma. Most of its 800-plus pages are crammed with arguments for and against particular institutions and mechanisms, and attempts to reach reasoned judgements about the most effective means of achieving the stated ends. Had the recommendations of the Campbell Report been held as articles of faith by its authors, the document would have been considerably shorter. There would have been no need to defend the recommendations with meticulous argument and appeal to evidence; a simple credo would have sufficed.

The public nature of the Campbell Inquiry and the accessibility of the Campbell Report itself stand against claims that financial deregulation was foist on an unsuspecting public by a group of faceless 'econocrats'. Moreover, before the major recommendations of the Committee were adopted, they were reviewed by two governments of diverse political persuasion, the latter establishing a second public inquiry with the specific brief of reviewing the recommendations of the Campbell Report in light of that government's *social priorities*.

The decision to deregulate Australia's financial markets was taken on the advice of economic rationalists, but only after considerable public scrutiny of the arguments and evidence brought forward in the Campbell Report and the report of the Martin Review Group. The economic rationalists may not have been right as often as they wished, but no-one can fairly claim to have had no opportunity to consider the arguments and raise public objection to the rationalist agenda for financial markets in a democratic forum, either prior to the onset of reform or subsequently.

Perhaps the criticism is not that the Campbell Committee was not objective and rational in its deliberations but that, in reaching its conclusions, the Committee implicitly or explicitly relied on the prescriptions of modern economic analysis that are subjective and value-laden. There is no doubt that the Campbell Committee drew substantially on the methodology and conclusions of neoclassical economic theory. In this sense, those who criticise economic rationalism in the reform of the Australian financial system attack head-on the application of economic principles to the analysis of financial markets and how to improve their operation.

There are many deep and engaging arguments concerned with the possibility of investigating economic phenomena in a manner that is completely free of the subtle prejudices and value judgements brought by the investigator. Are the facts we observe objective or do we see merely what we want to see or what our training/upbringing forces us to see? Such arguments have a long history in economic thought and are well represented in the formal literature of the discipline.[5] Needless to say, the arguments are unresolved; furthermore, they have not prevented economists from continuing to observe, analyse and comment upon economic phenomena, notwithstanding the philosophical doubts about what they are doing.

Very few critics of economic rationalism base their criticisms on such philosophical considerations, although some clearly do. Those who do tend to come from within the profession and are thoroughly conversant with the strengths and weaknesses of the discipline. Nevertheless, it remains true, for better or for worse, that the views of the critics within the profession are shared by a minority. There is a mainstream culture within the global economics profession from which the economic principles underpinning economic rationalism are drawn. This does not readily mean that these principles are infallible, but rather that they happen to represent, at this point in the history of the discipline, the majority or mainstream view of the profession. Those who reject economic rationalism therefore reject the application to public policy of principles drawn from mainstream economic knowledge.

To be fair to the critics, most would not see themselves rejecting all of modern economics when they bridle at economic rationalism. The objections of many critics boil down to a deep suspicion of the free market as a mechanism for enhancing the material wellbeing of Australians. What they find objectionable is the mainstream neoclassical economist's predilection for the free market as a mechanism for enhancing economic welfare. It is this preference that they suspect has no basis in objective truth but merely reflects the blind prejudice or narrow self-interest of a particular caste of individuals who worship the market. Critics of economic rationalism distrust the market; whereas for the most part, modern economic analysis is pro-market, hence the case for modern economic analysis is so much the worse in the eyes of their detractors.

Opposing the critics of economic rationalism is then a matter of refuting their claim that the economist's preference for market mechanisms is mere prejudice, and establishing the counter-claim that the preference is soundly supported by theory and evidence. To do so in detail would take us well beyond our current brief; indeed, to make a convincing case, one would need to refer to a wide spectrum of economic literature. In fact, to convince any one of the validity of this claim requires them to spend long hours in disciplined study of articles and books written by economists.

Even after such an exhaustive study of the economics literature, one could reasonably remain unconvinced that the pro-market stance of much modern economics is more than the cultural or class prejudice of its practitioners. In this event, the only response is that such views remain (for the time being at least) in the minority — perhaps understandably so if the conspiracy theory is correct. The intellectual weight of many critiques of economic rationalism would be much greater, however, if more of the critics would undertake such an extended study of economics.

Despite acquiescence by the Campbell Committee towards market solutions, it did not blindly accept the superiority of deregulation, regardless of context. The Committee was only too well aware that the 'theory of the second best' (Lipsey & Lancaster 1956) undermined any general claim for the optimality of deregulated financial markets while other markets elsewhere in the economy were subject to continuing intervention. Most notably, the Committee recommended the imposition of *stronger* regulations on banks to improve their prudential soundness. In its recommendations concerning the safety and soundness of the financial system, the Committee was anything but pro-market and was criticised at that time for this alleged lapse in consistency.[6]

As Valentine (1991, p. 39) explains, the Campbell Committee approached each regulation on its merits and conducted a separate cost-benefit analysis. A recommendation to remove a regulation was made only if the economic costs of maintaining it were judged to exceed the economic benefits. Where the cost-benefit calculus showed otherwise, the regulation was upheld, or a recommendation made for it to be strengthened. This is hardly a dogmatic or ideological approach to reform; it is, indeed, standard rational economic analysis at work.

The inevitability of financial deregulation

A theme common to opponents of financial deregulation is the choice between continued (or even strengthened) financial regulation and deregulation. It was the baleful influence of economic rationalists that induced the Australian government to take the unwise and unnecessary decision to deregulate.[7] This view conveniently ignored the fact that *all* of the major Western democracies and many of the minor ones experienced some degree of financial deregulation or liberalisation during the 1980s. This includes countries like France and Sweden that are not noted for their fondness of free-market economics.[8] In the French case,

> The central bank and the Ministry of Finance argued that the French financial system was hampered by inefficiencies reflected in modest competition and negative real interest rates. . . . It was simply realised that interest rates in the French economy were neither playing their role in the allocation of resources nor as an instrument of monetary policy'. (Bisignano 1991, pp. 253-4)

As for Sweden, 'The system which was structured to help finance the government by artificially holding down long-term interest rates and directed at providing privileged finance to the housing sector, ultimately ended up retarding the growth and health of its banking industry' (Bisignano 1991, p. 258).

A variety of pressures were brought to bear on financial institutions and markets around the world in the 1970s and 1980s. While the details differ from case to case, a number of common experiences can be identified.[9] Many countries found that regulations imposed on banks induced rapid growth in non-bank financial institutions that distorted the allocation of financial resources and eroded the effectiveness of monetary policy. The growing sophistication of financial markets, spurred by developments in information technology and the increasing internationalisation of financial activity, combined to reduce the effectiveness of many domestic financial regulations that either became redundant, or gave rise to obvious distortions as markets attempted to take evasive action.

It is not sufficient to show that there were common international pressures and a common response. Could it be that all these countries were similarly affected by rationalist paranoia and none were sufficiently strong-willed to resist the pressure to conform? In other words, they all had a choice to maintain financial regulations but none of them took it. Bisignano draws attention to differences in the experiences of different countries according to whether or not they indulged in 'reform procrastination'. He cites the case of Norway that resisted the pressure to deregulate until, when finally forced by developments in its financial system, did so in a rush. The shock of sudden deregulation in the mid-1980s gave rise to a 'classic central bank induced credit expansion' (Bisignano 1991, p. 265) and a wave of bank failures and mergers that reduced the number of savings banks in Norway from 322 to 150. The experience of the US could also be described as an instance of *crisis deregulation*. In this case, massive losses incurred by thrift institutions as a result of inappropriate deposit interest-rate ceilings and the deposit insurance arrangements set in place by the US government left little alternative to deregulation. The costs of failing to address this regulatory debacle more promptly are still being counted.

It is naïve to suggest that deregulation of financial markets was a matter of preference, exercised by devotees of market forces who sought universally and virtually simultaneously to overthrow the yoke of government intervention. Developments in financial markets rendered the decision to deregulate inevitable (both here in Australia and overseas). Countries that tried to resist the pressure for change have found their post-deregulation experience more turbulent than others, which, like Germany, 'bent with the breeze' and deregulated early. In the words of Greenbaum and Boot in their review of financial deregulation in the US:

> macroeconomic instability, financial innovation and increased competition from foreign and domestic financial institutions characterised the 1970s and 1980s, and provided a compelling environmental explanation for banking deregulation. Thus, the relaxation of selected regulatory restrictions in banking should not be seen as merely another symptom of the contemporary political dogma. (Greenbaum & Boot 1992, p. 635)

It is also clear from international experience that the decision to deregulate was taken by governments seeking to restore a measure of control over their financial systems. In all countries, regulations were imposed on financial markets for a variety of reasons. Regulations provided a source of cheap finance for the central government and helped the government direct financial resources towards favoured groups within the community.[10.]

A consideration of overriding importance, however, was the desire of governments everywhere to influence the path of economic activity through macroeconomic stabilisation policy. This required, among other things, an ability to influence the volume of borrowing and lending being undertaken through the financial system. In periods of strong economic growth, a government might seek to restrain the volume of borrowing from financial intermediaries to finance new investment projects and consumption, while in less buoyant economic times, it might seek to stimulate activity in the real economy by easing conditions in credit markets.

In the days when commercial banks accounted for the bulk of financial activity, the most direct approach to controlling the aggregate volume of private borrowing and lending was to regulate the banks' ability to raise funds and make loans. This was achieved through a raft of direct controls, including ceilings on deposit interest rates, reserve ratios and quantitative and qualitative lending 'guidance', largely administered by central banks. The conformity of experience of financial deregulation throughout the developed world is less surprising when one realises how alike were the standard devices used by monetary authorities of different governments to achieve their goals for credit growth.

The process began to lose its effectiveness as alternative means for meeting the demand for credit developed outside the banking system. This was certainly the experience in Australia but it is repeated in other countries with a wide variety of institutional structures. Bisignano (1991, p. 258) points out that such a model fits the Swedish and US experiences particularly well. With the growth of alternative forms of intermediated finance ('non-bank' financial intermediaries) and direct finance, the link between the growth of the borrowing and lending activity of banks and the aggregate volume of financial activity began to weaken. The more banks were obliged to reduce their lending, the more non-banks and direct financiers would expand theirs. The process also worked in reverse, with an expansion of bank lending tending to displace lending by non-banks and direct financiers. The result was that central banks had progressively less influence over the total volume of borrowing and lending, although they never lost the ability to control the balance-sheet activity of banks.

In order to restore their influence over aggregate financial activity, central banks around the world *sought* financial deregulation. The traditional emphasis on controlling the quantity of financial activity directly was replaced by an indirect method of control, focusing on the price at which credit would be made available.[11] If price was to become the preferred method of manipulating conditions in financial markets, financial prices (i.e., interest rates and exchange rates) would have to be free to find their market-clearing levels. This required that traditional impediments to price rationing in financial markets, including regulations on interest rates and foreign-exchange controls, be removed.

The alternative strategy of extending existing controls on banks to cover non-bank financial intermediaries was not viable and, significantly, was not sought by the monetary authorities. While the banks had lost ground increasingly to non-banks, both forms of intermediated finance experienced increasing competition from mechanisms of direct (i.e., non-intermediated) finance. This was facilitated by the development of securitisation and the increasing tendency of large corporates to access financial markets directly through their own treasury divisions. To extend the regulatory net beyond the banks to incorporate non-banks would simply have exacerbated the trend towards non-intermediated finance and moved financial activity beyond the reach of the monetary authorities altogether — at least so long as they relied on direct controls on financial intermediaries. The move to indirect controls, imposed via movements of interest rates and exchange rates, ensured that the influence of the monetary authorities was felt throughout the financial system, whether borrowing and lending was direct or via an intermediary. The extension of influence sought by the authorities could only be achieved if financial markets were deregulated.

Lest there be any doubt that financial deregulation has restored the potency of monetary policy, one need look no further (in Australia at least, although the British experience is similar) than the depth of the recent recession. Whatever the underlying factors might have been, a proximate cause of the 1990/91 recession was the application of tight monetary policy over an extended period (OECD 1992; Access Economics 1992). During the 1970s (the latter part of the regulated era) the government tried time and again to bring inflation under control via largely unsuccessful attempts to tighten monetary policy. The first major experiment in monetary tightening since deregulation has helped to produce an annual inflation rate in 1992 of 0.3 per cent, the lowest figure in several decades. It has also produced record levels of unemployment. The implementation of monetary policy may be more complex in a deregulated environment (Blundell-Wignall & Browne 1991; Marzouk 1990) and the timing of its impact on the real economy less certain, but of its potency, once it has begun to bite, there can be no doubt.

Monetary authorities the world over are not known for their readiness to abandon measures of control over financial institutions and markets. Deregulation of financial markets represents no lapse from this stance. Central banks and finance ministries pressed for deregulation precisely because it promised to restore a measure of influence over domestic financial conditions that had steadily eroded during the regulated era. They sought merely to change their *modus operandi*, not their guiding philosophy. Those who firmly believe that the only safe financial market is a controlled financial market need not fear deregulation. Without it, monetary authorities would have been in a far less powerful position to influence financial markets than they are today.

There is a second reason why it is misleading to depict financial deregulation as the wholesale abandonment of 'proper' control over the wanton proclivities of the free market. 'Deregulation' is a one-sided description of reforms in financial markets over the 1980s. Accompanying deregulation has been substantial 're-regulation', both in Australia and elsewhere in the developed world (Litan 1992). 'Liberalisation' is a better description of events since, notwithstanding the easing of some regulations while others have been strengthened, the net result is still freer rein for market forces than has applied at any time since World War II.

The most obvious area in which regulations have been tightened and/or new regulations introduced is in monitoring the safety and soundness of financial institutions. Prudential regulation and supervision of financial institutions was a very relaxed affair in most countries during the regulated era. This was because regulations imposed for monetary-policy purposes simultaneously provided a measure of prudential security by constraining the choices banks and other financial institutions could make in their borrowing and lending decisions. The removal of monetary regulations created a vacuum, and left much greater scope for institutional autonomy than most monetary authorities thought desirable (Thompson 1991). This was also the firm view of the Campbell Committee in Australia that, as noted previously, combined recommendations for widespread deregulation with proposals for revamped prudential regulation and supervision of banks.[12]

The emergence of the Bank for International Settlements (BIS) prudential standards on bank capital adequacy in 1988 and their subsequent adoption by all the major Western countries, including Australia, signifies the international nature of this development. There are already some dissenting voices claiming that the BIS standards are too stringent and will engender a repeat of the experience of disintermediation during the latter days of the regulated era. On the other hand, the BIS, in conjunction with member central banks, is working on a similar set of standards to cover banks' exposure to interest-rate risk.

From the very outset of financial deregulation, it was recognised that removing controls on banks would expose them to greater risk. The concern, as evident in the Campbell Report, was to provide sufficient freedom for banks to compete effectively, with one another and with non-banks, without exposing the financial system to undue risk. A new trade-off of aggregate risk and return in the financial system had to be found, and the process of deregulation plus simultaneous re-regulation — 'liberalisation' — was designed to achieve just such a trade-off (Vives 1991).

There was never any intention, certainly not in official circles, of abandoning regulation altogether and moving into a regime of 'free banking', whatever the merits such a regime may offer (Dowd 1989). To characterise financial deregulation as a reckless dismantling of all controls in order to allow the untrammelled forces of the free market to hold sway is to misread completely both the intention and the outcome of the process as it actually took place, here in Australia as well as overseas.

The outcome of deregulation — paradise or pandemonium?

In October 1990 the then Treasurer Paul Keating commissioned the House of Representatives Standing Committee on Finance and Public Administration, under the Chairmanship of Stephen Martin, to undertake a major review of all aspects of the performance of the Australian banking industry since deregulation. The Martin Inquiry presented its report to Parliament in November 1991. One month later the Industry Commission presented a report on the 'Availability of Capital in Australia' that had been referred to the Commission by the Treasurer in December 1990. The two reports focused clearly (the former more broadly than the latter) on whether financial deregulation had delivered the benefits to the Australian community that were held out by the Campbell Committee a decade earlier.

Both reports concluded that the outcome of financial deregulation was broadly as predicted by the Campbell Committee, but that there had been substantial transitional problems. In the words of the Martin Committee:

> The Committee's assessment is that much of what was envisaged of deregulation has occurred. The efficiency of banks has increased and they have taken market share from other financial intermediaries that had benefited from regulation. Finance has become more widely available, though customers have had to pay a market price for it, including a component to reflect risk. Product range has increased and banks have increased their responsiveness to customers.
>
> However, deregulation has not delivered some of the benefits envisaged. While competition has been strong (perhaps too strong) in some sectors, particularly in the large-business sector, it has not been strong in the retail market. The failure of the market to deliver better

information to consumers and to price better for some products indicates that the retail [market] has still to realise the full benefit of deregulation. (HRSCF & PA 1991, p. 457)

The Industry Commission commented that:

The extensive deregulatory changes of the 1980s have meant that there are few barriers to entry to any segment of the finance sector. The result is an extensive, sophisticated and competitive capital market containing a range of intermediaries providing a diverse range of services (IC 1991, p. 223)

and further,

Financial institutions, particularly banks, have experienced transitional problems in adjusting to financial deregulation, but the benefits of deregulation are already apparent and should increase with time. (IC 1991, p. xv)

Other studies of the outcome of financial deregulation that echo these views include Ackland and Harper (1990), Harper (1991), Valentine (1991), Milbourne and Cumberworth (1991) and Twrdy (1991). Authors who draw the opposite conclusion, that financial deregulation had imposed net costs on the Australian community rather than net benefits, include Stretton (1987), Reinecke (1988), Fitzgerald (1990), Jones (1991) and Alford (1992; 1993).

For the purposes of this discussion, one should perhaps discount those supporters of deregulation who belong to the mainstream economics profession. This would include the authors of the Industry Commission report. Such individuals would be bound to support deregulation (so the critics might argue) since they subsist on a professional diet of economic rationalism and cannot, or will not, sanction any suggestion that rationalist economic policy might have failed. Granted the exclusion of such 'sympathetic' witnesses from court, it is therefore highly significant that the Martin Committee should have concluded so resolutely in favour of deregulation delivering most of its promised advantages.

No member of this Committee was a practising professional economist; indeed, a number of members were known by repute and party allegiance to be hostile towards 'free-market' economics. That such a group of individuals should endorse a report (with only one dissenting opinion on foreign-bank entry) whose conclusions were contrary, in at least some cases, to their natural political inclinations speaks highly of the professional integrity of the Committee and the quality of the advice set before it. It is difficult (although clearly not impossible) for prejudice to hold out against strong and persuasive evidence to the contrary. Members of the Martin Committee were persuaded by the weight of evidence and argument, not by predisposition and prejudice, to conclude in favour of deregulation.

If the support of a sceptical group of non-economists is accepted as valid, it becomes difficult to sustain the case that the Campbell Committee (also a committee, incidentally, without a single professional economist among its membership), and other proponents of deregulation, had no real concern for the welfare of the Australian people but sought to pursue a rationalist policy agenda on purely ideological grounds. This claim is either wrong outright, and there is in fact a connection between the adoption of rationalist reform in financial markets and the realisation of significant benefits for the Australian community, or else it is the happiest and most unlikely of coincidences.

But to say that deregulation conferred *net* benefits is not to say that the process was without costs. None of the assessments written by acknowledged economic rationalists has denied that deregulation imposed costs on the community as the adjustment to the new financial environment took place. Indeed, the process is continuing and further costs may yet be incurred. The focus should be on the net result of costs and benefits, and others, apart from economic rationalists, appear to be convinced that such net benefits exist. Economic rationalists admit that financial deregulation did not usher in paradise, but they reject the claim put forward by the critics that it gave rise to pandemonium.

It must be conceded that some of the costs of financial deregulation were not foreseen by its proponents, including the Campbell Committee. Valentine, a former Senior Adviser to the Committee, points out that the Committee 'oversold' the benefits of interest-rate deregulation on the cost and availability of housing finance. Moreover, the Committee failed to foresee the dramatic deterioration in the quality of loan portfolios of banks and non-banks that occurred during the rush to claim market share in the newly deregulated environment. A number of these failures have been subsequently redressed through re-regulation, especially the creation of the Australian Financial Institutions Commission to oversee the affairs of non-bank financial institutions. These developments (opposed by some rationalists) are further evidence that public policy in the financial arena is far from driven by a single-minded pursuit of rationalist purity.

Despite the acknowledged excesses of the 1980s there has been no official call to 'turn back the clock' on financial deregulation. Again, the Martin Committee, while critical of the failure of deregulation to promote competition in financial markets to the extent anticipated by the Campbell Committee and others, concludes that 'there should be no winding back of the deregulatory changes that have occurred' (p. 458). The Committee strongly endorses the need for continuing government involvement in a deregulated financial system 'to ensure that markets work efficiently and competitively and that the financial system remains safe and sound' (p. 458). Such a role would ensure the provision of adequate information to consumers, the prevention of monopoly and the supervision of prudential standards.

This is well within the bounds of a mainstream rationalist interpretation of the proper role for government in economic affairs and is certainly consistent with the role for government envisaged by the Campbell Committee in its blueprint for a deregulated financial system. The notion that economic rationalism in financial markets ever called for the complete abandonment of government intervention in financial markets is simply untrue.

A final area in which critics of economic rationalism seek to asperse financial deregulation is by attributing to deregulation the macroeconomic disturbances of the late 1980s and early 1990s, notably, the asset price inflation and the subsequent deep recession from which Australia is only now slowly emerging. In framing their explanations the critics tend to argue fallaciously that, because these events occurred *after* financial deregulation, they occurred *on account of* financial deregulation. Monocausal explanations are almost always incorrect, especially in the social sciences, and it is unrealistic to ascribe a complex phenomenon such as the business cycle to the single cause of financial deregulation.[13]

The full story of the late 1980s in Australia has yet to be written. The accounts that have emerged so far certainly attribute a role to financial deregulation, but it is a supporting role rather than a leading part. No doubt, financial deregulation facilitated the inflow of financial capital from outside Australia and encouraged the rapid growth of bank lending. It also exposed inadequate risk-assessment procedures adopted by banks and their corporate clients. The view that this, and this alone, was responsible for the rapid escalation of asset prices in Australia ignores the importance of distortions in the tax system and the fact that asset price inflation was an international phenomenon. It also makes no allowance for the role of monetary policy that, as some have argued (and others disputed), dropped a lighted match on economic tinder already dry from the effects of financial deregulation.

Similarly, the onset of recession cannot fairly be ascribed *in toto* to financial deregulation. It is true that financial deregulation allowed the current-account deficit to expand as it facilitated the import of capital to Australia.[14] The fact that the government chose to respond to higher levels of imported savings by dramatically tightening monetary policy, a response that a significant number of economists regarded as inappropriate and one the government itself now admits was overdone, can hardly be blamed on financial deregulation. Nor is the reimposition of controls on capital flows, especially international capital flows, the solution to what critics perceive as an ever-increasing burden of foreign debt.[15] The Economic Planning Advisory Council, expressing concern about Australia's external adjustment, rejects calls to reintroduce financial regulation on the grounds that it would be 'almost impossible to implement in today's capital markets . . . [and it] would involve a cost in terms of investment and growth' (Whitelaw & Howe 1992, p. 41).

The seriousness of Australia's macroeconomic problems is acknowledged by economic rationalists and 'anti-rationalists' alike. Such formal analysis of these problems as has been conducted to date identifies financial deregulation as a contributing factor. But the full explanation is more complex and, as a result, reimposing financial regulations would be of little assistance. In fact, the view of those who acknowledge the contribution made by financial deregulation to our present travail (in other words, who are not blindly pro-deregulation) is that re-regulation of financial markets would make it harder to achieve our macroeconomic objectives.

For most of our economic history, Australians have enjoyed the fruits of highly productive primary industries selling commodities into world markets hungry for raw materials. Our wealth was such that we could afford economic policies, including the tariff, whose rationality was open to question. Like the Europeans and Japanese of today, we could thumb our noses at the economic costs of widespread government intervention in, and protection of, our industries. Non-economic considerations dominated the political agenda.

In the last two decades the changing world economic environment has come to our attention. The declining importance of primary commodities in world trade and the consequent decline in our terms of trade have begun to affect our standard of living. There has been a realisation that we can no longer afford the luxury of ignoring economically expensive institutions, policies and practices — at least, not if we are to maintain a standard of living commensurate with other developed countries. The desire of the Australian people for their wealth to continue to grow at rates at least equal to those of our international peers has produced a reorientation of the national political focus. Economic considerations are now atop the political agenda.

'Economic rationalism' represents the incorporation into public policy of principles designed to enhance the efficiency of the Australian economy, and hence to promote its capacity to create material wealth. Some more conservative elements in Australian society decry the change of focus and lament the displacement of non-economic considerations by the economic. Many economic rationalists share the conservatives' concern that traditional non-economic objectives, including a degree of egalitarianism in the make-up of Australian society, may be compromised in the application of their policies. They fear, however, that the failure to sustain the wealth-creating capacity of the Australian economy, by eschewing rationalist reforms, may present a greater threat to non-economic goals. The hope is that, by regaining our economic security, we will once again be able to afford the luxury of trading off marginal improvements in economic performance against the achievement of particular social objectives.

Financial deregulation is the application of rationalist economic policy to financial markets with the intention of improving the performance markets so that they would play their part in revitalising the growth of the Australian economy. Experience to date points to both costs and benefits, although the majority view is that the latter outweigh the former.[16] Financial deregulation may not have been a spectacular success, but relative to the alternative of continuing with costly and inefficient regulatory intervention, it has probably achieved as much as we should have expected, if less than we actually hoped for.

Notes

1 It is not that 'rationalist' economic policy had never been applied to the Australian economy prior to the 1980s. One obvious example is the across-the-board tariff cut of 25 per cent that occurred in the mid-1970s. The point is that the economic policies of the first and subsequent Hawke governments and the current Keating government represent the most comprehensive attempt to apply orthodox microeconomic policy in a consistent and widespread manner.

2 See Fitzgerald (1990), Pusey (1991), Horne (1992) and Carroll and Manne (1992).

3 Precisely why economic rationalists should hold to such a dogma in the face of alleged evidence to the contrary is rarely explained. Unlike a religious conviction, there is no equivalent of Holy Scripture which rationalists hold out to be an infallible revelation of God's truth (as much as they might admire the writings of Adam Smith). It is sometimes suggested that economic rationalism serves the interests of the ruling

class and that its half-truths and fabrications have no purpose other than to keep the underclasses in their place — certainly not to discover objective truth. This is a dangerous doctrine for a critic of economic rationalism to espouse because it bears more than a passing resemblance to the self-interested behaviour that economic rationalism itself posits as a characteristic of human decision-making in an economic context.

4 See, for example, AFSI 1981, p. 10.

5 McCloskey (1985) is a recent and well-known example.

6 See, for example, Hogan (1982).

7 See, for example, Alford (1992, p. 781).

8 Indeed, in recent times, even socialist countries, including China (Weicai 1986), have moved (in some cases dramatically) to adopt market-oriented reforms to their economic and financial systems.

9 For a review of the Australian experience, see Harper (1986), Grenville (1991) and Industry Commission (1991, pp.14-17). On financial deregulation in Europe, see Steinherr (1990), Bisignano (1991) and Miles (1992); in the US, see Wojnilower (1991) and Greenbaum and Boot (1992); and in the Pacific Basin, see Cargill et al. (1986). For a general international overview, see International Monetary Fund (1991).

10 For a detailed discussion of these points in the context of the OECD countries, see Bröker (1989).

11 Macfarlane 1991) discusses this process in greater detail.

12 This is not to say that the previous framework of monetary regulations was proof against prudential concerns, as the demise of the Bank of Adelaide in 1979 illustrates.

13 Ironically, 'anti-rationalists' accuse rationalists of making the same mistake when they (allegedly) ascribe all economic ills to the baneful influence of government.

14 Although as Makin (1992) points out, the import of foreign capital facilitated the growth of assets in Australia to an extent which exceeded the accompanying increase in foreign liabilities. In other words, national net worth increased as a result of the current-account deficit.

15 EPAC (1991) argues that a multiplicity of factors, apart from financial deregulation, can be held responsible for the rapid growth of private debt in the 1980s. The resurrection of financial regulations could not, by itself, be expected to halt further accumulation of debt, let alone reduce the outstanding balance.

16 Note, in particular, the recent study by Lowe (1992), from the Economic Research Department of the Reserve Bank of Australia, which concludes that:

> the liberalisation of Australian financial markets has improved resource allocation and made possible a faster rate of economic growth than would have been possible had the regulated system continued. (p. 38)

References

Access Economics 1992, *Origins of the 1990-91 Recession in Australia*, EPAC Background Paper no. 18

Ackland, R. and Ian R. Harper 1992, 'Financial Deregulation in Australia:

Boon or Bane?', *Microeconomic Reform in Australia*, ed. P. Forsyth, Allen & Unwin, Sydney, pp. 45-71

Alford, K. 1992, 'Econotalk: The Case of Financial Deregulation', *Meanjin*, vol. 51, no. 4, pp. 766-84

Alford, K. 1993, 'From Belts and Braces to Bells and Whistles: Reviewing the Case for Deregulation', *National Economic Review*, forthcoming

Australian Financial System Inquiry 1981, *Final Report*, Australian Government Publishing Service, Canberra

Bisignano, J. 1991, 'European Financial Deregulation: The Pressures for Change and the Costs of Achievement', *The Deregulation of Financial Intermediaries*, ed. Ian Macfarlane, Reserve Bank of Australia, Sydney

Blundell-Wignall, A. and Browne, F. 1991, 'Macroeconomic Consequences of Financial Liberalisation: A Summary Report', *OECD Economics and Statistics Department Working Papers*, no. 98

Bröker, G. 1989, *Competition in Banking: Trends in Banking Structure and Regulation in OECD Countries*, OECD Publications, Paris

Cargill, T. F., Cheng, H. S. and Hutchinson, M. M. 1986, 'Financial Market Changes and Regulatory Reforms in Pacific Basin Countries: An Overview', *Financial Policy and Reform in Pacific Basin Countries*, ed. H. S. Cheng, Lexington Books, USA

Dowd, K. 1989, *The State and the Monetary System*, Philip Allan, UK

EPAC 1991, *The Surge in Australia's Private Debt: Causes, Consequences, Outlook*, background paper no. 14

Fitzgerald, T. 1990, *Between Life and Economics*, Boyer Lectures, Australian Broadcasting Corporation, Sydney

Greenbaum, S. I. and Boot, A.W.A. 1992, 'Deregulation of American Financial Markets', *The New Palgrave Dictionary of Money and Finance*, ed. P. Newman, M. Milgate and J. Eatwell, Macmillan Press, New York

Harper, Ian R. 1986, 'Why Financial Deregulation?', *The Australian Economic Review*, first quarter, pp. 37-49

— 1991, 'Competition: Choice and Diversity, Gainers and Losers', *The Deregulation of Financial Intermediaries*, ed. Ian Macfarlane, Reserve Bank of Australia, Sydney

Hogan, W. P. 1982, 'Financial Exegesis: Reviewing the Australian Financial System', *Economic Papers*, vol. 1, no. 1

Horne, D. ed. 1992, *The Trouble With Economic Rationalism*, Scribe Publications, Australia

House of Representatives Standing Committee on Finance and Public Administration 1991, *A Pocket Full of Change: Banking and Deregulation*, AGPS, Canberra

Industry Commission 1991, *Availability of Capital*, AGPS, Canberra

International Monetary Fund 1991, *International Capital Markets: Developments and Prospects*, World Economic and Financial Surveys, Washington, D.C.

Jones, E. 1991, Submission to House of Representatives Standing Committee on Finance and Public Administration (Martin) Inquiry into Banking, vol. 6, pp. 1389-439

Lipsey, R. G. and Lancaster, K. 1956, 'The General Theory of Second Best', *Review of Economic Studies*, vol. 24, no. 63, pp. 11-32

Litan, R.E. 1992, 'Financial Deregulation and Re-regulation', *The New Palgrave Dictionary of Money and Finance*, eds P. Newman, N. Milgate and J. Eatwell, Macmillan Press, New York

Lowe, P. 1992, 'The Impact of Financial Intermediaries on Resource Allocation and Economic Growth', Research Discussion Paper 9213, Reserve Bank of Australia

Macfarlane, I. 1991, 'The Lessons for Monetary Policy', *The Deregulation of Financial Intermediaries*, ed. Ian Macfarlane, Reserve Bank of Australia, Sydney

Makin, A. 1992, 'Capital Market Integration and National Net Worth', Department of Economics Discussion Paper no. 98, University of Queensland

Manne, R. and Carroll, J. 1992, *Shutdown: The Failure of Economic Rationalism and How to Rescue Australia*, Text Publishing, Australia

Marzouk, G. A. 1990, 'Deregulation and Macroeconomic Policy in Australia', Centre for Applied Economic Research, Paper no. 27

McCloskey, D. 1985, *The Rhetoric of Economics*, University of Wisconsin Press, USA

Milbourne, R. and Cumberworth, M. 1991, 'Australian Banking Performance in an Era of Deregulation', *Australian Economic Papers*, vol. 30, no. 57, pp. 171-91

Miles, D. 1992, 'Deregulation of European Financial Markets', *The New Palgrave Dictionary of Money and Finance*, eds P. Newman, N. Milgate and J. Eatwell, Macmillan Press, New York

OECD 1992, *Economic Surveys: Australia*, Paris

Pusey, M. 1991, *Economic Rationalsim in Canberra: A Nation-Building State Changes its Mind*, Cambridge University Press

Reinecke, I. 1988, *The Money Masters*, Heinemann

Steinherr, A. 1990, 'Financial Innovation, Internationalization, Deregulation and Market Integration in Europe: Why Does It All Happen Now?', *Financial Institutions in Europe Under New Competitive Conditions*, eds D. E. Fair and C. de Boissieu, Kluwer Academic Publishers

Stretton, H. 1987, *Political Essays*, Georgian House, Melbourne

Thompson, G. 1991, 'Prudential Lessons', *The Deregulation of Financial Intermediaries*, Ian Macfarlane ed., Reserve Bank of Australia, Sydney

Twrdy, K. 1992, 'Has Financial Deregulation Improved the Efficiency and Competitiveness of the Banking Sector?', thesis submitted at Macquarie University

Valentine, T. 1991, 'What the Campbell Committee Expected', *The Deregulation of Financial Intermediaries*, ed. Ian Macfarlane, Reserve Bank of Australia, Sydney

Vives, X. 1991, 'Regulatory Reform in European Banking', *European Economic Review*, vol. 35, pp. 505-15

Weicai, W. 1986, 'China's Economic and Social Reform', *Financial Policy and Reform in Pacific Basin Countries*, ed. Hang-Sheng Cheng, Lexington Books, USA

Whitelaw, R. and Howe, J. 1992, 'Australia's External Constraints in the 1990s', EPAC Research Paper no. 1, AGPS, Canberra

Wojnilower, A. 1991, 'Some Principles of Financial Deregulation: Lessons from the United States',*The Deregulation of Financial Intermediaries*, ed. Ian Macfarlane, Reserve Bank of Australia, Sydney

Comments

I n 1985/6 the Hawke-Keating government issued 16 new bank licences. These banks were established with an initial capital base of $2 to $3 billion. In order to make reasonable return on this shareholder funds, they had to be able to lend about 20 times the initial equity investment. The injection of $40 to $60 billion into bank credit from the newly licensed banks combined with the removal of controls on foreign borrowing led to the creation of a potentially unlimited supply of credit. In the three years to June 1990, credit grew 67 per cent or about 20 per cent a year.

The intensified competition between financial intermediaries for market share led to a collapse in lending standards. The injection of excessive supplies of credit led to an asset-price boom rather than a wages explosion (thanks to the discipline of the unions through the Accord process). Lending and borrowing decisions were based on anticipation of continued asset-price inflation rather than consideration of potential cash flows generated by the assets purchased.

The tax system magnified the distortions opened up by financial deregulation in a way that was not possible prior to deregulation when the banks competed on the basis of the quality of their lending portfolio rather than market share because the supply of credit was constrained. 'Nominal' rather than 'real' interest expenses and receipts were counted as costs or income for tax purposes which meant that the component of nominal interest that was compensated for inflation was fully taxed or allowed as income even though it was, in reality, early repayment of capital. The favourable tax treatment of interest expense over interest receipts, (as well as the differential tax treatment of borrowings abroad and domestic borrowing), encouraged debt-financed takeovers, loading companies with debt as defence of takeover and foreign borrowings rather than domestic borrowings. According to Chicago economist David Dale, quoted in Paul Kelly's *Age of Uncertainty*:

> In Australia external borrowing was encouraged by a financial liberalisation programme which caused the number of merchant banks to increase from 44 to 108. Because of the depression prevailing in many of Australia's traditional primary producing industries during the 1980s, the banks could not make loans to finance new capital intensive resource projects. So they went to work engineering a boom in speculative corporate takeover activity which has since been followed by a wave of

bankruptcies . . . it is obvious, in retrospect, that the critical factor attracting capital to Australia was not a boom in export generating investment; rather it was the interaction if an overdeveloped financial sector with open asset markets and surplus global liquidity.

Financial deregulation became the means by which a high proportion of the new, rapidly expanding business of the 1980s that were dependent on borrowed money for their expansion and might have been expected to play an important part in the restructuring process in the 1990s were bankrupted. Deregulation also became the conduit by which many of Australia's prime corporate assets were transferred to foreign control and created a huge debt that in one way or other, is the responsibility of all Australians without funding very much by way of wealth-producing assets that might help pay that debt.

The disastrous consequences for Australia's economic sovereignty might have been reduced if the monetary authorities had seen the poisonous interaction between the tax system and inflation which meant that the interest expense on borrowings to finance the takeovers were being met largely by accessing the general and takeover tax base and expectations by both borrower and lender that repayment of principle would come out of asset inflation rather than improved cash flows. The authorities should have tightened up the tax system especially through the introduction of an effective provisional tax on interest receipts on foreign borrowings; measures to prevent artificial schemes to separate income from expense so that all interest expense rather than interest expense net of dividends was deductible from other incomes and changing the tax treatment of interest expense and receipts from 'nominal' to 'real'. By not taxing only the 'real' component of interest receipts and not allowing only the 'real' component of interest expense as a deduction for income tax purposes, the tax system subsidised borrowers at the expense of savers.

The authorities response was higher and higher interest rates to try and 'wring inflation out of the system' or 'take the tough decision' rather than ameliorate the consequences of the interaction of high inflation and financial deregulation. The abolition of foreign exchange controls meant that authorities lost control over supply of credit. Until deregulation and the abolition of exchange control monetary policy operated primarily by credit rationing and to a lesser extent, the price of credit.

Deregulation meant that interest rates became the main means of monetary restraint. Thus for a given level of restraint, interests rates had to be higher than in a situation where the authorities had an influence over both the price and the supply of credit. Financial deregulation must assume a major part of the responsibility for the much wider swings in the business cycle than had occurred hitherto. Higher interest rates 'crowded out' more cautious investors in favour of the paper entrepreneurs. The high interest rates forced up the exchange rate, and made export and import competing industries uncompetitive.

The efficiency of capital markets as allocations of scarce savings to the most productive forms of investment was probably undermined by the breakdown in the long-term relationships between banks and their customers as a result of intensified competition between the providers of credit. According to Joseph Bisignano of the Bank of International Settlements, 'the extension of credit requires a transfer of inflation from borrower to lender and a monitoring of the credit quality of the borrower' which is extremely difficult, if not impossible, in an intensely competitive environment where customers are encouraged to shop around. (As an example of the times, in 1987 Warwick Fairfax was able to arrange a line of credit of $1 billion from the ANZ for the privatisation of Fairfax without the presentation of a business plan on the basis of a telephone call and the threat to take his business elsewhere.)

The result of excessive competition between the banks and inadequate supervision by the RBA was huge financial costs in the form of some $30 billion in non-performing loans, the failures of SBV and SBSA, and the closure of the first significant deposit-taking institution, Pyramid, since the 1890s. All the costs of these failures have not been borne by shareholders or depositors in the case of Pyramid; all Australians are taxed for these failures in the form of higher borrowing costs and lower deposit rates.

The abolition of foreign-exchange controls and the floating of the dollar created a foreign exchange market with a turnover of $16 to $18 billion a day largely divorced from the financing of international trade. Is all this speculative activity directed to getting a sustainable long-term exchange rate? The exchange rate bears very little relationship to fundamental values relating to Australian trade or the real purchasing power of the $A compared to other currencies because the stock of funds available to influence the value of the $A overwhelm the flow of funds generated by trade and the need to finance imbalances. Australia is about twentieth (and falling) in terms of ranking in international trade while the $A is the fifth or sixth most important currency in terms of volume traded.

The big mistakes associated with financial deregulation were the licensing of additional banks, inadequate supervision of the financial system by the RBA and the abolition of exchange controls. Exchange controls did not prevent speculative short-term capital movements, but they dampened their amplitudes. The case was never convincingly made by the Campbell or Martin Reports or the monetary authorities that exchange controls could not have been made to work more efficiently by being tightened up.

The major economic problem of the 1980s has been the failure of orthodox financial policies to engineer expansion of investment. 'Financial capital' has crowded out 'industrial capital'. Exchange controls are not a 'sufficient condition' for expansion of productive investment.

The bottom line in measuring the effectiveness of 'financial deregulation in the 1980s is its impact on the productivity of the other sectors of the economy that it serves. Over the past decade financial services share of GDP has increased from 8 to 9 per cent to 11 to 12 per cent of GDP, or, by some $8 to $12 billion a year. This increase in resources consumed by the financial sector has occurred without any discernible expansion in the productivity of the industries it served. In fact, quite the opposite happened. Productivity growth in industries subject to the discipline of takeover fell during the 1980s while productivity growth of GBE's not subject to this discipline accelerated. Privatisation will put the assets of GBEs 'into play' in the 1990s in much the same way that corporate assets were put 'into play' in the 1980s. Without fundamental reforms of the financial sector based on an understanding that the financial sector exists to serve the 'real' economy rather than vice versa, the financial services sector of the economy will live off privatisation in the 1990s in much the same way as it lived off takeovers in the 1980s, with some meagre returns.

Kym Anderson

International Trade and Australian Protectionism

From the early years of the Federation Australia had been highly protectionist towards its manufacturing sector while providing relatively little assistance to most of its primary industries. The past two decades, however, have seen a considerable lowering of manufacturing protection (with the notable exception until recently of textiles, clothing and cars). Moreover, there is bipartisan support for a continuation of that reform programme which, if completely implemented, would mean that by the turn of the century Australia's tariffs on imports, and other forms of government assistance to industries, would be close to zero.

Not surprisingly, these reforms are opposed by the producers who expect to lose directly from it. But there are others whose incomes are not directly affected who also question the wisdom of this policy reform, especially in the current climate in which unemployment has risen to unprecedented levels and per capita output has ceased to grow. This essay seeks to reassess the arguments for and against continuing the tariff reductions during the current recession and beyond. That reassessment first requires a review of the facts concerning the changing intersectoral structure of protection and other forms of industry assistance in Australia over time compared with other countries. The economic reasons for implementing the reform are reviewed. I will then examine the reasons most frequently given in arguing the case that Australia should delay or abort the tariff reform programme and/or replace the old with new forms of industry assistance. Even with the most generous of interpretations I find it difficult to see merit in those arguments for maintaining import tariffs or for adding new forms of assistance, despite the possibility that some jobs will be lost and the output of some firms will decline. This view is based not just on economic theory but more importantly on empirical evidence of how markets — political as well as economic — work in

Australia. I will conclude with the proposition that Australian society would be better off completing this aspect of its economic reform as soon as possible so that attention can focus more sharply on reaching consensus on how to reform other welfare-reducing policies.

Australian protection and other industry assistance

During the nineteenth century the Australian colonies were economically very distant from the centre of industrial activity in Europe. High transport costs provided local manufacturers with considerable natural protection; directly from imports and indirectly in the sense that they acted as an export tax so fewer resources were attracted to Australia's primary-export industries. It is therefore not surprising that at the time of Federation the average level of import tariffs was low in Australia compared with other high-income countries (see column 1 of Table 1). But as the real cost of intercontinental sea freight fell (North 1958) so did the Australian manufacturers' natural protection. That made those who had vested interests in protection in Victoria even more adamant that an Australian Federation would adopt high tariffs, bringing them into sharper conflict with free-trade interests in NSW. It is not surprising that trade policy was a major issue in the early years of Federation; two of the original three national political parties were called the Free Trade Party and the Protection Party, the third being the Labor Party. Yet, by the end of the first decade Australia had become clearly protectionist, the Free Trade Party had given up its commercial policy and fused with the Protection Party in an anti-Labor coalition. The Labor Party had also opted for protection, believing this would generate higher profits for manufacturers from whom workers could then extract a higher wage. Soon after its formation after World War I, the Country Party also came out in support of protection for many goods. This consensus allowed protection to be strengthened or at least maintained for more than half a century. As Table 1 shows, even as early as 1925 Australia's tariffs on manufactures averaged well above those of most other high-income countries; but that difference was greater still by 1970, partly because Australia had stood apart from the multilateral agreements to reduce manufacturing tariffs that resulted from a series of GATT trade negotiations in the 1950s and 1960s.[1]

Following a change to a Labor government in 1973, Australia's tariffs were cut by 25 per cent, and their average level has been steady or falling ever since. As a result, the effective rate of assistance to manufacturing in the early 1990s averaged less than half that of the early 1970s — or less than a third if the exceptionally highly protected

Table 1 Average manufacturing tariff rates, various industrial countries, 1902, 1925, and 1970 (%)

	1902	1925	1970
Australia	6	27	23
Belgium	13	15	na
Canada	17	23	14
Denmark	18	10	na
EEC-6[a]	na	na	8
France	34	21	na
Germany	25	20	na
Italy	27	22	na
Japan	10	13	12
Netherlands	3	6	na
New Zealand	9	na	23
Norway	12	na	11
Sweden	23	16	7
Switzerland	7	14	3
United States	73	37	9

na not available
a Belgium, France, West Germany, Italy, Luxembourg, and the Netherlands
Source: Anderson and Garnaut (1987, Table 2.1) based on the League of Nations, *Tariff Level Indices*, Geneva, 1927 and the GATT, *Basic Documentation of the Tariff*, Geneva, 1972

sub-sectors such as textiles, clothing and footwear, and motor vehicles and parts are ignored. If the reductions announced in March 1991 are further implemented, those rates will fall another two-thirds before the end of the decade (see Figure 1).

In the meantime the dispersion of industry assistance in the agricultural and mining sectors have also been reduced substantially: assistance to the agricultural sector has been reduced by about a third, and that to mining has continued to be close to zero. The past two decades have seen a remarkable reduction in the distortions to incentives facing producers of tradables in Australia. We now have the promise of Australia returning, by the late 1990s, to being one of the world's more open advanced economies. As the data on the share of GDP traded in Figure 2 suggests, it was in the mid-nineteenth century, particularly in light of the relatively high natural protection that transport costs provided Australian manufacturers then instead of being one of the most protected as it had become by the early 1980s.[2] Much has been written about why Australia adopted and held on for so long to a protectionist trade policy, and there is substantial

Figure 1
Effective rates of assistance to Australia's manufacturing and agricultural sectors, 1968 to 1990 with projections to 2000

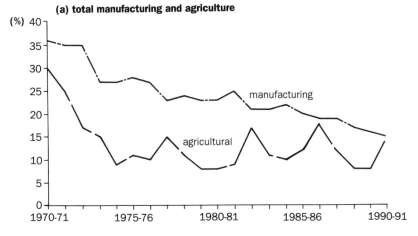

(a) total manufacturing and agriculture

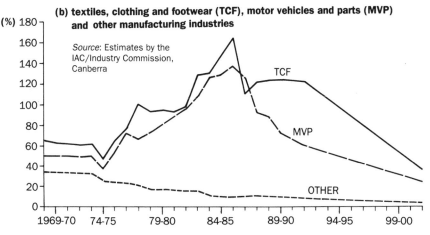

(b) textiles, clothing and footwear (TCF), motor vehicles and parts (MVP) and other manufacturing industries

Source: Estimates by the IAC/Industry Commission, Canberra

literature on the reasons for its recent reversal.[3] But it is not my purpose to review or extend that political economy literature. Rather, it is to examine the pros and cons of the recent and continuing liberalisation. We begin with its advantages to Australian society, as perceived by those who advocate reform.

The perceived benefits of trade liberalisation

Any student of economics has learnt in their principles course about the economic gains from exploiting one's comparative advantage through trade. Just as each of us sees the virtue of specialising in one set of tasks and exchanging the rewards of our labour with other households' specialisation in a different set of tasks, so it is between nations. Individuals benefit materially from such voluntary exchanges, otherwise they would not participate. The gains are larger the more scope there is for exploiting economies of scale in production and marketing, again at both household and national levels. But at the national level the gains are larger still the less competition there would be between firms in the absence of trade. Since in autarchy competition and scope for exploiting economies of scale are greater the larger the domestic economy, it follows that smaller economies such as Australia's would enjoy above-average benefits from trade liberalisation. Recent empirical studies inspired by the latest regional economic integration initiatives in Europe suggest that a large proportion of the comparative-static gains from trade liberalisation there would result from the pro-competitive effects of closer market integration through removing trade barriers (Winters 1992).

The benefits from freeing markets come not just from these static gains from trade. Recent eonomic models have also been able to incorporate more fully the beneficial effects of trade liberalisation on economic growth, with initial estimates suggesting that in the long term these effects could be several times larger than the conventionally measured comparative-static gains from trade-policy reform (Baldwin 1989; 1992). These recent endogenous growth analyses help to explain why so many econometric studies show a strong positive correlation between openness and economic-growth rates (Balassa 1978; Nishimizu and Page 1992). It is not surprising that Australia, having chosen to be highly protectionist and to delay its participation with other OECD countries in the post-war tariff reductions, progressively slipped down the rank ordering of countries in terms of per capita income. According to Maddison (1982), Australia was ranked as the world's highest-income country in the late nineteenth to early twentieth century, with an average income in 1870 that was about 40 per cent higher than the next country, the UK. But over the next hundred years its per capita output grew slower than in any other industrial country. It wasn't until World War 1 that Australia lost its first place to the US; by 1950 it had slipped to third, by 1970 to seventh, and by 1990 to eighteenth (as measured by the World Bank at official exchange rates — see Table 2).[4]

While no-one would suggest that the only, or even the prime, objective of policy is to ensure that Australia performs well on such league tables a large majority probably place a reasonably high weighting on that goal. As more and more Australians became aware during the 1970s and 1980s

Figure 2
Trade orientation and the GDP of various industrial countries, circa 1870 and 1984

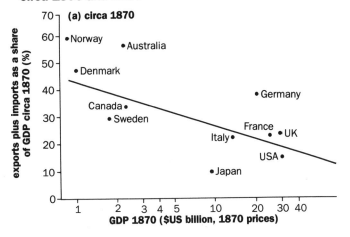

(a) circa 1870

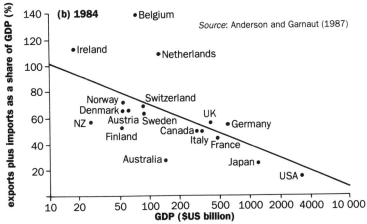

(b) 1984

Source: Anderson and Garnaut (1987)

of Australia's relatively poor economic growth performance, calls to reassess the country's economic policies became louder. They intensified further with the gradual dissemination of more information (a) on the degree of intersectoral skewness in industry assistance (as revealed progressively by the publication of the Tariff Board/Industries Assistance Commission/Industry Commision estimates of effective rates of assistance, and (b) on the large economic costs and often adverse distributional consequences of Australia's choice of trade and other industry assistance policies (as revealed very effectively by the general equilibrium analyses of the Impact Project — see Powell and Snape 1992).

Kym Anderson

Table 2 Ranking of high-income countries by GDP per capita, 1950 to 1990[a]

1950	1970	1990
1 United States	1 United States	1 Switzerland
2 Canada	2 Sweden	2 Luxembourg
3 AUSTRALIA	3 Canada	3 Japan
	4 Switzerland	4 Finland
	5 Denmark	5 Sweden
	6 Germany, GDR	6 Norway
	7 AUSTRALIA	7 Denmark
		8 Germany
		9 Iceland
		10 United States
		11 Canada
		12 United Arab Emirates
		13 France
		14 Austria
		15 Netherlands
		16 Belgium
		17 Italy
		18 AUSTRALIA

[a] At current prices converted to $US at official exchange rates
Source: World Bank, *World Tables 1992*, Washington, D.C., 1992, and earlier editions

Tolerance of high protection was also weakened as awareness of two other developments increased. One was the inevitability of Australia's increasing comparative disadvantage in an ever-widening range of manufactures as second- and third-generation newly industrialised economies in East Asia followed Japan's impressive example. China's dramatic penetration of Australia's market for clothing and other labour-intensive manufactures in the 1980s showed the futility of continuing to try to compete with such low-cost suppliers, while at the same time Northeast Asia's increased demands for Australian resource-based goods was a sharp reminder of the positive aspect of trading with the resource-poor, rapidly industrialising economies.[5]

The other development in the 1980s that affected Australian attitudes to protection was the 1986 launch of the eighth round of multilateral trade negotiations under the GATT. The Uruguay Round would, for the first time, include temperate farm products on the agenda. Thus an opportunity arose (as it happened, through the formation of the Cairns Group of non-subsidising, food-exporting countries) for Australia to take the lead in arguing for reductions in agricultural protectionism, particularly by Northeast Asia and Western Europe. But to do so without at the same time showing a willingness to remove Australia's own protectionist policies would have been unacceptably hypocritical.

Notwithstanding these arguments, numerous counter-arguments have been offered as to why Australia should temporarily or permanently reverse or at least slow its trade liberalisation programme. We now turn to examine some of the more common of those counter-arguments, as well as to the so-called 'new' arguments for industry assistance.

The (in)validity of arguments for reversing or slowing the tariff cuts

Numerous justifications on 'public-interest' grounds have been given in the past for Australia's highly protectionist policy, but virtually none of them apply today. For example, the argument that protection is necessary to foster infant industries was never strong since there were always more efficient ways to overcome whatever the problem was perceived to be.[6] Even if it had been valid in the early days of the Federation, it could hardly still be claimed to be necessary to help industries nearly a century later. Other justifications are resurfacing in the current recession. Three of the main ones are discussed below, namely, that tariff cuts (a) worsen the current-account deficit, (b) reduce the demand for labour (thereby adding to unemployment and to the downward pressure on real wages), and (c) reduce the industrial base and make the economy more vulnerable to fluctuations in export earnings. As well, there is a brief discussion of why the reform programme should be so inflexible and so extreme.

tariff cuts worsen the current-account deficit

The apparent logic of avoiding tariff cuts when there is a current-account deficit seems very appealing. What needs to be understood is that as well as the direct effect of encouraging imports, a tariff cut simultaneously improves the relative profitability of the country's export industries. It is an empirical question as to whether import growth would exceed export growth in the short to medium term (depending on the speed of adjustments by producers and consumers to the relative price changes), but with a flexible exchange rate and over the longer term there is no reason to expect the current-account deficit to be affected either way by a tariff cut, *ceteris paribus*. This is a straightforward implication of the Lerner (1939) symmetry theorem published more than fifty years ago.

tariff cuts reduce the demand for labour

In the early years of the Federation much was made of the argument that the provision of tariff protection to an industry would raise the demand for labour. These arguments, which included references also to its positive effect on immigration and its effective redistribution of income from wealthy landowners to poorer workers, were incorporated in a major report to the Australian government just prior to the depression (Brigden 1929). When the depression hit the natural policy reaction was to raise tariffs in the hope that this would slow the loss of jobs.

Immigration and income redistribution are handled with more direct policy instruments today, but what about the effect of protection on labour demand and wages? Again, it is easy to understand people not looking beyond the direct employment effect to see the negative indirect effect on labour demand in other sectors producing tradables, and therefore not realising that the aggregate employment effect is an empirical question. The seminal paper by Stolper and Samuelson (1941) suggested that, in the case of a country such as Australia that has relatively abundant capital (they called it 'land') compared to labour, an import tariff would, in the long run, boost the aggregate demand for labour and thereby put upward pressure on real wages. The Stolper-Samuelson theorem was less applicable to Australia than their article implied, not least because their analysis assumes that factors of production are perfectly mobile between domestic sectors but completely immmobile internationally. If one adopted the more realistic assumption that land is specific to the primary sector, then theory cannot tell us whether real incomes of workers will rise or fall, because the extent of the change in the price of a worker's consumption bundle has to be taken into account (Cassing 1981). Moreover, both labour and capital have been highly mobile internationally such that immigration could increase and/or aggregate capital inflows could slow or reverse following the imposition of a tariff, either of which could be enough to prevent real wages from rising (although stricter immigration quotas these days rule out the first option except by government design). Trade theory therefore provides no basis for assuming that a tariff increase will raise real incomes of workers and/or reduce unemployment.

But what about a tariff *decrease?* Given that wages in Australia tend to be sticky downwards, is it not possible that more jobs would be shed if tariffs are reduced further? The answer is possibly yes for the industries having to face less protection from import competition. However, three points need to be kept in mind.

First, if those job losses are in industries whose comparative disadvantage is increasing over time, as with labour-intensive manufacturing, then job losses will continue even if protection is maintained; protection needs to be ever-increasing for job losses to be avoided. Secondly, it is necessary to adopt an economy-wide perspective and realise that the job losses in the presently less protected sector may be more than compensated for by the number of jobs that will emerge in other more profitable sectors. And thirdly, the faster the economy grows, the fewer number of jobs lost and the larger and faster the number of new jobs created. This underscores the importance of trade-policy reform being accompanied by labour market and other growth-inducing microeconomic reforms.[7]

Which sectors would expand their job offerings as a result of reform is a moot point. As Max Corden (1979) points out and as ORANI modelling results have been able to indicate in some detail (see Powell and Snape 1992), most of those new jobs are unlikely to be in Australia's capital-intensive rural, mining and primary processing sectors (even though there would be some expansion there relative to what otherwise would have been the case). Rather, they would be in sectors producing non-tradables and services — which are where the vast majority of workers currently have and always will have their jobs — as well as in manufacturing firms that have found niche markets at home or abroad.

Furthermore, it is also necessary to consider the counterfactual situation of what employment levels would be in protected industries if their protection levels were retained. In this respect it is instructive to look at employment in Australia's textile, clothing and footwear (TCF) industries compared with that in other labour-intensive manufacturing industries. In the 1970s especially both groups suffered losses in profitability due to real-wage hikes and increased import competition from East Asia, but the former group enjoyed substantial increases in protection in the latter 1970s/early 1980s when protection for most other (and particularly other labour-intensive) industries was being reduced. Yet, as Table 3 shows, during that period employment fell almost as much in those favoured TCF industries as in other labour-intensive industries and far more than was the case for other manufacturing. The data suggests that the huge increase in TCF protection not only was unable to prevent large job losses in those industries — even though the subsidy equivalent of that protection was much more than the wages being paid — but it would have added to the job-loss difficulties of other labour-intensive industries as well. And since workers in the latter industries earn below-average incomes, and TCF protection (because it is effectively not only a producer subsidy but also a consumer tax) imposes a disproportionate burden on poorer households; their welfare has been doubly bruised. Admittedly, further job losses could add to social tensions in areas where unemployment is high. But this is not sufficient reason for retaining tariffs. That policy option is likely to be much less costly and have fewer adverse distributional consequences than bringing a halt to tariff reform, because the producer subsidy component of a tariff is equivalent to a subsidy to all workers in the industry (not just those in depressed regions) as well as to all owners of the industry's capital (which may, incidently, include foreigners). That option also has the advantage of focusing attention on the cost of such protection since the subsidy payments have to appear in the annual budget papers.

tariff cuts would make for a less balanced, more vulnerable, dependent economy

It is probably true that because of Australia's protection policy the manufacturing sector grew more rapidly in the first half of this century

Table 3 Changes in effective assistance and employment levels in selected Australian manufacturing sub-sectors, 1973 to 1983

	Effective rates of assistance (%)		Changes in rates of effective assistance (%)		Changes in employment (%)	
	1973-74	1982-83	1973-74 to 1977-78	1977-78 to 1982-83	1973-74 to 1977-78	1977-78 to 1982-83
Textiles, clothing and footwear	51	135	38	42	-24	-14
Other labour-intensive manufacturing	35	20	-10	-5	-30	-23
Other manufacturing	25	19	-6	0	-12	-6

Source: Anderson and Garnaut 1987, Table 6.2, based on IAC estimates of effective rates and ABS employment data

and has remained larger than it otherwise could (Anderson 1987). The desire to have a larger manufacturing base partly reflected a public interest in having an economy whose structure was not unlike that of other advanced industrial countries despite Australia's rich endowment of natural resources per worker.

Public sympathy for protection on these grounds arose because many people believe that the Australian economy rendered little assistance to the manufacturing sector and has an export structure that is narrowly based on primary products that tended to be subject to wide fluctuations. Neither of those perceptions is accurate. The first overlooks the services and non-tradable sectors. Yet, services in Australia currently accouint for three-quarters of GDP, four-fifths of employment and a fifth of exports. The possibilites for Australia to earn a larger proportion of export income from tourism, education and a host of other sevice activities as well as from sophisticated manufactures in niche markets has only just begun to be explored. Already, those efforts are showing up in the export data. Services have increased their share of Australia's exports from 16 to 20 per cent since the mid-1980s. The share of manufactures (excluding processeed primary products) in total exports rose from 10 to 16 per cent over those years (see Table 4, and Swan and Zeitsch 1992). There are also industries that produce non-tradable goods and services, demand for which would expand as incomes rise following trade liberalisation. Since by definition non-tradables have to be produced domestically, their expanded production to satisfy this extra demand would at least offset and may more than compensate for any net reduction in manufacturing activities in urban areas brought on by tariff reform.

The main reason that the second perception, that a free-trading Australia would be more vulnerable to fluctuations in its international terms of trade, overlook the fact that protection cuts increase the share of GDP that is traded and ensures that exports come from a wider range of industries than otherwise. Protection cuts are likely to make the economy's export earnings more rather than less stable through time. Indeed, the export composition data in Table 4 suggest this is already happening. It is true that self-sufficiency in highly protected products would decline, on an economy-wide scale, self-sufficiency in some of the less-protected products Australia currently imports may well increase — the measure of vulnerability is not so obviously negative. Insofar as our being free-trading increases the probability of other countries opening up their markets to our exports (for example, via the Cairns Group's efforts for a successful conclusion of the Uruguay Round of GATT) also adds to the probability that trade

Table 4 Contribution to exports of goods and services by sector, Australia, 1984 to 1992 (%)

	Rural products	Minerals and metals	Other merchandise	Services	Total
1984-85	31	43	10	16	100
1985-86	32	42	10	17	100
1986-87	30	39	12	18	100
1987-88	30	38	13	19	100
1988-89	29	38	12	20	100
1989-90	26	41	14	19	100
1990-91	22	43	15	20	100
1991-92	23	41	16	20	100

Source: Australian Bureau of Agricultural and Resource Economics, *Agricultural and Resources Quarterly,* September 1989 and December 1992.

reform would leave the Australian economy less, rather than more, vulnerable.

In short, reducing protection does not mean Australia regresses backwards to being more dependent on foreigners buying a small range of our primary products. On the contrary, it means progress and enjoyment of the fruits of greater interdependence with other economies. Australia has matured from its colonial dependence on Britain when it rebelled and went against the trend of other OECD countries by raising instead of lowering its protection levels (and suffering for it like many ex-colonies in the third world), to a period now when it is increasingly acknowledging the virtues of a broader international interdependence. One doubt that remains is whether it is sensible to continue pushing reform to its completion during a recession.

that reform should be more flexible and less extreme

Being 'more flexible' and 'less extreme' may be desirable in many circumstances but in the case of trade and other industry assistance policies it is far from desirable. Such action will only prolong the agony and is likely to make the present value of the benefits smaller (notwithstanding the risk of greater unemployment in some regions in the immediate term). Reducing tariffs to a maximum of 10 or 5 per cent rather than to zero simply means that the gains from reform will be less, particularly if the remaining differences in effective rates of assistance between industries are still significant. And excluding certain sectors only makes adjustment more difficult for others. The difficulties facing the manufacturing sector in the mid-1970s following the 25 per cent tariff cut of 1973 (coupled with real wage hikes, exchange-rate appreciation and intensified competition from Asia) led to the same calls for a halt or reversal of tariff cuts then as we have heard during the recession of the early 1990s (Gruen 1975). The government then responded by oiling only the squeakiest wheels; resulting in assistance that was highly skewed in favour of a few industries and at the expense of the vast majority of manufacturers (see Table 3) and other tradable sectors. I have great difficulty in seeing the justice in such selective redistribution.

The most important reason for sticking to the announced timetable and taking the reforms to their logical conclusion of zero tariffs has to do with politics. If industries are convinced the government will not respond to lobbying pressure, they will cease their investments in tariff lobbying and divert more resources to furthering their international competitiveness. Lobbying for protection is most obvious in the lead-up to elections by industries located in marginal electorates. The assistance given to Kodak during the 1990 election campaign and the three-year postponement of sugar-tariff reductions announced just prior to the 1993 elections are clear cases in point. If the use of tariffs and other trade-policy instruments were to be outlawed and any lobbying has to be directed toward more direct forms of government assistance, the greater transparency of the latter is likely to ensure that the cost and other adverse consequences of such intervention will be smaller than those of trade policies.

The questionable validity of the 'new' arguments for industry assistance

The new arguments for industry assistance put forward have drawn in part on the strategic trade literature that sprung up in the US during the late 1970s and early 1980s. But these arguments too suffered badly when scrutinised from a practical point of view, especially for small economies such as Australia (Grossman 1990).[8] First, the perspective of many of the protagonists is, as Banks (1992) puts it, a 'firm's eye view' that ignores the indirect economy-wide effects. In that respect the arguments have the same flaws as that for tariffs. And secondly, the 'picking of winners' deserving of support is fraught with the usual danger that government failure will be worse than the supposed market failure the intervention is meant to overcome. Government failure can come at the bureaucratic level (involving not just administrative costs but also the costs of making mistakes in deciding how much to give whom); and it can also come at the political level at which deals between politicians and vested interests are struck. In short, the 'new' arguments for industry assistance have little more practical validity than the traditional arguments for tariffs and other forms of selective assistance.

That conclusion is amplified by the experiences of East Asia. Much has been made of the fact that governments intervene in the highly successful economies of East Asia and that in particular some of those economies do not practice completely free trade (Wade 1990). At least two points need to be made in response to the claim that 'what was good for the goose will be good for the gander'. One is that the counterfactual for those economies is not known, they may well have grown even faster had their governments intervened less. The other is that the quality and type of intervention matters. The economies of South Korea and Taiwan, for example, did not grow rapidly under the import-substitution policies that were in place in the 1950s. It was only after those protection policies were replaced in the early 1960s with more outward-oriented policy that those economies boomed. It is true that the latter regimes included policies that promoted export industries, but as a whole the regimes remained biased toward import-competing industries (Hong and Krause 1981). What distinguishes them from the policy regimes of many other countries apart from their agricultural policies is that the extent of distortion to the inter-industry structure of incentives was reduced to relatively small levels (as Australia is currently trying to do) and the changes in that pattern of distortions over time has been such as to facilitate structural adjustment in line with changes in their comparative advantages. The latter contrasts markedly with Australia's attempts in the past to use protection policies to prevent or at least postpone adjustment to permanent changes in our competitiveness in labour-intensive manufacturing.

The argument that we should copy or counteract other countries' trade policies may appear to have more validity in cases where the international price of an industry's product is significantly reduced by those policies abroad. If the price-depressing policies are immovable even in the long term (e.g., via commercial diplomatic efforts), they should be considered a permanent part of Australia's trading environment from which we benefit (if the relevant items are importables) or are worse off (if Australia is still a net exporter, as with dairy products and sugar). The same might be said for short-term actions or policies overseas (dumping or temporary subsidies), assuming Australia's private sector has access to borrowing to tide them over. In both situations but more so in the latter, a case may be made for intervention (e.g., anti-dumping or countervailing duties, as allowed by the GATT) on the grounds that domestic interest groups would be more inclined to support a liberal trade policy if the government were prepared to provide offsets in these 'unfair' situations (see Brennan and Pincus 1992). Once that type of policy response is allowed in principle, there is the risk that it will be demanded for normal protectionist reasons as well as has been the case in Australia (Banks 1990).

Should losers from tariff reform be compensated?

As with antidumping and countervailing duties, reasonable people can and do argue the case for using some of the benefits from tariff reform to compensate the losers (see Pincus in this volume). The most compelling reason for doing so is purely political, namely, to reduce opposition to the reform. But there are several compelling reasons not to compensate as well. One is simply the injustice of compensating for this but not other policy changes (or for a poor season or a downturn in the international price for an industry's output). Another is that if the government promises compensation following any policy reform, this increases the incentive for lobbyists to seek assistance policies because there will be the additional payoff of compensation should assistance be withdrawn in the future. There is also the risk that lobbying efforts will be devoted to securing compensation in the form of elaborate structural adjustment schemes that turn out not to encourage permanent adjustment. In 1973/74, for example, textile workers who were displaced by the tariff cuts of 1973 were given several months' pay by the government. Employers laid off workers for that period with the understanding that the same workers would be hired again once a reversal of the protection cut had been secured, as indeed it was. Ideally, general safety nets should be in place to provide social insurance for all unforseen shocks rather than specific ones for a particular policy change. Apart from anything else, there is the difficulty of identifying who has been hurt by a specific policy action as distinct from all the other changes in the economy

The difference between so-called economic rationalists who believe in the virtues of free trade and those who believe that Australia should slow or reverse its adopted programme of tariff cuts is not that the former has a narrower perception of what determines individual and social welfare. Rather, it is arguable that the main difference is that the latter group has an insufficient understanding of the indirect effects of protection policies and the availability of superior policy instruments for achieving society's objectives that are less costly and more transparent. The good news is that the degree of misunderstanding is steadily diminishing in Australia. This fact — reflected in the growth in community support for trade liberalisation during the past quarter century — is a result of the increased dissemination of pertinent information on the costs and uneven income redistributional consequences of protection compared with the lesser adverse effects of more direct policy instruments. Bodies such as the IAC and the Industry Commission and the associated Impact Project have made enormous contributions in improving our understanding of the indirect and economy-wide effects of trade and other industry assistance policies. Not surprisingly, other governments and international agencies are looking favourably at the idea of setting up similar transparency institutions elsewhere — which is ironic since the Australian government is currently undermining morale in the Commission by proposing that it be relocated away from the policy arena in Canberra!

Even if tariffs are phased down to zero by the end of the 1990s, Australia still may not be a free-trading nation. The history of tariff reductions in other industrial countries is overlapped with a history of rising non-tariff barriers (NTBs). While the latter may have simply slowed rather than reversed the trade-liberalising effects of the tariff cuts, NTBs are typically both more covert and uneven in their impact across industries than has been the case with tariffs. One of the more worrying developments in the global trading system recently has been the increasing use of anti-dumping and countervailing duties in periods of downturn in an economy — a development of which Australia has been a part (Banks 1990; Industry Commission 1992). This is mentioned not as an argument against the phasing-out of tariffs but simply as a word of caution against complacency. Alternative policy instruments that will be sought by vested interests seeking industry assistance will not always be less inefficient and/or more equitable than tariffs. This suggests that Australia will have a continuing need for its Industry Commission in the years ahead as tariffs are gradually phased out. But it also follows that the sooner tariffs are abolished, the sooner attention can focus more sharply on NTBs and other policy areas needing reform.

Notes

1 For details of Australia's protection policies to the 1970s, see Lloyd (1978) and the references therein.
2 The least-squares regression lines in Figure 2 slope downwards because larger economies tend to be more diversified and have less need to trade internationally.
3 See, for example, Anderson and Garnaut (1987), Capling and Galligan (1992) and the references therein.

4   The use of purchasing-power parity (PPP) rather than market exchange
    rates would provide a less worrying picture, but only slightly. Unfortu-
    nately PPP estimates are available only for a subset of countries and for
    recent decades, so a complete comparison is not possible. See Dowrick
    in this volume.
5   Details of those developments are provided in Garnaut (1989).
6   If it was believed that there was an imperfection in the capital market
    whereby banks would not lend to new industries, the first-best policy would
    be to improve the capital market. See Baldwin (1969) and Corden (1974).
7   It has been acknowledged that one of the positive indirect economic
    effects of tariff reform is that it puts more pressure on the government
    and unions to reform labour markets.
8   For a range of views by trade economists on that literature's relevance
    to the virtues of free trade, compare Bhagwati (1989) and Baldwin (1992)
    with Krugman (1987).
9   While it is not conclusive that NTBs have less than offset tariff cuts, the
    extent of increase in the shares of GDP traded is supportive of that view.
    Between 1968 and 1990, for example, merchandise exports plus imports
    as a share of GDP rose from 34 to 46 per cent in Western Europe, from
    10 to 19 per cent in North America, from 21 to 29 per cent in Asia and
    from 22 to 34 per cent globally (Anderson and Norheim 1993).

References

Anderson, K. 1987, 'Tariffs and the Manufacturing Sector', *The Australian
    Economy in the Long Run*, ed. R. Maddock and I.W. McLean, Cambridge
    University Press, Cambridge
Anderson, K. and Garnaut, R. 1987, *Australian Protectionism, Extent, Causes
    and Effects*, Allen & Unwin, Sydney
Anderson, K. and Norheim, V. 1993, 'Is World Trade Becoming More Regional-
    ized?' *Review of International Economics*, vol. 1, no. 2, pp. 91-109
Balassa, B. 1978, 'Exports and Economic Growth, pp. Further Evidence',
    Journal of Development Economics, vol. 5, no. 2, pp. 181-9
Baldwin, R. 1989, 'On the Growth Effects of 1992', *Economic Policy*, no. 9,
    pp. 247-81
— 1992, 'Measurable Dynamic Gains From Trade', *Journal of Political
    Economy*, vol. 100, no. 1, pp. 162-74
Baldwin, R. E. 1969, 'The Case Against Infant Industry Protection', *Journal
    of Political Economy*, vol. 77, no. 3, pp. 295-305
— 1992, 'Are Economists' Traditional Trade Policy Views Still Valid?' *Journal
    of Economic Literature*, vol. 30, no. 2, pp. 804-29
Banks, G. 1990, 'Australia's Antidumping Experience', PRE Working Paper
    no. WPS 551, The World Bank, Washington, D.C.
— 1992, 'A Comment on Determining Industry Policy', *Australian Journal
    of Management*, vol. 17, no. 1, pp. 153-60
Bhagwati, J. N. 1989, 'Is Free Trade Passé After All?' *Weltwirtschaftliches
    Archiv*, vol. 125, no. 1, pp. 17-44
Brennan, G. and Pincus, J. 1992, 'Economic Rationalism Revisited: The Case
    of Countervailing Duties', paper presented to the 1992 Conference of
    Economists, University of Melbourne, 8-10 July

Brigden, J. B., Copeland, D. B., Dyason, E. C., Giblin, J. F. and Wickens, C. H. 1929, *The Australian Tariff: An Economic Enquiry*, Melbourne University Press, Melbourne

Capling, A. and Galligan, B. 1992, *Beyond the Protective State: The Political Economy of Australia's Manufacturing Industry Policy*, Cambridge University Press, Cambridge

Cassing, J. 1981, 'On the Relationship Between Commodity Prices and Factor Owners' Real Positions', *Journal of Political Economy*, vol. 89, no. 3, pp. 593-5

Corden, W. M. 1974, *Trade Policy and Economic Welfare*, Clarendon Press, Oxford

— 1979, 'Tell Us Where the Extra Jobs Will Be', *Bank of New South Wales Review*, no. 30, pp. 1-5

Garnaut, R. 1989, *Australia and the Northeast Asian Ascendency*, AGPS, Canberra

Grossman, G. M. 1990, 'Promoting New Industrial Activities: A Survey of Recent Arguments and Evidence', *OECD Economic Studies*, no. 14, pp. 87-125

Gruen, F. H. 1975, 'The 25 per cent Tariff cut: Was it a Mistake?' *Australian Quarterly*, vol. 47, no. 2, pp. 7-20

Hong, W. and Krause L. B., eds 1981, *Trade and Growth of the Advanced Developing Countries in the Pacific Basin*, Korea Development Institute Press, Seoul

Industry Commission 1990, *Strategic Trade Theory, pp. The East Asian Experience*, AGPS, Canberra

Industry Commission 1992, *Annual Report 1991-92*, AGPS, Canberra

Krugman, P. R. 1987, 'Is Free Trade Passé?' *Journal of Economic Perspectives*, vol. 1, no. 2, pp. 131-44

Lerner, A. P. 1936, 'The Symmetry Between Import and Export Taxes', *Economica*, vol. 3, no. 11, pp. 306-13

Lloyd, P. J. 1978, 'Protection Policy', *Surveys of Australian Economics*, vol. 1, ed. F.H. Gruen, Allen & Unwin, Sydney

Maddison, A. 1982, *Phases of Capitalist Development*, Oxford University Press, London

Nishimizu, M. and Page, J. M. 1991, 'Trade Policy, Market Orientation, and Productivity Change in Industry', *Trade Theory and Economic Policy*, ed. J. de Melo and A. Sapir, Basil Blackwell, Oxford

North, D. C. 1958, 'Ocean Freight Rates and Economic Development, 1750-1913', *Journal of Economic History*, vol. 18, no. 4, pp. 537-55

Powell, A. A. and Snape, R. H. 1992, 'The Contribution of Applied General Equilibrium Analysis to Policy Reform in Australia', General Paper No. G-98, Impact Project, Monash University, Clayton, January

Swan, P.L. and Zeitsch, J. 1992, 'The Emerging Australian Manufacturing Export Response to Microeconomic Reform, *Australian Journal of Management*, vol. 17, no. 1, pp. 21-66

Stolper, W. and Samuelson, P. A. 1941, 'Protection and Real Wages', *Review of Economic Studies*, vol. 9, no. 1, pp. 58-73

Wade, R. 1990, *Governing the Market: Economic Theory and the Role of Government in East Asian Industrialization*, Princeton University Press, Princeton

Winters, L. A., ed. 1992, *Trade Flows and Trade Policy After '1992'*, Cambridge University Press, Cambridge

Vince FitzGerald

Comments

The core of Kym Anderson's essay, reached after a tour of the past background to the current debate, takes each of five arguments or propositions commonly raised against tariff cuts (e.g., that tariff cuts reduce the demand for labour) and sets out a rebuttal.

The essay's primary audience is presumably the sort of people who would attend a conference such as this — those engaging with, or interested in, the intellectual debate, particularly economists themselves. The five propositions however, are ones which have had wide currency in popular discussion and in media coverage of the debate.

It would be easy to conclude, looking at media coverage of the last two to three years, that despite a spirited defence from a few, the economic rationalist position is in retreat and the anti-economic rationalist assault is succeeding, and that it is only a matter of time before the basic political consensus around the relevant policies breaks down.

I don't think that nearly as many people in the wider Australian community oppose the tariff cuts as is supposed. Rather, I think that surprisingly many people have an understanding of the positive results the cuts are intended to achieve, and actually believe that they are likely to have such effects.

A piece of evidence for these brash assertions is a Morgan Poll released at the end of November 1992 that showed 41 per cent nationally supported cutting motor vehicle tariffs to near zero levels by 2000, 40 per cent opposed the move, and 19 per cent were undecided. There was an almost even split, 40—40 and 41—41 in NSW and Victoria respectively, with clear Queensland and WA majorities for the cuts outweighing equally clear majorities against the cuts in SA and Tasmania. More encouraging was a very strong majority: 42 per cent to 34 per cent nationally who thought that the cuts would result in a more efficient car industry; only in SA was there a narrow margin the other way.

I think that this level of understanding of the issues speaks volumes for the efforts of those such as the Industry Commission who have patiently educated the public over the years.

My problem with this paper is that while most economists will read it as a confirmation of their views, it does not go very far on engaging the debate with those who hold different but reasonable views and are prepared to debate them in relation to evidence; nor does it seem to me to offer much material to contribute to the public debate.

Figure 1
ETM Exports (Original Prices)

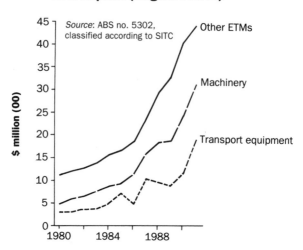

There are, I would concede, well-based concerns held by some in the community, that
- tariff cuts will cause at least employment displacement for some time, even if aggregate employment in the distant future is not significantly affected. In a recession especially, when anyone losing a job is apt to be in the dole queue a long time, this type of concern need to be sensitively addressed; and
- tariff cuts may worsen the current account over some uncomfortably long-short to medium run. For a country heavily in debt this is again a concern that needs addressing

The essay's answer to the former is to cite trade theory (the Stolper-Samuelson theorem, etc.) and observe that employment has fallen almost as much in the highly protected TCF sector in past years as in other labour-intensive industries. There is no substantial canvassing of the issues this poses in the current climate. On the possible current-account impact, there is no discussion of the empirical evidence at all, just a reference to Abba P. Lerner's 1939 theoretical result on the symmetry between import and export taxes.

Not everyone outside the profession takes the view implied in Anderson's essay, that any flexibility in reform programmes 'will open the floodgates', 'simply open the door to abuse by influential interest groups'. That is a rigid but respectable position; however, to put it forward as unarguable truth seems to me to be avoiding full

Figure 2
Sample of 401 new manufacturing exporters

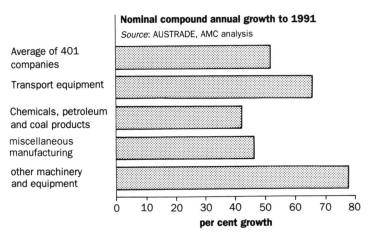

Nominal compound annual growth to 1991
Source: AUSTRADE, AMC analysis

engagement in the strongest *intellectual* forces now ranged against the pure free-trade position.

I think there is a serious intellectual debate still running around the world over trade and industry politics. Robert Manne remarked yesterday that he recalled Paul Krugman commenting in *The Economist* that he had become, in the light of increased globalisation and more complex production and markets, pervasive spillovers and so on, a 'cautious activist' on issues of government intervention. Krugman is now advocating a 'modest industrial policy, say $10 billion of subsidies annually for industries for which a strong case for external economies can be made'. Anderson makes a brief reference to the strategic trade theory literature but his discussion does not take into account some recent contributions that tend to move the debate on trade and industry policies from the premise that 'all government interventions are bad' to something more constructive like 'in what specific circumstances might government intervention be justified?'

I think Anderson could have covered Gene Grossman's 1990 OECD paper that he cites in more depth, since Grossman probably provides the best recent survey of this new debate. Jon Stanford's book *Industrial Policy in Australia and Europe* argues for a 'middle way' and presents arguments that are to my mind much more worthy of engagement than the extreme anti-economic rationalist assertions that at least one speaker put forward yesterday. Stanford says,

Opposition to generalised policies of intervention does not need to be based on religious grounds, nor should one attempt to rewrite history to prove that intervention is always damaging, if only to the human spirit. Neither does it mean that the only alternative is a pure *laissez-faire* approach.

Stanford, like Grossman, believes that the evidence rules out any *general* case for intervention, but does not necessarily rule out intervention in specific instances. Stanford also sugggests that output subsidies and trade barriers (tariffs, etc.) are unlikely to be the best instruments, rather, intervention should focus on particular activities that can generate positive spillovers such as research and development.

I also share in Michael Porter's assertion that technological change is a key factor in raising living standards over the longer term and that this dynamic obervation suggests that 'we should not be totally indifferent as to what sectors and activities claim valuable productive resources'. Others may agree with any implication for sectoral assistance and consider that it at most may support *generic* government support for say, education and research. I think Stanford's objective is the same as that of most mainstream economists — maximising national welfare and I think we should now be engaging more in the debate on 'what after tariffs?' — to which the answer may be 'not much, and very critically and sparingly applied', and less in further debate on 'tariffs or no tariffs?'

I believe that mainstream economists, provided that they widen their focus to look more thoroughly and rigourously at important dynamic phenomena such as globalisation of production and markets will win the debate in Australia. The current process of economic adjustment is demonstrably working in the sense of raising Australian manufacturing industry efficiency and viability and showed that the old tariff debate has outlived its welcome.

Empirical evidence has shown us that over the five years to 1990/91 the share of muanfactures in commodity exports rose from 16.7 per cent to 23.8 per cent within which STMs rose from 8 per cent to 10.5 per cent while ETMs rose from 8.8 per cent to 13.3 per cent. The extremely encouraging recent survey conducted by McKinsey's for the AMC found some 400 small and medium-sized firms whose exports had grown by 50 per cent per annum compound for five years to the point that they now collectively account for the some billions of dollars of export trade — a significant proportion of the nation's total — and much of it achieved in the competitive Asian-Pacific area. Moreover, while some of the exports can probably be attributed in part to specific interventions (e.g., export facilitation in the motor-vehicle industry), in many cases they plainly cannot, not does 'fire-sale' behaviour in response to recessed domestic demand appear to be a major factor, since the companies' export successes date from well before the onset of the recession. Finally, I understand that the report found that the major issues for the firms concerned were microeconomic reforms, not tariffs. Other evidence has shown that many aspects of the Australian manufacturing industry has become much more internationally competitive under the current policies and that includes global and technology-intensive industries such as telecommunications equipment.

Mainstream economics and empirical evidence will, I believe, determine the outcome of the current debate over trade and industry policies, and in the process will marginalise extreme anti-rationalist assertion. While Anderson's essay raises many valid points, I would have liked to see him delve further into many of the issues that he raises.

Judith Sloan

Labour-Market Reform: an Economist's Perspective

The anti-economists: hoist by their own petard

Those who are opposed to the ideas of 'economic rationalism' will often refer to the labour market as a special case where economic theory has no place because the labour market is not like the market for cabbages. In terms of the latter proposition, this is quite true, the labour market does not behave as a spot-auction market. The bulk of labour-market arrangements are characterised by long-term attachments between buyers and sellers. This realisation does not rule out the importance of economics in general, or price in particular when analysing the labour market and industrial relations.

Indeed, anti-economists and corporatists are often hoist by their own petard when advocating policies that assume that prices/wages do matter a great deal in the labour market. A clear case is wage-subsidy schemes designed to assist the unemployed. If employers require subsidies to be encouraged to recruit individuals from the unemployment queue, this surely indicates that wages are above market-clearing levels for these individuals. If this were not the case, why would there be a need to provide subsidies? Similarly, the Prices and Incomes Accord, a central part of which has been to restrain the course of real wages, has been predicated on the assumption that employment and inflation are directly affected by real-wage movements.

Even among economists, there is often a backing-away from industrial-relations reform, the labour market being seen as a special case, or alternatively labour-market reform is seen as a second-order issue (see Mitchell 1991). For instance, Hancock (1987, p. 106) has argued that:

> it is irrelevant to test the performance of the Australian industrial relations system . . . against the the characteristics of the competitive market of economic theory. The overwhelmingly important attribute of the com-

petitive market is the absence of power; whereas the raison d'être of industrial relations systems is precisely the management of power.

He proposes that the way forward lies with better operation of the conciliation and arbitration system. In a similar vein, Dabscheck (1992, p. 309) maintains that the original vision of Australia's system of conciliation and arbitration as a 'new province for law and order' has 'stood the test of time' as a conceptual proposition and 'has been an all-pervasive feature of Australian industrial relations'. It is not clear which test the arbitration system has passed, nor why the historically inherited system should be retained. The point is, many academic economists, particularly those working in industrial-relations departments, essentially concur with Dabscheck.

The effect of Australia's arbitration system on relative wages has been assessed by a number of economists. There was the early work of Brown, Hayles, Hughes and Rowe (1978) who measured inter-occupational wage differences in three cities across the world, including Adelaide, and found a high degree of similarity. Norris (1986) also concluded that international comparisons of wage relativities indicate that Australia's pattern is broadly similar to, albeit slightly more compressed than, other developed economies. But as Blandy and Sloan (1986, p. 3) have argued, if 'the system has no discernible influence compared with a 'market' outcome . . . the retention of the system becomes difficult to defend'. There is no case for tax-payers to fund a dead-weight loss.

A related but reverse point concerns the regional disparity in earnings that might be expected to emerge in an unregulated labour market, compared with the outcomes of the arbitration system. Certainly, in a competitive labour market with complete information and zero mobility costs, one would expect a very high degree of uniformity in the pay levels of those in the same occupations with the same qualifications. This proposition is often used as a basis to defend the degree of wage uniformity across regions that arises out of the workings of the arbitration system. But economists would be the first to admit that information in the labour market is not perfect and that significant mobility costs exist. A dispersion in occupational earnings is likely to exist and will not necessarily disappear over time. A study by DEET (1993) demonstrates that the regional segmentation of the Australian labour market is large. A fitter in Kalgoorlie would not be expected to earn the same as a fitter in Footscray in an unregulated labour market. Yet, through the arbitration system, particularly the federal award system, a high degree of uniformity is imposed on occupational earnings although over-award payments can bring wages *up* to market levels.

The irony is, anti-economists often advocate policies that are squarely based on the proposition that prices/wages do matter. Similarly, some of the research on the effects of the arbitration system implies that the system is in effect a dead-weight loss and should therefore be abolished — an implication rarely drawn by anti-economists. On the contrary, the competitive labour-market model is often used to defend the uniformity in pay and conditions arising from the system of legal awards, when in fact most economists would argue that because of imperfect information and high mobility costs, a degree of regional disparity in occupational earnings is likely to be an equilibrium outcome.

The contribution of economic theory

This section outlines the contribution of economic theory to the analysis of the labour market and industrial relations. It has been argued that modern labour economic theory informs us about the operations of labour markets and points to appropriate policy directions. There have been a number of exciting new streams of labour-market analysis over the past three decades or so. These start from the premises that relationships between workers and their employers generally extend over years; that the employment relationship is essentially 'idiosyncratic' [sic] (see Williamson, Wachter and Harris 1975) in the sense that the identities of workers and employers matter and that productivity is endogenous, not a given. While it is difficult to group all the different (overlapping) theories and ideas, some of the new developments include: theories focusing on on-the-job training (dating from Oi (1962) and Becker (1962)), implicit contract theory and relational contracting theory (incorporating transactions-costs theory).

Some of the main ideas of these theories follow (see Brook 1990). On-the-job training is very important in many jobs, it is an investment activity for both workers and employers. Where the training is firm-specific, the investment is valuable so long as trained employees remain working for the firm that has provided the training. In other words, both workers and employers have strong incentives to defend their investments by continuing the employment relationship. Arising from high levels of on-the-job training, long-duration jobs are common since there are substantial transaction costs for both workers and employers if the employment contract is terminated.

In effect, a 'hostage situation' exists since workers lose if they are laid off but employers lose if workers quit. Unions, particularly enterprise unions, can play a useful role in monitoring and balancing the situation.

Moreover, as employers gain from having a reputation as a 'good employer' (employees will carry a greater share of training costs), unions can be important in terms of verifying this reputation and informing prospective employees (see Okun 1981; Gorringe 1987).

Trade unions can also enhance productivity by providing a 'collective voice' for individual employees, enabling them to channel grievances to employers (Freeman and Medoff 1984). Fear of retribution might otherwise discourage employees from communicating their grievances and frustrated workers may quit. Unions can increase job duration and encourage firm-specific training by providing a 'collective voice'. Economic analysis points to both good and bad effects of trade unions, the latter associated with their monopoly supply of labour.

In many production situations, it is either impossible or extremely costly to assess the contribution of individual employees to output. Worker effort and team work are often instrumental in determining levels of labour productivity. Trust between workers and employers becomes a very important factor in instances when monitoring and close supervision aren't always possible. Internal labour markets (with long-duration jobs and accepted paths of promotion) and reward methods such as profit-sharing become economically efficient for employers to ensure that workers maximise their efforts. Notions of fairness are significant in engendering this trust, as will employee participation and the sharing of objectives within workplaces (Blandy 1989).

Workers' investment in human capital cannot be broken up and diversified like the capital of businesses. Workers are likely to be more risk averse than the owners of firms. Employers may therefore chose to insure their employees against the potential vagaries in their income levels associated with variations in the demand for the firms' products. As a result, wages are likely to be relatively sticky (see Sloan and Wooden 1984). This is so even without the presence of unions.

These are some of the characteristics of modern labour economic theory. They may come as a surprise to some readers: there is a 'touchy-feely' aspect to many of them and a considerable overlap with modern management ideas. Yet, they are based on rigorous analytical work and empirical verification. The exchange of labour services for money is still a trade just as the labour market is still a market. (It is now recognised that in many product markets, long-term relationships between sellers and buyers are very important and new theories based on 'customer markets' have been developed.) Price plays a part, particularly at the entry ports of internal labour markets but also in terms of providing appropriate incentives for training, although notions of fairness are also important. And unions are not necessarily seen as damaging.

Where labour-market issues are concerned, the public is often ill-informed and unaware of the major theoretical developments that cast aside the assumptions of labour as a commodity under strictly competitive conditions. In other words, a 'straw man' is often created by those who wish to discredit economic analysis by refusing to acknowledge these new ideas.

Defining the debate

The state of the intellectual debate about industrial relations and the labour market has not been trivial in terms of policy directions. While there has been fairly widespread acceptance of the need for economic reform in other markets, the labour market is still seen as a special case. This would appear to be the present position of the federal government — the labour market is a special (non-market) case that requires special (non-market) policies.

On one side of the debate are those who argue that the current system of industrial relations in Australia is quite adequate, and that the required changes to labour-market arrangements can be made within the existing framework of compulsory arbitration and legal awards. Developments from the mid-1980s have demonstrated the flexibility that can be achieved within the system (McDonald and Rimmer 1988; Rimmer and Zappala 1989), so the argument goes; it is not necessary to 'throw out the baby with the bath water'.

By contrast, others maintain that the pace of change in the labour market has been unacceptably slow; that change is often far too expensive and risky and on balance, it can be argued that the labour market has been re-regulated rather than deregulated over the past decade (Sloan 1992). This latter proposition is based on a number of policy-related measures that have been introduced by government that constrain various aspects of employee-management relations and/or carry additional imposts for employers. The only real alternative is to abandon the system of compulsory arbitration and in its place, introduce a light form of regulation based on employment contracts and some minimum conditions.

It is important to recall that Australia has in the past maintained a close link between the protection of product markets and the regulation of the labour market. Most of the initial work of the Commonwealth Conciliation and Arbitration Court under president Henry Bournes Higgins was granting excise exemption certificates to local producers who could demonstrate that 'fair and reasonable' wages were being paid (Plowman 1992). This process became more refined when tariffs became tailor-made under the auspices of the Tariff Board and arbitrated wage increases were used as the basis for adjusting tariff rates.

The unwinding of this arrangement probably goes back to 1967 when the Conciliation and Arbitration Commission granted large wage increases to metal workers (of the order of 17 per cent) on the basis of work value. The very size of the increase called into question the ability of the Tariff Board to offset the implied cost disadvantage by adjusting tariffs. The case for Australia becoming a world-competitive economy without a high tariff wall has only been slowly accepted. John Carroll, for example, believes that the circumstances that brought about the relative economic prosperity of the the 1950s and 1960s should now be emulated. The reality was, protection led to the relative impoverishment of its citizens, but this was disguised by Australia's ability to feed off the relative efficiency of its agricultural and later, its mining sector, as well as the favourable terms of trade that existed then. As the terms of trade have trended down (indeed over the entire century), this 'equilibrium' became unsettled. In any case, it left Australia vulnerable to external shock in terms of variations in commodity prices, the export basket being almost completely dominated by commodities.

Nostalgia can be a powerful force in terms of moulding opinions. However, given that we cannot replicate the circumstances of the 1950s and 1960s, we must carefully identify the labour-market arrangements that will maximise the benefits of economic internationalisation and guarantee an equitable distribution of the gains. If there was to be a backing-away in the future from product-market liberalisation, 'all bets will be off' as far as labour-market reform is concerned. There has been realisation among most key members of the federal Labor government and the ACTU that modified industrial relations and wage determination processes are required in the 'brave new world' of an internationalised economy. Not surprisingly, there have been largely successful attempts to control the agenda in a way that the central role of trade unions is maintained. Nevertheless, the realisation of the need for change has been fairly pervasive.

Admittedly, there has been change in industrial-relations since the mid-1980s. That productivity would become a central criterion in wage fixing could not have been predicted in 1983, for instance. Initially the form of change was highly controlled by the Industrial Relations Commission, with maximum rates of pay established and the 'no-extra-claims commitment' extracted as a condition for the payment of wage increases. Recent developments have involved a less controlled form of enterprise bargaining, with the major conditions being that workers are not 'disadvantaged' and that agreements be struck with a single bargaining unit. The process of change has been incremental to the system of conciliation and arbitration with registered unions continuing to be central and protected and awards remaining in force. Despite this shift towards a more decentralised form of wage determination and the focus on productivity, there has been nothing in macro-level indicators of labour-market outcomes, particularly in terms of productivity growth, to suggest that benefits have been substantial (Sloan 1992; 1993).The future role of National Wage Cases is ambiguous.

An alternative reform agenda would incorporate enterprise bargaining 'from the ground up' or holistic enterprise bargaining that replaces industrial awards and the abolition of compulsory arbitration. All terms and conditions of employment could be negotiated subject to certain specified minimum conditions in terms of hourly pay and other conditions such as annual leave and sick leave. There would be no necessary prescription in terms of the level at which bargaining would occur; thus individual contracting could be encompassed within this understanding of enterprise bargaining. At the same time, trade unions would in all likelihood continue to play an important role in enterprise bargaining, particularly for workers employed at large workplaces and currently strongly unionised. However, enterprise bargaining could occur without trade unions. At the same time, there would be no single-party access to tribunals and endpoint arbitration would only happen with mutual agreements of the parties. In other words, compulsory arbitration would be abolished along with other protective devices that assist trade unions — preference clauses in awards is a clear example — and employers' associations.

Enterprise agreements achieved under this reform agenda would be entered into voluntarily without duress, but substantial trade-offs in conditions will be allowed (subject to minimum wages and conditions). The agreements would have the force of law, be of fixed duration and have set procedures to deal with grievances that arise during the course of the agreement. Penalties will be enacted for non-compliance.

These are the two main alternatives. The first embraces a form of bargaining undertaken by registered trade unions and is essentially an addition to the bank of awards. The main features of the system of conciliation and arbitration remain intact. The alternative version by contrast, involves agreements supplanting awards — awards and the system of compulsory arbitration would cease to exist. Clearly, it is speculative as to which of the two will produce superior results. The point here is that economics *is* useful, both in terms of enabling empirical assessments of different models (particularly using international comparisons) and providing theoretical insights.

The Kennett reforms: the Employee Relations Act 1992

An essay on economics and industrial relations in Australia must necessarily deal with the Kennett reforms enacted through the Employee Relations Act 1992. The Kennett legislation is based on a contract view of labour-market arrangements, freedom of association and the abolition of compulsory arbitration. In terms of these three factors, there is a degree of coherence in the new policy direction. While there is a distinct possibility that the Kennett reforms will be scuttled by the transfer of state award employees into the federal jurisdiction, it is useful to use economics to analyse the proposed changes.

The basic idea behind the reforms is that employees, with or without bargaining agents, and employers are best-placed to work out employment arrangements that will suit their needs. This contrasts with the award system that applies to a number of employers of which only some employers may have had a say in creating, and of which employees certainly have had none. The charge that employees will be 'exploited' without the protection of the award system can be countered by pointing to the incentives employers have to defend their investments in the firm-specific training embedded in workers, as well as maintaining a trusting and committed workforce and reputation as 'good employers' — ideas emanating from economic theory. To be sure, there will be some employers who may wish to reduce wages. (Minimum wage conditions will limit this process.) The upside is, new jobs may be created, or, at the very least, some may be saved.

It is likely that there will be a number of 'shonky' employers who will treat their employees in harsh and unjust ways. The truth is that 'shonky' employers exist even under the award system: they violate award standards and the policing system is far from perfect. In any case, the notion that the arbitration system can deliver high wages (magic puddings notwithstanding) sits uneasily with the fact that a large number of countries in the world provide their workers with superior wages and better conditions to those in Australia, and this is achieved without an award system. High wages are achievable without compulsory arbitration!

This does not mean there are no flaws in the Kennett reforms — and this an admission from a rational economist. The prescriptive approach taken by the Victorian government in relation to leave-loading and penalty rates is inconsistent with the policy thrust of enterprise-based bargaining, since these matters should be left for negotiation at the enterprise level. Moreover, the legislation is unnecessarily restrictive in terms of the right to strike (which should be a legitimate course of action when agreements are being negotiated) and the criminality associated with breaches of the legislation is unwarranted. Breach of employment agreements should be dealt with under civil and not criminal law. More generally, the new policy direction has had a disturbing 'kick heads' flavour which is quite contrary to the literature in this area. 'Winning the hearts and minds' of workers is a vital ingredient of successful business. If Australia is to be world competitive, a co-operative and committed workforce will be required. Flat hierarchies, employee participation and trusting arrangements should be key features of the workplace. The combative approach is likely to be counterproductive, especially in the medium term.

Finally, there is the issue of transition arrangements that should be put in place when moving from a system of legal awards and compulsory arbitration to one based on voluntary employment contracts. In New Zealand, employees under the Employment Contracts Act 1991 were given the choice of remaining under the terms and conditions of the award by which they had been covered (awards were however abolished), or changing to an employment contract. This way, existing employees could be made no worse off by the change. This facet of the New Zealand experience has been important in terms of promoting a degree of acceptance to the new approach and raises the general point of establishing an appropriate transition arrangement when moving from a system of compulsory arbitration and awards to a less regulated, enterprise-based system. This aspect has not been handled well in Victoria.

My principal aim has been to demonstrate the relevance of economics to the analysis of the labour market and industrial relations. 'Workers are not commodities', 'The labour market is not like the market for cabbages.' These are statements with which most economists would agree. The labour market is not at all like a spot-auction market — day labour is in fact rare these days! Yet it is still a market, where exchange takes place and prices/wages matter. There are some special features of the labour market, including the fact that jobs generally last for years and that productivity is 'endogenous' — a fancy term used by economists to mean 'growing from within'. In this context, worker effort, team work and morale, for example, all impact on productivity. There are a number of new streams of labour economic theory that accept the special features of the labour market and draw out the implications.

The irony is, a number of those who are strongly opposed to the ideas of so-called 'economic rationalism' are often hoist by their own petard. The advocacy of wage-subsidy schemes and incomes policies such as the Prices and Incomes Accord is based on the premise that wages/prices do matter. Similarly, the argument that relative wages are little affected by the workings of the arbitration system implies that compulsory arbitration can easily be dispensed with — an implication rarely drawn by the anti-economists.

The debate about industrial-relations reform and the future of the arbitration system now centres on whether or not the required changes can be delivered with the key features of the system remaining intact. One point-of-view is that the existing system, based on compulsory arbitration and legal awards, is sufficiently flexible and responsive to accommodate the requirements of an internationalised, competitive economy. According to this view, labour-market reform must be gradual and consensus-based, and trade unions should continue to have a central role. The alternative view is radical reform that involves abolishing compulsory arbitration which has been so inextricably linked to product market regulation and dismantling the award system and the protective devices that affect unions (and employers' associations). What is required is a light form of labour-market regulation based on employment contracts and a small number of minimum conditions.

What is a rational economist's view of the Employee Relations Act 1992 introduced by the Kennett government in Victoria? In a central sense, the thrust of the new legislation is embedded in modern economic theory that stresses the importance of building strong and trusting relationships between employers and employees, the latter which may be represented by trade unions. A contract-based approach to employee relations where employees and employers work out wages, working conditions and work organisation to suit their particular requirements can be seen to be consistent with these new economic theories. At the same time, the prescriptive approach of the Victorian government in relation to leave-loading and penalty rates is inconsistent with the basic premise of enterprise-based bargaining.

References

Becker, G. 1962, 'Investment in Human Capital: A Theoretical Analysis', *Journal of Political Economy*, 70, Part 2 Supplement, pp. 9-49

Blandy, R. 1989, 'The Industrial Relations Revolution', *Labour Economics and Productivity*, vol. 1, no. 2, pp. 139-148

Blandy, R. and Sloan, J. 1986, 'The Dynamic Benefits of Labour Market Deregulation', *ACC/Westpac Discussion* Paper 3, November

Brook, P. 1990, *Freedom at Work: The Case for Reforming Labour Law in New Zealand*, Oxford University Press, Auckland

Brown, W., Hayles, J., Hughes, B. and Rowe, L. 1978, 'How Far Does Arbitration Constrain Australia's Labour Market?', *Australian Bulletin of Labour*, vol. 4, no. 4, pp. 31-9

Dabscheck, B. 1992, 'Enterprise Bargaining: A New Province for Law and Order?', in *Contemporary Australian Industrial Relations*, eds Dabscheck, B., Griffin, G. and Teicher, J., Longman Cheshire, Melbourne

Department of Employment, Education and Training 1993, *Natural Labour Markets in Australia*, AGPS, Canberra

Freeman, R. and Medoff, J. 1984, *What Do Unions Do?* Basic Books, New York

Gorringe, P. 1987, A Contracting Theory View of Industrial Relations, Centre of Policy Studies, *Discussion Paper*, D117, June

Hancock, K.. 1987, 'Regulation and Deregulation in the Australian Labour Market', *Australian Bulletin of Labour*, vol. 13, no. 2, pp. 94-107

McDonald, T. and Rimmer, M. 1988, 'Award Structure and the Second Tier', *Australian Bulletin of Labour*, vol. 14, no. 3, pp. 469-91

Mitchell, W. F. 1992, 'Wages Policy and Wage Determination in 1991', *Journal of Industrial Relations*, vol. 34, no. 1, pp. 153-61

Norris, K.. 1986, 'The Wage Structure: Does Arbitration Make Any Difference?', in *Wage Fixation in Australia*, ed. J. Niland, Allen & Unwin, Australia

Oi, W. 1962, 'Labor as a Quasi-Fixed Factor', *Journal of Political Economy*, 70, pp. 538-55

Okun, A. 1981, *Prices and Quantities: A Macroeconomic Analysis*, The Brookings Institute, Washington D.C.

Plowman, D. 1992, 'Industrial Relations and the Legacy of New Protection', *Journal of Industrial Relations*, vol. 34, no. 1, pp. 48-64

Rimmer, M. and Zappala, J. 1988, 'Labour Market Flexibility and the Second Tier', *Australian Bulletin of Labour*, vol.14, no. 4, pp. 564-91

Sloan, J. 1992, 'Until the End of Time: Labour Market Reform in Australia', *Australian Economic Review*, 4/92, pp. 65-78

—— 1993, 'The Economics of Enterprise Bargaining', *Economic and Labour Relations Review*, forthcoming

Sloan, J. and Wooden, M. 1984, 'Labour Markets for the Microeconomic Perspective: Implicit Contract Theory', *Australian Economic Review*, 3/84, pp. 120-9

Williamson, O., Wachter, M. and Harris, J. 1975, 'Understanding the Employment Relation: The Analysis of the Idiosynchratic Exchange', *Bell Journal of Economics*, 6, pp. 250-78

Joe Isaac

Comments

I do not propose to dwell on what 'economic rationalism' means. The debate brings to mind what Alfred Marshall (Keynes 1933, pp. 207-8) said over 100 years ago and which Keynes paraphrased eloquently in the preface to the various Cambridge Economic Handbooks Series (e.g. Robinson 1931, v) on which we were brought up in the 1930s and 1940s:

> The Theory of Economics does not furnish a body of settled conclusions immediately applicable to policy. It is a method rather than a doctrine, an apparatus of the mind, a technique of thinking, which helps its possessor to draw correct conclusions.

In the spirit of this dictum, an economist who is trying to understand labour-market problems or is having to advise on how to make it work efficiently, should collect, examine, and classify relevant facts about the labour market, bring out the relevant economic instruments to analyse such material and then draw appropriate conclusions for policy. Such policy may or may not involve regulation, that would depend on the characteristics of the particular labour market. International experience could also be drawn upon, cautiously, as a guide.

I suspect most of us who are familiar with labour economics will agree that an efficient labour market is a labour market that would facilitate the market to be cleared, wage inflation to be minimised and labour to be efficiently allocated. More importantly, interruptions to work would be minimised and harmony at the workplace enhanced. We may also be asked to establish minimum pay and conditions as a 'safety net' to protect sections of the workforce against the superior bargaining power of employers. Appropriate fiscal, monetary and international trade policies would be critical to the achievement of labour-market objectives.

However, this very simple statement of objects and method hides difficulties for policy formulation because of the special characteristics of the labour market. Sloan has mentioned many of these, but I should like to emphasise three things. First, work has social as well as economic significance to the worker, and workers are subject to group pressures and values. Secondly, custom, practice and notions of 'fairness' are important factors in the operation of labour markets; they are not easily overridden by purely economic consideration. Thirdly, the existence of unions introduces a countervailing economic power to that of employers by making possible a collective approach in the determination of pay and conditions; but the 'monopoly' view of unions oversimplifies the objects and behaviour of unions.

It is the complexity of the labour market that makes it difficult to decide on the nature and extent of any regulation needed to make it work more efficiently. It is not that 'economic theory has no place' in labour-market analysis or that the effect of price should be ruled out. Rather, if economic theory is to be a reliable basis for achieving defined policy objectives, it should incorporate the institutional factors affecting the demand and supply of labour. Sloan's recital of the significant modifications which in effect have to be made to the competitive neoclassical theory bears out this point. I therefore find Sloan's objection to Keith Hancock's proposition difficult to understand. Solow (1986, S33) once remarked that

> Someone once defined an economist as a parrot trained to repeat 'supply and demand, supply and demand'. There are many worse things you could teach a parrot to say . . . but I want to suggest that, in the case of the labour market, our preoccupation with price-mediated market-clearing as the 'natural' equilibrium condition may be a serious error.

What I have said so far applies, more or less, to the labour markets of many Western countries. The peculiarity of the Australian labour market is the existence of a network of legally constituted tribunals that mediate in the settlement of industrial disputes by compulsory conciliation and arbitration. The system spawns a large number of agreements and awards, the latter mostly on minimum pay and conditions that employers may exceed.

The role of the arbitration system has been a perennial source of controversy, but its alleged rigidity is greatly exaggerated. The system is capable under certain conditions of formulating and applying a national wage policy to deal with macroeconomic objectives and more recently, with microeconomic reform. I say 'certain conditions' because what the system can do to achieve certain policy objectives depends very much on whether the main parties and governments are prepared to work within the limits of the principles of such policy. In short, its regulating power, or more accurately, its facilitating power, depends on a largely compliant and consensus-minded institutional environment. The highly structured centralised system that operated for most of the period from 1975 to 1987 was an economically rational response to the highly inflationary consequences of sectional, pattern-setting wage increases. The changed economic environment since 1987 has moved the system from giving primary emphasis to keeping wage inflation in check through synchronised national wage adjustments to giving primary emphasis on a decentralised basis to encouraging changes in work practices in order to stimulate productivity. A considerable change in the attitude of the main players has taken place. What has been possible in recent years by way of decentralised adjustments conditional on workplace reform would have been unrealistic ten years ago.

In the context of the present circumstances, Sloan identifies two schools of thought. One would maintain a substantial part of the present system of decentralised wage determination and operate under a centralised umbrella of principles. Enterprise bargaining and agreements would be encouraged; but for those not covered by agreements, there would be awards that provide minimum wage rates and basic conditions as a kind of safety net. The alternative approach is a system in which 'a light form of labour market regulation based on employment contracts, and a small number of minimum conditions' would prevail, compulsory arbitration would be discontinued, and agreements would ultimately displace awards.

While admitting that 'it is speculative as to which of the two reform agendas will produce superior results' from her various criticisms of the arbitration system, it is fair to infer that Sloan probably has her heart set on the second approach. It is true that the present system does not appear to be yielding substantial productivity outcomes. But what is the evidence that the system has been a retarding force? The Commission itself has complained that despite its strenuous efforts to encourage workplace reform through award restructuring, substantial reform has occurred only in some workplaces. The evidence from surveys and case studies does not show that the system has been an obstacle to productivity growth. Workplace reform depends essentially on the initiative and resourcefulness of management and it is here that the problem mainly lies.

To say that a 'contract-based approach . . . can be seen to be consistent with the new economic theories' adds nothing to the argument. The same could be said of the existing system. A significant feature of the reform agenda is that enterprise bargaining could occur without trade unions. So far as the larger firms are concerned, given the density and spread of union membership, it is highly likely that employers will continue to deal with unions under enterprise bargaining. The prospects for workplace reform will be no better than they are now. Dismantling the award system would be relevant mainly to small firms where union presence is sparse. Without the countervailing power of collective action, individual bargaining would in most cases be a euphemism for unilateral determination by the employer — subject to market pressures and the minima prescribed by legislation. What these minima would be over time, who sets them and on what criteria has not been spelled out. This is perhaps the most important difference between the two options. On the basis of the tardiness with which firms and small firms in particular have embraced workplace reform, there is no warrant for a conclusion that individual bargaining will lead to higher productivity.

In summary, the complex nature of labour markets calls for the use of judgement, based on imperfect and changing data to decide on a policy direction for efficiency that is consistent with the equity norms of the markets. A doctrinaire view in favour of more or less regulation could well turn out to be economically irrational. On the data available, I would be inclined to take an incremental rather than a radical approach to labour-market reform. Hence I would support the first of the two courses mentioned. The present system has proved to be sufficiently flexible and responsive to the requirements of an internationally competitive economy; industrial action, for example, has been at a low level for the last decade. The present system would also meet the social objective of a safety net more effectively than the alternative proposed. The latter system is at best unnecessary for higher productivity; and at worst, disruptive to that object by unsettling long-established institutions. Moreover, should wage inflation re-emerge with economic recovery and lower unemployment, the system could provide the basis, if the parties so desired, for a centralised anti-wage inflationary policy. It would be a mistake to dismantle the system unnecessarily when it has this potential. But then my judgment could be wrong.

References

Keynes, J. M. 1933, *Essays in Biography*, Macmillan, London

Robinson, E. A. G. 1931, *The Structure of Competitive Industry*, Nisbet, London

Solow, Robert M. 1986, *Economica* 53, S23-S24

Privatisation and Market Forces: Their Role in Infrastructure Provision

The importance of infrastructure to economic growth is a matter of debate. Recent studies have attempted to show that infrastructure investment is associated, both over time and across geographical regions, with higher levels of income and productivity (Munnell 1990). These results are vulnerable on a number of counts: they say little about the direction of the causation; and the conclusion they draw would only be valid were the marginal return on infrastructure investment higher than that on other types of investment — which these studies typically do not find to be the case.

Some light has been thrown on this issue by economic historians. While traditionally, great importance has been ascribed to the development of the railroads as a factor in nineteenth-century growth, a re-examination of the data found that the so-called 'transport revolution' had not significantly raised national income. Recent work takes into account the indirect effects of reductions in transport costs and suggests that the impacts may indeed have been significant — but the extent of the gains depended to a considerable degree on the efficiency with which the railroads were operated. In the UK, for example, national income at the turn of the century is estimated to have been some 3 per cent lower than it would otherwise have been because of the large productivity gap separating British railroads from their US counterparts (Foreman-Peck 1991).

The state of infrastructure in OECD countries, and the quality of the services that it provides, are widely viewed as a matter for concern. This essay examines the major issues that are involved in the provision of facilities and services in transport and communications, and the production and distribution of the products generally produced by public utilities. This is not the only possible definition of infrastructure, which is often thought of as also including schools, universities, hospitals, and more broadly public facilities for health and recreation. But these particular activities share a number of characteristics that make it useful to treat them together:

• The capital stock in each case yields services that enter directly into the production processes of virtually all goods and services and into the consumption of the vast majority of households.

• They are characterised by very significant scale economies, generally associated with investment decisions that are lumpy and hard to reverse, a high ratio of fixed to variable costs, and hence marginal opportunity costs that, up to the point where congestion arises, are far below the average cost of provision.

It is in relation to these activities and services that the chief concerns about inadequate investment within OECD economies have been expressed.

Efficiency in provision and utilisation

While there is little reason to believe that recent years have seen a significant fall-off in infrastructure investment, this does not mean that the recent and current investment programmes can be viewed as satisfactory, either in total or in their make-up. There is strong evidence that infrastructure in the OECD countries is poorly managed and utilised so that communities do not secure a return on new infrastructure investment that is commensurate with its opportunity cost. Two interrelated problems are involved: first, prices that do not adequately reflect costs and therefore give rise to distorted consumption and investment decisions; and governance structures that shield the suppliers of infrastructure services from the disciplines of competition, and hence reduce the pressure to innovate and to cut costs. These factors will be considered in turn.

The considerable pricing distortions are most strikingly apparent in the transport network and especially in road access. Roads provide two broad sets of 'products': the capacity to handle traffic flow measured by the number of vehicles that can travel on a particular road at a given average speed; and durability, that is, the capacity to absorb vehicle weight without damage to the road surface (Winston 1991). Each road-user places demands on these dimensions of road capacity, and hence imposes costs on other users through congestion, and on the supplying authority through wear and tear. Negative externalities are also generated through noise, the emission of pollutants and accidents.

By and large, road-users are not charged directly for the use of specific stretches of road — except for France and Italy where motorway tolls in

1987 accounted for over 10 per cent of revenue. Rather, charges for road use are levied indirectly, typically through taxes on fuels and vehicles, while at the same time, in virtually all countries, subsidies are granted to transport modes that compete with the road network or at least with private vehicle use of that network. Most countries including Australia have taxes on fuels and vehicles exceed public outlays on roads but most countries raise revenues largely by charging on the basis of some average cost of usage spread over the population of users rather than by facing each user with charges that are systematically related to the marginal system costs which that user's transport choices give rise to.

In practice, the impact of these average cost charges on transport choices is far from unambiguous. There is, however, little reason to believe that they reduce road congestion, and it is clear that they bear little relation to costs arising from damage.

This is partly because fiscal subsidies and concessions may bring the effective tax rates on car ownership and use to well below the nominal rates implied by fuel and registration charges. In the UK for instance, tax concessions provided to company cars have created strong incentives for companies to shift employee compensation from taxable income towards payment in the form of vehicle use. As a result, estimates suggest that only 20 per cent of automobile commuters received no employer subsidy in the latter part of the 1980s while 40 per cent of peak-hour trips into London occurred in company vehicles. Similar fiscal concessions have favoured motor vehicle use in the US, Germany, and the Netherlands (Nijkamp, Vleugal and Van Ghent 1990).

Charges are not structured so as to discourage transport decisions that impose the highest costs (Goodwin and Jones 1989). Even when viewed in terms of average (rather than marginal) costs, the charges do not fall most heavily on the most socially costly forms of transport, whether in relation to types of vehicle or the timing of trips. For example, charges for lorries frequently recover a far lower share of the costs these vehicles impose than do the charges on passenger cars: a study for Switzerland found that in 1985, charges for heavy trailers recovered less than 10 per cent of the road costs attributable to these vehicles. while charges on passenger cars recovered from 50 to 120 per cent of costs (Perret and Jaccard 1989). In the US, the system of taxing lorries on the basis of the number of axles induces truck owners to opt for higher weight per axle vehicles, thereby sharply increasing the road damage these vehicles impose (Winston 1991).

The charges do not fall most heavily on the use of vehicles at the socially most costly periods of the day or week. Fuel taxes appear to have their greatest impact on the amount of discretionary travel rather than on peak-time driving; while annual registration taxes probably increase vehicle use at peak, as owners seek to amortise the fixed charge through more intense use of their vehicle, so that the net effect on congestion is very limited and may well be perverse. Charges are not systematically related to congestion, so that they do not serve as an efficient rationing device.

Three consequences follow from the marked discrepancies between the structure and level of charges and that of costs. First, when faced with a marginal private cost of travel that remains far below the marginal social cost, users have dramatically increased the amount of their travel by car. Total vehicle kilometres travelled in the OECD area doubled from 1970-90, with the greatest increases being in peak-hour traffic. Given that even relatively minor increases in peak-time vehicle density can sharply reduce average speed — one study for the US shows that each additional vehicle entering the typical highway during peak-hour adds an hour's delay to the sum total of travel time of all other commuters — the result has been to raise the extent of congestion and the severity of its costs. Estimates for France, for example, suggest that in the Paris region alone, the dead-weight loss associated with traffic congestion currently amounts to around 7 billion francs annually — or some $US100 per resident in the area (Bonnafous 1993). In the US, peak-hour traffic now exceeds capacity on half of the urban interstate roads and on a third of main arterial roads; congestion cost estimates for 1988 were nearly $US300 per resident in the large urbanised areas. A recent UK estimate puts the annual cost of congestion in urban areas at £3 billion — approximately equal to 7 per cent of the cost of distributing goods (Cottell 1992).

Secondly, attempts to offset the below-cost pricing of car use by subsidies to public transport have proved largely ineffectual, if not counter-productive. There is evidence that suggests that these subsidies have less impact on the modal split of travel than on the overall number of trips; that they reduce the perceived cost of travel by more than they alter the relative net cost of alternative transport modes. As a result, they do not seem to reduce first-car ownership and use (income effects may even serve to increase it), while raising total distance travelled. Moreover, even to the extent to which they do displace some work trips, the impact on congested roads is very largely offset as the initial reduction in the time cost of travel stimulates replacement traffic, so that any net effect on the social costs of road transport is minimal.

Thirdly, in the US and Japan at any rate, the low cost of travel has interacted with distortions in markets for land and housing to skew the pattern of resitential growth towards low-density sreas. In out-of-pocket terms, travel costs households less than land; and tax and land-use policies typically raise the price of high-density housing above social cost while keeping that of additional transport below it. As a result, households can increase disposable income by opting for housing on the suburban fringe and in the process impose social costs through the greater demands placed on utility trunk-lines (acccss to these typically being priced at less than avoidable cost) and on the transport system (Peiser 1989).

Japan presents an extreme example. Land prices have been kept artificially high by a tax system that encourages the holding of urban land for agricultural purposes. Despite recent reforms, land consolidation is still penalised by heavy taxes on capital gains. This, and transport prices that are well below social cost have induced a shift in the residential pattern towards the urban fringe. As a result, the land area of the largest conurbation (Tokyo) increased by 170 per cent over the period from 1960 to 1980, as the share of the conurbation's population living at more than 30 kilometres from the city centre went from 25 to 36 per cent. The high costs involved in extending the infrastructure to these areas — further raised by the difficulty of securing the land needed for public works — has meant that those living on the urban fringe are poorly served in terms of facilities such as parks, sewerage and macadamised roads. Transport congestion has increased dramatically; over a third of suburban commuters now face more than an hour's journey each way either on public transport that operate at close to or even above 100 per cent load, or on roads where congestion levels (measured as time spent in traffic line-ups that start, stop and crawl for more than 30 minutes) have about doubled since 1980 (Hebbert and Nakai 1988).

The failure to charge users the marginal costs they impose generates excess demands on the transport system — and concomitant demands for greater investment in roads. But the roads, though the most conspicuous instance, are by no means unique in this respect, since price distortions remain a pervasive feature of service provision by public utilities.

Governance structures: the effects of restricting competition

These price distortions are largely explained by governance structures that create few incentives for allocative, productive or dynamic efficiency. Notably in Europe, the regulatory arrangements for public utilities still shield infrastructure suppliers from effective competition. This accounts for pricing structures that reflect costs very poorly, cost levels that are far above world-best practice, and innovation that lags behind technical opportunity significantly.

Each of these effects of the governance structures can be illustrated by experience in telecommunications — a sector that all non-European OECD countries have now opened to full, facilities-based competition but where broad-reaching monopolies, covering two-thirds or more of industry revenues, persist in all these European countries except the UK, Sweden and Finland. Three factors characterise service provision in the countries where competition remains curtailed.

First, prices continue to bear little relation to the underlying costs of service, and this has the effect of distorting both consumption and investment decisions. In particular, local charges are typically set at or below cost, while there are very high price-cost margins on long-distance and international services that make up the difference. At the same time, prices for the long-distance services are themselves severely distorted, since they rise steeply with distance even though costs are only weakly distance dependent.

The overall extent of the misalignments can be assessed by comparing rental and connection charges to the charge for a five-minute peak rate long-distance call. Studies suggest that on average, a local line should cost (on a fully distributed cost basis) some $US250 a year to provide; a peak time long-distance call covering some 300-500 kilometres, about $US0.12-0.15 a minute. Were the price structure purely cost based, the monthly rental would be some 30 times the cost of a five-minute peak time long-distance call. Recent data has suggested that in the countries where monopoly regimes remain in place, the gaps between prices and costs are greatest and the trend to rebalancing prices towards costs is weakest.

There are valid economic reasons for fixing relative service prices to attract the largest possible number of connected customers since the value of the network to each user generally rises with the number of users who can be contacted. The practical extent of the cross-subsidies observed in monopoly environments goes far beyond what could be accounted for on these 'network externality' grounds. In effect, for the externality to justify rentals that cover barely 50 per cent of access costs (as is the case in France), the existing users would have to gain nearly as much from each additional user as would the marginal user. And yet, traffic studies do not find a rise in the willingness to pay for calls as already mature networks expand. Rather, the primary effect of the subsidies is to encourage an excess demand for access lines, most recently by families seeking a second line in their primary residence or a line in a holiday home; markets where access demand is highly price elastic. Since providing local access accounts for around 70 per cent of system capital costs, this excess demand adds sharply to the network provider's capital expenditures.

Secondly, costs themselves remain high by comparison with world-best practice. State-owned service providers in particular have enjoyed subsidised access to capital, and since they are insulated from competition, have had few incentives to deploy efficiently their use of capital. This has been reflected in economic rates of return on invested assets which, for the European carriers, are well below the opportunity cost of capital, and in low levels of capital and total factor productivity (McKinsey Global Institute 1992).

Thirdly, the monopoly context has distorted the pace and direction of innovation. The protected service providers have tended to emphasise innovations that are aimed at the broad public rather than at narrowly defined customer segments; exploit network-wide economies of scale; and are technology, rather than marketing, intensive. They have also discouraged the development of private networks through regulatory and pricing barriers, which in the US, the UK and Japan have acted as a test bed for product and service innovations as well as a source of market contestability to the point where the number of high-capacity leased circuits in continental Europe is less than a tenth that in North America (Cleevly 1992). These factors have slowed telecommunications advancement; the monopoly carriers effectively offer to their customers only a third of the advanced options and services made available by their US counterparts (McKinsey Global Institute 1992).

Overall, the governance structure has acted to increase the costs of service provision, and hence the volume of resources required. Added to the inefficiencies that arise partly independently from price distortions, the effect has been to further accentuate the difficulties economies face in trying to ensure that their infrastructure is adequate, appropriate and efficiently used.

Directions for reform

The pressures on infrastructure investment in the OECD countries are likely to continue to rise in the future. In the absence of reform, rising incomes will continue to expand usage for those services that are already greatly underpriced and subject to severe congestion. Left unchecked, demand for road use is likely to increase rapidly as car densities rise towards saturation (broadly expected to involve between 550 and 650 cars per thousand population, as against a current OECD level of 400 per thousand), as car ownership by women and the elderly moves closer to that of prime-age men, and the continued growth of single-earner families further raises labour-force participation rates and the number of sole-passenger trips (Banister 1992, Bonnafous 1993). In the absence of reforms, congestion will likewise be more acute at airports, adding to the already high costs of congestion-related delays (Morrison and Winston 1989). Current US forecasts highlight the conflict between the continued strong growth of demand and the increasingly tight planning constraints on airport expansion — with gate capacity unlikely to increase at all in the next five years at a third of large airports, and likely to increase only marginally at another fifth (US General Accounting Office 1990). Congestion problems are even more acute at Narita airport in Japan, where the number of take-offs and landings rises by over 5 per cent annually, and in the most congested European airports, notably in Germany.

Environmental concerns will continue to increase provision costs for large parts of the infrastructure industries. These costs relate in the first instance to the investments and changes in production processes needed to meet new environmental standards and regulations — as for example with the decommissioning of nuclear-power plants, the need to modify water-treatment plants to meet effluent standards, and the impact of noise regulations on the transport system. But their greatest impact is probably on the delays and uncertainties that affect the design, construction and operation of infrastructure. Delays place an enormous strain on demand forecasts and on the ability to plan and control costs; they increase the risk premium that must be built into the infrastructure provider's cost of capital, and they greatly increase the risk of welfare losses arising from chronic mismatches of capacity and demand.

Thirdly, the development of new technologies will create pressures to scrap existing plant and install new plants, even in cases where the prospective rate of return on such investment is low. In telecommunications, for example, some analysts argue that existing network facilities should be upgraded rapidly to allow distribution of broadband services (such as interactive video) to the home — even though doing so would cost over $3 000 per subscriber (some three times the cost of the installed base), while even a more limited up-grading (which increased the capacity of the current transmission network by a factor of around 2.5) would cost $300 per subscriber line (Egan 1992). As a recent report to the Canadian government notes, the economic viability of these investments is highly questionable (Report of the Co-Chairs of the Local Networks Convergence Committee 1992); yet they have developed a strong constituency of support. A similar situation has arisen in Europe, where there are strong pressures to upgrade railway systems to handle high-speed trains, even though the cost of doing so is estimated in Germany to exceed $20 million per kilometre — some 40 per cent more than the cost of providing for an equivalent increase in capacity by air.

To expand infrastructure capacity in ways that respond to the strongest pressures (which is the most likely outcome in the absence of reform) is simply not efficient. It leaves untouched many of the existing chronic problems where there is compelling evidence that demand rapidly expands to take up additions to capacity and it would involve committing additional resources to areas where current resources are poorly used. Rather, policy should act to ensure greater efficiency and effectiveness throughout the infrastructure system, with three main ingredients of reform: putting prices for infrastructure onto a more rational basis; increasing the role of the private sector in infrastructure provision; and managing better the support provided to services that are considered socially desirable even though they are not commercially viable.

Rational pricing

Failure to charge users of infrastructure the costs they impose artificially increases infrastructure demand and skews investment decisions. There are several reasons for thinking that significant economy-wide gains would be secured by a shift to pricing on a commercial basis.

First, recent analysis and experience suggests that price elasticities of demand for infrastructure services are higher than has convention-ally been assumed, notably when adjustment lags are taken into account. Thus, international studies suggest that though the elasticity of demand of road traffic with respect to tolls is of around 0.3 in the short term, longer-term elasticities may be twice or three times as great. Similarly, traditional estimates of demand elasticities for tel-ecommunications services typically did not take account of long adjustment lags and of return-traffic effects (where each call in one direction stimulates calls on the return stream); doing so brings the price elasticity of demand for long-distance service from the conven-tional estimate of 0.6 to over 1.0 and of international traffic from just under 1.0 to closer to 2.0.

These relatively high elasticities imply that the misallocation effects of current price structures are significant — and that bringing prices more closely into line with costs would prove effective in shifting demand onto a basis that better reflects consumers' estimates of the value of the services provided (Kraus 1989). These presumptions are borne out recently by two instances. One is the result of experiments in road-charging carried out in Hong Kong, in Bergen and in Milan. In all of these, the congestion-suppressing effects of use-based prices proved high both in absolute terms and relative to the efficacy of alternative traffic-control strategies (such as restrictions on parking) (Goodwin and Jones 1989). A second indication is the significant gains in consumer surplus that have occurred from price-rebalancing in telecommunicstions — with a recent estimate for the UK finding that the price changes following the privatisation of BT and the opening of the market to competition yielded a net welfare gain equivalent to almost half a percentage point of UK's GDP (Attenborough, Foster and Sandbach 1992).

Secondly, bringing prices into line with costs would trim investment programmes and raise the rate of return on investment as consumers who valued the resources they had previously consumed at less than the cost of providing them shifted their consumption to other goods and services, and increases in capacity for which proven willingness to pay could not be established were therefore no longer made. The combined effects of more economically efficient consumption and investment would be considerable — with an estimate for the US suggesting that cost-based pricing of roads would provide an annual net welfare gain of around $8 billion (in 1982 dollars), of which some $2 billion would come from the increased efficiency of investment; while cost-based pricing of airport use would yield an annual net welfare gain of some $11 billion, two-thirds of which would come from more efficient investment in runways (Morrison and Winston 1989).

Thirdly, cost-based pricing would reduce the need for subsidies from taxation. Financing these subsidies involves an excess burden arising from tax-induced distortions in consumption and production choices. In the US, for example, it has been estimated that each $1 in subsidies may cost $1.20 to provide. In those parts of the infrastructure where long-run marginal costs are constant or increasing, efficient prices would generate sufficient revenues to cover the full costs of provision — as would be the case for roads where diseconomies of scope between the provision of traffic-handling capacity on the one hand, and of load-bearing capacity on the other, generate nearly constant unit costs to the joint product. In contrast, in those parts of the infrastructure where costs decrease with scale — as in the local reticulation networks of the classic public utilities — the revenues raised by prices based solely on marginal costs would often though not always fall short of total costs; but even here, the gap would be more efficiently dealt with through two-part tariffs (which would secure the greatest contribution from those with the greatest willingness to pay for the service) rather than through the blunt instrument of subsidies financed by taxes falling on the community as a whole (Mitchell and Vogelsang 1991).

Fourthly, pricing in line with full social costs would internalise, and hence help reduce, the many environmental diseconomies associated with the use of infrastructure. The most conspicuous example is that of roads. Estimates for France suggest that the externalities associated with road usage — including costs of accidents and congestion — impose annual costs equivalent to over 18 per cent of GDP (Quinet 1992), and broadly similar orders of magnitude have been reported for other countries (OECD 1992).

Fifthly, technological change is reducing the costs involved in metering usage and undertaking billing and collection. In the road network, the development of low cost electronic vehicle identification (EVI) technology has sharply reduced the need for toll booths; and even where booths are used, widespread reliance on electronic payment systems means that the costs of charging are likely to fall to less than 5 to 10 per cent of the efficient toll (Quinet and Morancay 1990). Equally, charging for electricity, gas and water is being revolutionised by developments in automatic meter reading technology, which allows complex signals to be sent from the control point in the billing system to the customer's premises. Besides lowering significantly the costs of securing and processing billing information, the tying in of the signalling system to the equipment at the customer-end makes possible real-time pricing of capacity and hence permits fuller capacity utilisation. In telecommunications, the increased intelligence now built into the information systems used for call processing and for billing has encouraged service providers to develop far more complex pricing and charging options, tailored to the demand patterns of diverse customer groups. The fact that virtually all modern private branch exchanges and even many residential handsets now have the ability to perform automatic (least cost) routing and carrier optimisation means that customers can respond fully to these price signals.

All of this means that the gains from appropriate pricing of infrastructure are likely to be very large, even after taking fully into account the actual costs of operating the charging systems involved. Hence the case for an early transition to more rational pricing systems is compelling.

Using market forces

Better pricing structures for infrastructure would help and be helped by a greater reliance on market forces in shaping the development of the infrastructure system. This would involve using competition in the product market to ensure that prices and costs stay in line with world-best practice and disciplining private capital markets as a means of allocating and monitoring risk more effectively.

A number of countries have made significant moves in recent years to open markets that were previously regulated to competition. The trend has gone furthest in the UK, the US, Japan and New Zealand where virtually all of the traditional utility markets have been liberalised. Major steps have also been taken in Australia through the deregulation of the airlines and telecommunications industries. There are beginnings of a co-operative process with the US to open markets for electricity and natural gas, and in Canada, Sweden and Finland, which have opened their telecommunications sectors to competition. The evidence to date points to significant efficiency gains from the process. Over the period 1979-84 total factor productivity growth in the UK public sector including enterprises that were privatised rose from 0.1 per cent annually to 3.7 per cent from the period 1984-90 (Kay forthcoming), while impressive improvements in technical, allocative and dynamic efficiency have been found in case studies of the deregulation of the airlines (Morrison and Winston 1989), railroads (Friedlander, Berndt and McCullough 1992) and telecommunications (Crandall 1991; OECD 1992; Schmalensee and Rohlfe 1992). Moreover, the evidence suggests that the efficiency benefits achieved in those countries that have liberalised have greatly exceeded those in the countries where monopoly structures have been retained — with current unit costs being up to one-half higher in the monopolised telecommunications markets than in their competitive counterparts (McKinsey Global Institute 1992) and total factor productivity growth rates, adjusted for output growth, being a third higher in those markets for air transport that have been liberalised.

In practice, liberalisation has generally been paralleled by at least partial privatisation of the service providers where these were previously government-owned. There are good reasons to believe that the transfer from public to private ownership has contributed significantly to the benefits achieved. Three factors appear to have been especially important in this regard. First, productivity improvements in government-owned firms appear to be less durable. The initial and substantial gains made at the time of liberalisation proved difficult to maintain as political interference was resumed, and as the power to manage, even of commercially oriented boards, was weakened. Privatisation makes political interference more difficult, particularly when governments have to bind themselves vis-à-vis to foreign investors with respect to the content and transparency of the regulatory process. This means that the initial gains are less subject to later erosion.

Secondly, private owners bring a greater ability and willingness to monitor the firm's performance. These benefits appear to be most fully secured when the firm's ownership structure involves not only a core group of owners that can exercise fairly close control but also equity which is widely traded: where this is the case, privatisation leads to the development of expertise among equity analysts in analysing and diffusing information about the firm. This makes for a governance structure with simpler, clearer and more efficiency-oriented objectives than those which characterise public ownership, and with effective means of assessing the extent to which those objectives are being met.

Thirdly, privatisation shifts the risk associated with the firm's performance away from taxpayers as a whole. Ideally, after privatisation, these risks should fall on those best placed to bear them, namely the equity-owners who can insure against risk both by monitoring the firm's performance and by diversifying their portfolio. How far this transfer of risk actually takes place depends to a significant extent on any regulatory arrangements put in place, notably with respect to price-setting. Partly to avoid the risk simply being transferred back to consumers through cost-plus price regulation, a number of countries — notably the UK, the US and Australia — have shifted to 'price cap' arrangements in which the regulated firm commits itself to a given rate of reduction in the real prices charged to customers, placing the risks associated with cost growth on the holders of equity, and providing them with a sharper incentive to cut costs. The evidence so far suggests that these incentives have proved highly effective — with a recent study finding that in the case of AT&T, the shift to price-cap regulation led to a near doubling in the rate of total factor productivity growth (Schmalensee and Rohlfe 1992).

The opening of markets to competition when accompanied by privatisation has led to significant gains in infrastructure efficiency.

Admittedly, competitive markets are not always achievable, since there are cases where the technical characteristics of the product limit the scope for rivalry in its provision. Even in those cases, however, benefits can be achieved by the reform of regulatory arrangements and of ownership structures.

There has, in particular, been increased interest in the scope for 'yardstick' competition in the supply of services considered to be local natural monopolies. This involves two basic features: that the supply of the service in each local area is carried out by a different corporate entity; and that the regulated prices set in each area, rather than reflecting the cost performance of the service supplier in each area, are based on the average cost performance of the group as a whole. Such a structure has the advantage that it provides the supplying firms themselves, as also the regulators and the public, with a yardstick for assessing each firm's performance, and that the prices set create incentives for each firm to strive for above-average performance. Experience in telecommunications and in water supply suggests that localised structures such as these lead to no loss of economies of scope or scale, and indeed, that the local enterprises have higher levels of productivity than their nationally unified counterparts (Ergas, Ralph and Sivakumar 1990; Shin and Ying 1992). Arrangements along these lines have now been implemented for water and electricity supply in the UK.

These locally segmented service markets also provide a natural venue for the injection of private funding. In the transport system, for example, increased reliance is being placed on securing private sector equity, typically on a project-specific basis, for major ventures such as the construction of motorways, bridges, tunnels, and urban rapid transit networks; a striking instance is the Channel Tunnel linking the UK with France. The long lead times involved in such projects, and the difficulties involved in accurately assessing costs and demand over the course of a project's life, create large risks. Allowing full or partial private ownership may help spread these risks across global equity markets, while providing a governance structure for the project itself that is less vulnerable than direct public sector provision to inefficiencies in design, construction and operation.

These benefits are not secured merely by obtaining private equity. Rather, experience suggests that certain conditions be met: the rights to undertake such projects must be allocated on a competitive basis, the regulations surrounding these rights — for example, in terms of price-setting or in the provision of implicit or explicit government guarantees — must not be such as to effectively remove the risk from equity-owners and market-place disciplines should, whenever possible, be maintained

— for example, by preserving a toll-free minor road in parallel to a pro-profit toll motorway. These have been important elements in the success of the French motorway system (Quinet and Morancay 1990; Gerardin 1990); and they figure, though to a very varying degree, in some recent infrastructure privatisations.

Uneconomic services

A transition to cost-based pricing within a context of greater reliance on market competition and private ownership may give rise to concern about the effects on particular classes of consumers. These concerns may be all the more acute because the provision of infrastructure services has often been characterised by significant (though almost always very opaque) cross-subsidies, augmented in some cases by direct fiscal transfers. The opposition which would in any case be provoked by the prospect of these subsidies being wound back is accentuated by the belief that the services provided are 'essential' and that price changes can therefore have large income effects relative to their effects in inducing substitution.

In practice, the greatest transfers that occur in a monopoly environment are probably not between different groups of consumers but from consumers to the producers of the services. Insofar as transfers from consumers to producers are reduced by price reforms and levels of efficiency are raised, charges in general can be brought down. This effect, as well as the effects of restructuring, will largely influence the way in which demand responds to reform. Given, however, that 'social' concerns may nonetheless have to be taken into account, four factors need to be borne in mind in doing so.

First, the actual cross-subsidies between customer groups — for example, between those in densely and sparsely populated areas — may be significantly smaller than is claimed. Thus, in telecommunications, the conventional estimates of cross-subsidies rely on a comparison of fully distributed access costs with access revenues; but from an economic point of view, the relevant comparison is between the avoidable cost of providing a subscriber with service and the avoidable revenue generated by that customer both through access and the calling both from and to that customer.

A study done for Australia using data disaggregated to 5 000 exchange units highlights the difference this can make: on the conventional approach, 47 per cent of customers and fully 90 per cent of exchanges were considered to be loss-making at then existing charges: but using an avoidability approach, the loss-making proportion was below 3 per cent of customers and 25 per cent of exchanges (Bureau of Transport and Communications Economics 1989). Given the reasonable expectation that a similar result holds for other countries (McKinsey Global Institute 1992), there is little likelihood of liberalisation undermining universal access to the service.

Secondly, even to the extent to which there are significant subsidies between customer categories, the incidence of these on income distribution may be more complex than generally thought. Again in telecommunications, studies suggest that a subsidy to access may be of special value to relatively high-income households, both because these have the highest incidence of second lines and because it escapes income tax. In the case of Australia, it was found that the access subsidy provided a pretax equivalent transfer of $A350 a year in 1989 to households in the highest income decile and of $A200 a year to households in the three lowest income deciles. At the same time, the high prices charged for long-distance service (largely in order to fund the access subsidy) may well suppress a great deal of traffic from low income households, since these have higher price elasticities of demand. The net welfare effect of the overall transfers — and of reducing them — is not necessarily shared in favour of the poor.

Thirdly, the redistributive effects of introducing economically efficient pricing depend on the use made of the extra revenues thus generated. The distributional impact of introducing road charges, for example, could be at least partly offset by using the additional revenue to reduce motor vehicle registration taxes — or to lower effective tax rates on low income groups as a whole.

To the extent to which income distribution goals are being pursued, these can be best achieved through direct measures, rather than through the questionable means of cross-subsidies. This shift towards more direct forms of assistance has played an important role in the reform of transport in the UK and of telecommunications in the US and Australia; the evidence on the impacts of these reforms points to clear gains from the targeted programmes in terms of greater transparency, improved monitoring of value for money (including through competition for the right to provide the subsidised service) and reduced leakage of the assistance to those who do not need it. These gains have more than offset the administrative costs which the targeted programmes involve (Richard 1990, Mitchell and Vogelsang 1991).

With the OECD economies already devoting nearly a fifth of capital formation to infrastructure, the issues of efficiency and value for money should clearly be viewed as central. The allocation processes for infrastructure are notoriously imperfect, with powerful interest groups securing public funding for projects that yield doubtful returns. Substantial costs to society are imposed not only by inappropriate investment choices, but also by inefficiencies in construction, operation and management. These are associated with prices that do not reflect the services' calls on resources, with costs which are above best practice, and with inadequate incentives for suppliers to raise productivity and innovate in line with technical opportunity.

In itself, additional investment in infrastructure would not address these problems; rather they need to be tackled through reform. Some countries have embarked on this path, and the results to date have been encouraging. But there are some sectors where very little has been done; and where only the first steps have been taken. A more determined effort in this direction would save investment resources that are currently being squandered, and provide communities with a more robust basis of infrastructure for durable economic growth.

References

Attenborough, N., Foster, R. and Sandbach, J. 1992, 'Economic Effects of Telephone Price Changes in the UK', *Topics*, 8, National Economic Research Associates, London

Baasch, H. 1990, 'Denmark', ECMT, *Round Table 80, Systems of Road Infrastructure Cost Coverage*

Banister, D. 1993, 'Topic 1: Demographic Structure and Social Behaviour', ECMT, *12th International Symposium on Theory and Practice in Transport Economnics, Transport Growth in Question*

Bonnafous, A. 1993, 'Topic 1: Demographic Structure and Social Behaviour', ECMT, *12th International Symposium on Theory and Practice in Transport Economnics, Transport Growth in Question*

Bureau of Transport and Communications Economics Australia 1992, *Spectrum Management Reform*, September

Co-chairs of the Local Networks Convergence Committee 1992, *Convergence*, Minister of Supply and Services Canada

Congressional Budget Office 1992, *Auctioning Radio Spectrum Licences*, Congress if the United States, March

Cleevly, D. 1992, 'Private Networks in Europe', Working Paper Series, Columbia Institute for Tele-Information, Columbia Business Shool

Cottell, M. N. T. 1992, 'Planning for Roads — Getting the Traffic Moving', *Long Range Planning*, vol. 25, no. 3, pp. 70-8

Crandall, R. W. 1991, *After the Breakup: US Telecommunications in a More Competitive Era*, Brookings

Delepiere-Dramais, C. 1990, 'Belgium', ECMT, *Round Table 80, Systems of Road Infrastructure Cost Coverage*

ECMT (forthcoming), *Round Table 94, Privatisation of Railways: Methods and Obstacles*, Paris

Egan, B. L. 1992, 'Benefits and Costs of Public Information Networks: The

Case for Narrowband ISDN', Working Paper Series, Columbia Institute for Tele-Information, Columbia Business School, February

Ergas, H., Ralph, E. and Sivakumar, S. 1990, 'Reforming Australian Telecommunications: A Review of Issues and Options', MONICT Working Paper, Monash University, August

Foreman-Peck, J. (ed.)1991, 'Railways and late Victorian Economic Growth', *New perspectives on the late Victorian economy: Essays in quantitative economic history 1860-1914*, VCambridge University Press, pp. 73-95

Friedlaender, A. F., Berndt, E.R. and Mccullough, G. 1992, 'Governance Structure, Managerial Characteristics, and Firm Performance in the Deregulated Rail Industry', *Brookings Papers on Microeconomics*

Gerardin, B. 1990, 'France', in *ECMT, Round Table 81, Private and Public Investment in Transport: Possibilities and Cost*

Goodwin, P. B. and Jones, P. M. 1989, 'Road Pricing: The Political and Strategic Possibilities', *ECMT, Round Table 80, Systems of Road Infrastructure Cost Coverage*

Hebbert, M. and Nakai, N. 1988, 'How Tokyo Grows', *ST/ICERD Occasional Paper*, 11, Suntory-Toyota International Centre for Economics and Related Disciplines, LSE

Isard, W. 1942, 'A Neglected Cycle: The Transport-Building Cycle', *Review of Economic Statistics*, vol. 24, no. 4, November

Izquierdo, R. and Monzon, A. 1993, 'Topic 3: Infrastructure Capacity and Network Access', *ECMT, 12th International Symposium on Theory and Practice in Transport Economics, Transport Growth in Question*

Kay, John (forthcoming), 'Efficiency and Private Capital in the Provision of Infrastructure' OECD forum for the future, *Infrastructure policies for the 1990s*, Paris

Konvitz, J.W. 1985, *The Urban Millenium*, Southern Illinois University Press, Carbondale

Kraus, M. 1989, 'The Welfare Gains from Pricing Road Congestion Using Automatic Vehicle Identification and On-Vehicle Meters', *Journal of Urban Economics*, vol. 25, pp. 261-81

McKinsey Global Institute 1992, 'Service Sector Productivity', Report, October

Mitchell, B. M. and Vogelsang, I. 1991, *Telecommunications Pricing: Theory and Practice*, Cambridge University Press

Morrison, S. A. and Winston, C. 1989, 'Enhancing the Performance of the Deregulated Air Transportation System', *Brookings Papers on Microeconomics*, pp. 61-112

Munnell, A. H., (ed.) 1991, *Is There A Shortfall in Public Capital Investment?*, Federal Reserve Bank of Boston

Munnell, A. (forthcoming), 'An Assessment of Trends and Economic Impacts of Infrastructure Investment', OECD Forum for the Future, Infrastructure Policies for the 1990s, Paris

National Academy of Engineering 1988, *Cities and their Vital Systems. Infrastructure, Past, Present and Future*, National Academy Press

National Economic Development Office Construction Industry Sector Group 1992, *A New Approach to Road Planning*, London

Nijkamp, P. and Priemus, H. 1993, 'Topic 3: Infrastructure Capacity and Network Access', *ECMT, 12th International Symposium on Theory and Practice in Transport Economics, Transport Growth in Question*

Nordstrom, L. 1993, 'Topic 2: Economic Trends and Transport Specialisation', *ECMT, 12th International Symposium on Theory and Practice in Transport Economics, Transport Growth in Question*

OECD 1992, *Market and Government Failures in Environmental Management: the Case of Transport*, Paris

Peiser, R. B. 1989, 'Density and Urban Sprawl', *Land Economics*, vol. 65, no. 3, August, pp. 193-204

Perret, F. L. and Jaccard, P. A. 1990, 'Switzerland', *ECMT, Round Table 80, Systems of Road Infrastructure Cost Coverage*

Quinet, E. and Morancay, G. 1990, 'France;', *ECMT, Round Table 80, Systems of Road Infrastructure Cost Coverage*

Quinet, R. 1992, 'France', *ECMT, Round Table 86, Evaluating Investment in Transport Infrastructure*

Richard, J. 1990, 'UK', *ECMT, Round Table 81, Private and Public Investment in Transport: Possibilities and Cost*

Schmalensee, R. and Rohlfe, J. H. 1992, *Productivity Gains Resulting from Interstate Price Caps for AT&T*, National Economic Research Associates Inc., Washington D.C

Shin, R.T. and Ying, J. S. 1992, 'Unnatural Monopolies in Local Telephone', *Rand Journal of Economics*, vol. 23, no. 2

Turbo, M. 1993, 'Topic 2: Economic Trends and Transport Specialisation', *ECMT, 12th International Symposium on Theory and Practice in Transport Economics, Transport Growth in Question*

US General Accounting Office 1990, *Airline Competition*, August

Windmuller, T. 1992, 'Germany still plagued by congestion', *International Air Transport Association Review*, 5, October-November, pp. 15-16

Winston, C. 1991, 'Efficient Transportation Infrastructure Policy', *Journal of Economic Perspectives*, vol. 5, no. 1, Winter, pp. 113-27

Woroch, G. A. 1991, 'Technology, Regulation, and the Emergence of Competitive Access Providers', Working Paper Series, Columbia Institute for Tele-Information, Columbia Business School

Stephen P. King

Comments

The essay by Henry Ergas focuses on the provision of government infrastructure in OECD countries. He emphasises that while the level of infrastructure investment has been relatively stable across the OECD as a whole, distortionary pricing policies and poor production methods have hampered the efficiency of service delivery. Australia provides an excellent illustration of these problems. The lack of efficiency in Australia's public sector became increasingly apparent during the 1970s and 1980s. One source of these inefficiencies, as identified by Ergas, is distorted pricing. For example, Albon (1988) estimated that the welfare cost in 1985/86 due to distortions in Telecom's pricing of long-distance phone calls was $244 million.

Management and labour practices are another source of inefficiency. Despite recent improvements in the productivity performance of some government business enterprises, many fall well short of 'world best practice'. For example, in telecommunications, Swan (1990, p. 25) concluded that 'OTC is one of the world's best-performing carriers and Telecom Australia one of the worst'. Similarly, a 1990 comparison showed that Australian electricity utilities are only about 72 per cent as productive as privately owned utilities in the US (see Forsyth 1992).

Australian state and federal governments have typically responded to these problems through 'corporatisation'. This involves reforming a public utility so that its behaviour mimics that of a privately owned and operated firm. The Industry Commission suggests that corporatisation should include clarifying the utilities' objectives, separating out regulatory functions, making any community service obligations transparent, applying normal commercial legal and accounting requirements to the utility and removing any legislative barriers to entry (Industry Commission 1991, p. 12).

While few reform programmes have fulfilled all the requirements set down by the Industry Commission, many public utilities have been partially corporatised. Telecom, for example, has merged with OTC to form AOTC. It is externally regulated by Austel and is subject to CPI-X controls on the prices it may charge.[1] A private company, Optus, now provides competition on both domestic and overseas long-distance calls.

In energy, all state electricity authorities have undergone some form of corporatisation and rationalisation. This has included selling off ancillary operations such as coal mines (NSW) and privatising generating facilities (Loy Yang B in Victoria). The Kennett government in Victoria is continuing the reform of the state Gas and Fuel Corporation begun by the Kirner government and recently announced the sale of one of the corporation's retail trading subsidiaries.

In water supply, state governments are moving away from pricing and access schemes based on property value, historic claim or 'first come first served' towards user-pays systems. An example is the pricing scheme being introduced by the Melbourne Water Corporation. Traditionally, Melbourne's domestic water charges have been based on property value. In 1993/94, 55 per cent of these charges will be based on usage, with the aim of raising this figure to 75 per cent by around the year 2000.

Most of the reform in Australian utilities has involved corporatisation rather than privatisation. As Forsyth (1992, p. 20) notes, 'the enterprises which have been, or are planned to be, privatised are generally those which operate in fairly competitive markets . . . or are secondary producers'. Qantas, Australian airlines, the Commonwealth Bank and GIO all provide examples.

Ergas examines the problems of pricing road usage. He notes that user-pays systems for road usage are either rare or non-existent in most countries. Australia is no exception. Road tolls are rare. While petrol taxes and registration charges are often justified by the claim of infrastructure expenditure, actual expenditure tends to have little correlation with these payments. As Ergas notes, annual registration charges are sunk costs for 364 days a year, bear little relation to road usage and cannot effectively operate 'at the margin'.

Ergas's suggestion of increasing user-pays pricing through tolls may offer little satisfaction in urban areas. While tolls operate effectively overseas on some long-distance routes, anyone who has witnessed the peak period jam caused by the toll booths on Boston's turnpike extension would question their efficiency on major urban routes. In such cases, the time wasted by toll collection may far outweigh any social benefit derived from efficient road funding. For interurban travel in a country with as vast distances and low-density population as Australia, it is not obvious that toll collection would cover its cost except on a few major routes. Electronic vehicle identification may solve this problem in years to come, but it does not provide an immediate solution.

The size of the potential gains to be achieved by rational pricing in other areas may also be exaggerated. Efficient pricing is often at odds with the regulatory regime imposed on public or privatised utilities. This is especially so for 'natural monopolies' where competition is undesirable and, usually, illegal. While it is recognised that rate-of-return regulation can lead to inefficient production, price-cap regulation may lead to distorted pricing. If CPI-X regulation is used to limit the abuse of monopoly position, it may lead to distortions and cross-subsidies among the basket of goods to which the price cap applies. If the value of X is regularly revised on the basis of historic performance, the productive efficiency of the utility may be distorted as it attempts to influence the future value of X.

As Ergas recognises, privatisation can add credibility to a government's reform programme. Reform within the public sector may be shortlived. In contrast, it is far more difficult for a government to 'undo' a privatisation. Even so, the gains may be overstated. Governments often face enormous pressure to 'bail out' failing private enterprises. If the enterprise was a major utility providing electricity, water or sewage facilities to an entire urban area, the pressure would be overwhelming.

The reported productivity gains due to privatisation also need to be carefully scrutinised. As many commentators have noted, competition rather than privatisation may provide the key to enhanced performance. Reported cost savings may reflect differences in work practices, as for example with the operation of the Borallan prison in Queensland. Fictitious efficiency gains may also be generated by either selective privatisation or by operating public and private utilities under different sets of rules. For example, in his study of privatised prisons in the US, Donahue (1989) notes that many of the 'cost savings' of privatisation merely reflect the occupancy guarantees given to private prisons and differences in the prison population mix.

I agree with Ergas that far-reaching reform is necessary in infrastructure provision. In Australia we are only just beginning this process. However, neither the path that this reform should take, nor the gains that are achievable, are as clear-cut as Ergas suggests.

Note

1   CPI-X price regulation requires that the utility can only increase its prices by at most the level of the consumer price index (CPI) less a fixed percentage (X) in any year. The value of X is fixed in advance for, say, a five-year period.

References

Albon, R. 1988, 'The welfare costs of the Australian telecommunications pricing structure.' *Economic Record*, vol. 64, p. 102-12

Donahue, J. D. 1989, *The Privatization Decision: Public Ends, Private Means*, Basic Books

Forsyth, P. 1992, 'Public enterprises: A success story of microeconomic reform?' *CEPR Discussion Paper*, Number 278

Industry Commission 1991, *Annual report, 1990-91*. AGPS, Canberra

Swan, P. 1990, 'Measuring carrier efficiency - the facts.' *Australian Communications*, October, 1990, pp. 21-5

Allan Fels and Jill Walker

Competition Policy and Economic Rationalism

This essay aims to discuss the current and future role of competition policy in Australia. This is pertinent to the current debate about 'economic rationalism', since the latter is grounded in the belief that the market mechanism is the best means of delivering society's welfare goals as it is directed at improving the efficiency of the market mechanism. The general aim of Australian economic policy, particularly at the microeconomic level, is the efficient performance of markets. This includes allocative efficiency, x-efficiency and dynamic efficiency. Economic theory tells us that in general a market economy will promote these goals. Hence there is no general need for intervention. However, market failure may occur, *inter alia*, if there is a lack of effective competition. In these circumstances there is a case for intervention via competition policy, not to override the market mechanism, but to make it work better in achieving economic efficiency. Competition policy may also occasionally have a role in helping to deal with other kinds of market failure, such as those that stem from information problems. There are some situations in which the remedy for market failure may require regulation that overrides market outcomes, e.g. price regulation for natural monopolies. It is important that in addressing one market failure another is not created, that is, the costs of intervention should not exceed the benefits.

A significant part of competition policy, especially in trade-practices law, involves the paradox that government intervention is needed to make markets work better. This can pose a dilemma for economists (especially those at the very dry [high-fire risk] end of the economic spectrum), since they are traditionally sceptical of intervention. However, as Anderson and Blandy's survey shows, 43.4 per cent of Australian economics professors agree that 'trade practices law should be used

169

vigorously to reduce monopoly power in Australia', while a further 37.7 per cent agree 'with provisos'. Only 11.3 per cent positively disagree, with 7.5 per cent unsure.[1] This is of some significance to the claim that rational economists oppose government intervention.

Competition policy is not just trade-practices law. It includes policies that are specifically directed at promoting competition and policies that have an indirect impact on competition. Their impact may be on either market structure, influencing the incentives for competitive conduct, or directly on market conduct. This embraces a wide range of policy instruments concerning trade, intellectual property, foreign investment, tax, small business, the legal system, public and private ownership, licensing, contracting out, bidding for monopoly franchises and so on, as well as both the restrictive trade practices and consumer protection provisions of the Trade Practices Act (the Act). Some of these policies have an obvious direct effect on competition while others affect the general economic environment and ultimately the general climate of competition in the country.

Competition-policy questions occur at all levels of government. At the Commonwealth level recent examples include policies concerning telecommunications, aviation, wheat and pay TV. At state level competition policy includes issues concerning privatisation, deregulation of public utilities, agricultural marketing boards, the professions and many others. At local government level it includes issues such as contracting out. In some cases multilevel governmental decision making is needed, as has been increasingly recognised at recent federal-state conferences. The policy is not simply a series of measures that positively promote competition through bodies such as the Trade Practices Commission (TPC). A large element in competition policy is the removal of legislative obstacles to competition, e.g. deregulation affects market structure and the incentives for competitive conduct.

There is an increased recognition that competition issues are integral to a whole range of policy questions, a recognition that partly reflects the influence of economists in Canberra. There are more changes to come in the education and health sectors. Here one can foresee a possible clash of economics and anti-economic rationalism.

This essay largely focuses on trade practices law and the wider aspects of competition policy. Reference is made to fair trading and consumer-protection laws, particularly because these are an important part of the Act and the activities of the TPC. Some concluding comments are made about the relationship of competition policy to the debate about economic rationalism.

Some emerging major issues in competition policy

The focus of competition policy is shifting as the economic reforms of the last decade begin to bear fruit. This in turn affects the Act as a major instrument of competition policy. Several key issues can be identified.

First, national competition-policy priorities must be influenced by the government programme of gradually reduced protection and the growing exposure of Australian business to international competition. Reducing tariffs has been a major victory for economic rationalism, but international trade is by no means a complete solution to insufficient domestic competition; there continues to be a role for competition policy in trade-exposed markets. However, as more sectors are exposed to international competition, anti-competitive conduct is undermined. This is particularly relevant to the TPC's treatment of mergers. Since at least July 1991 the TPC has not opposed any mergers in the traded goods and services sector.[2]

Many of these industries depend on inputs from the non-traded goods and services sector. If they are to compete successfully in international markets, attention must be focused on maintaining or increasing competition between their suppliers. Deregulation and microeconomic reform have largely focused on industries such as waterfront and coastal shipping, telecommunications and domestic aviation. The change in the merger provisions of the Act from a dominance test to a substantial lessening of competition test is expected to impact on major mergers in important domestic industries, and possibly most of all, those areas currently undergoing deregulation, such as public utilities. Many non-traded inputs are still not exposed to the discipline of competition on their costs and prices, e.g., rural products subject to statutory marketing schemes, public utilities and professional services. Furthermore, much of the non-traded sector is fully or partially exempt from application of the Act.

The future direction of competition policy will depend on the adequacy of the Act to react to emerging issues as progress is made towards microeconomic reform and deregulation. This will more than likely mean universal application of the Act to many important areas of the economy not currently exposed to the disciplines of competition. The TPC has made clear in its statement of 'Priorities for 1992 and 1993' that testing the reach of the Act is one of its priorities. The TPC has also called for legislative measures to be taken at Commonwealth and State level to achieve universal applicability. The Hilmer Review (discussed later in this essay) is of great significance here.

Deregulation (especially of public utilities) poses major policy challenges. Industries such as telecommunications and airlines are being more heavily exposed to the market mechanism and others such as electricity will soon be exposed for the first time. Significant structural impediments to competition may remain since deregulation does not necessarily deliver a fully competitive market. The TPC is already beginning to encounter a new set of competition-policy issues. For example, deregulation of the financial sector has stimulated considerable supply-side competition and product innovation. However, there are considerable impediments to obtaining the maximum benefits from competition because of information impediments on the demand side of financial markets, particularly consumer-finance markets. In the aviation market, abandonment of the two-airline policy did not make the market contestable. International airlines were not able to compete in the domestic market, there remained problems of access to terminal space and restrictions on foreign ownership and investment deterred entry. Deregulation of many utilities will replace a government monopoly with a privatised natural monopoly. A free market will not in these cases deliver efficient outcomes. Competition policy must address the conditions and price of access to essential facilities as well as final consumer-pricing issues.

This leads on to the question of whether there is a need for a wider and perhaps more flexible set of regulatory instruments to deal with the issues raised in newly deregulated sectors, for example, the use of divestiture to reform the structure of industries either before deregulation or as a remedy for anti-competitive conduct, the encouragement of interstate trade and the use of administrative review mechanisms to deal with questions of the terms and conditions of access to essential facilities and final prices.

As long as the legal process remains a central instrument of competition policy, attention must focus on how to make that process more effective to achieve the goals of competition policy. This includes a whole range of issues, from questions of access and cost of the legal process, time taken to achieve a remedy, evidentiary issues and the nature of legal remedies available.

The Trade Practices Act

The Underlying Principles and Provisions of the Act

The Trade Practices Act 1974 was enacted to prevent anti-competitive conduct and encourage competition and efficiency in business that would result in greater choice for consumers in price, quality and service that would safeguard the position of consumers in their dealings with producers and sellers.

The Act is divided into two major parts: part IV deals with anti-competitive practices and part V deals with unfair trading practices. Recently there have been amendments to the Act that have resulted in two additional parts: part IVA which deals with unconscionable conduct; and part VA which is concerned with the liability of manufacturers and importers for defective goods.

Part IV of the Act deals mainly with the manifestation of anti-competitive conduct (anti-competitive agreements, price fixing, primary and secondary boycotts, misuse of market power, anti-competitive exclusive dealing, resale price maintenance, anti-competitive price discrimination) rather than address the structure of markets and hence the incentive for firms to engage in such conduct. The merger provision which include limited powers of post-merger divestiture for up to three years after a merger, are the major exception to this.

Part V of the Act contains a range of provisions aimed at protecting consumers and businesses who qualify as consumers. The consumer-protection provisions can largely be seen as a means of promoting fair competition by addressing problems of insufficient information in markets.

Competition generally promotes efficient market outcomes. The existence of other types of market failure, e.g. poor information, free-riding, economies of scale may create a conflict between competition and the achievement of economic efficiency. The authorisation process provides an avenue of administrative review to balance the costs and benefits of practices designed to overcome these market failures. This pre-empts the need for costly litigation. The 37.7 per cent of Australian economics professors who agree with the vigorous use of trade practices laws 'with provisos' no doubt had the authorisation process in mind. Authorisation cannot currently be granted for price agreements for goods, except for genuinely recommended prices if at least 50 parties are involved, misuse of market power, resale price maintenance or price discrimination.

The case for simplification

Part IV of the Act is quite long and complex. One suggestion is that consideration be given to the long-term proposal that part IV be simplified to say 'Any behaviour which substantially lessens competition in a substantial market for goods and service is prohibited unless authorised.'

The principle that underlies the proposal is an economic one. It should prohibit behaviour that substantially lessens competition, nothing more and nothing less, but authorisation should be possible if the economic benefits outweigh the detriment to competition.

It is worthwhile contrasting the Act with the key parts of the Sherman Act in the US and Articles 85 and 86 of the EEC Treaty, although it is recognised that the Sherman Act and EEC Articles are different in substance and procedure and that they do not stand alone. Nevertheless the basic competition legislation is expressed briefly but comprehensively in these two examples.

A more general wording may be more appropriate as the reach of competition law is extended to newly deregulated sectors of the economy where the requirements of competition policy may be somewhat different. It would be preferable to apply the same general competition law to all sectors of the economy rather than developing specific regulatory regimes where the focus on competition may be lost. The concept of the simplification proposed can be found in Part V of the Act and in particular Section 52. The application of this general prohibition on misleading or deceptive conduct seems to have worked well despite its generality.

Some argue that the simplified Act will cause more uncertainty as it would not contain a specific description of proscribed behaviour. However, the current Act is already complex, sometimes difficult to read and ambiguous. The brevity of the US Sherman Act and the EEC Articles 85 and 86 have not necessarily resulted in any greater uncertainty. The Act's approach of proscribing specific behaviour rather than laying down general precepts was adopted at its introduction in 1974. But nineteen years later, there is a body of experience and case law that makes clearer what forms of behaviour are of concern to competition policy.

One possibility would be to introduce a general two-line simplification of the Act but to retain more specific prohibitions, for example, the *per se* ban on price-fixing of goods and other specific prohibitions desired by the government, such as Sections 45D and 45E. Another possibility is to adopt the concept of a two-line Act as a guide against which all future legislative options would be evaluated.

The questions of whether the Act is purely economic or whether a mixture of economic and moral concepts would have significant ramifications for the issue of its simplification as suggested. If it is the latter then the simplification proposal may be less appropriate.

Universal coverage
The Act is currently limited in its operation by the Shield of the Crown, by the Constitution, which limits its application to corporations and

other companies engaged in interstate trade or commerce; by specific exemptions provided for by section 51 of the Act, including conduct specifically endorsed by legislation and by other specific provisions in the Act, such as exemption by regulation under section 172(2) and the special regime established for international shipping under part X of the Act.

Those areas of the economy that are fully or partially exempt from the operation of the Act include public utilities and government businesses, state rural marketing boards and some professions and occupations. For the most part, these activities are not directly subject to the pressures of international competition. They do, however, contribute significantly to the input costs of many Australian firms which are striving to compete internationally. Their activities also represent a significant element of consumer prices. Notwithstanding this they are, to some extent, insulated from the discipline of competition. The TPC's ability to act against anti-competitive and unfair practices is constrained by the limited application of the Act in some of the most important sectors of the economy.

There is no apparent underlying economic rationale for immunity from competition law when it comes to exemptions, they are the result of historical and constitutional factors. This deficiency was noted as long ago as 1976 by the Swanson Committee:

> We believe it to be extremely important that the Trade Practices Act should start from a position of universal application to all business activity, whether public sector or private sector, corporate or otherwise.[3]

A series of Industry Commission reports has highlighted the need for reforms and for more competition in the electricity, gas, rail and postal industries. Currently the Industry Commission is also reporting on ports and water. The radical recommendations (or expected radical recommendations) call for the comprehensive application of competition policy to virtually all facets of these industries to achieve the reform necessary for greater efficiency. The reports call for the full application of the Act but their policy prescriptions go far beyond this. Horizontal and vertical divestiture is called for in electricity and gas, as well as the promotion of interstate trade. In addition, some regulation is also seen as required in areas where natural monopoly exists. This relates to both 'access terms and conditions' issues and to prices charged to end users.

The question of universal coverage is currently the subject of an independent review. The Commonwealth and states have agreed on the principle of a universal competition policy. Fred Hilmer is heading a review charged with examining the appropriate way of giving effect to this principle, including whether universal application of the Act or some alternative is preferable, whether the Act needs to be amended to deal with the extended coverage and how to make the transition to a universal competition law regime. Universality is economically rational, but there are considerable political obstacles including the powers and revenues of State governments and interest group pressures.

Natural monopoly

As state governments proceed with deregulation, corporatisation and privatisation of public utilities, coverage of the Act will be naturally extended. This raises the question of whether the Act is, or could be, an appropriate instrument to deal with the particular problems of market failure arising in those industries which will continue to retain substantial elements of natural monopoly.

Traditionally there has been government intervention in these industries on the grounds of economic and social policy. Industries with natural monopoly characteristics have, at least until recently, been exclusively owned and operated by the public sector. Competition has played a very limited role in these markets. Too often legislation has extended the scope of monopoly well beyond the bounds of true natural monopoly. True natural monopoly areas have been mixed up with areas in which there is scope for competition. Yet, competition can often ensure that the monopolised industry maintains efficient production and minimises the scope for abuses of market power. Competition could be introduced by a number of mechanisms including contracting out, common carrier provisions and structural separation. The question then arises of how to regulate the true natural monopolies that remain after deregulation, privatisation and other pro-competitive measures.

There will be a role for pro-competitive regulation to limit the abuse of market power of a deregulated natural monopoly. Typically such regulation involves control over pricing and access to natural monopoly facilities such as transmission grids and natural gas pipelines. In seeking to achieve an efficient set of prices for natural monopolists, governments have tended to introduce surrogates for competitive behaviour such as cost-plus pricing or rate-of-return regulation. These methods have long been used in the US where public utilities have generally been privately run monopolies subject to government regulation. Both these methods have fundamental flaws, there are major problems to do with asymmetric access to information between the regulator and the regulated. Cost-plus pricing offers little incentive for cost efficiency, especially in industries where demand is relatively inelastic, while rate-of-return regulation creates incentives for over-capitalisation.

In response to these problems, price capping has become popular as an alternative means of regulation, that is, imposing a ceiling on prices using a formula that relates the rate of increase of prices to the Consumer Price Index minus a so-called 'X' factor based on an expected or targeted rate of productivity increase. The major advantage of price capping is that it provides incentives for cost minimisation, since the regulated firm benefits directly through increased profitability and it is far less reliant on information provided by the regulated firm. However, the more frequent are reviews of 'X' and the more closely it relates to achieved productivity performance, the more these advantages are reduced.

Another alternative is the 'light-handed' regulation which is characterised more by the monitoring of actual market outcomes than the establishment of complex and predetermined sets of financial or cost related benchmarks. Finally, in some industries 'yardstick' techniques can be applied in which prices of individual firms or individual regions are set on the basis of the actual or targeted average performance of an industry or nation as a whole, or even on the basis of world best practice prices (as in the case of petrol in Australia).

Pricing, while of central importance, is not the only problem associated with natural monopoly. The broader terms and conditions of access are also important. Barriers to entry can be raised when access to natural monopoly facilities is denied or frustrated, with the effect of limiting competition, e.g. problems of interconnection can severely affect the level of service which a second carrier can offer in competition with a vertically integrated natural monopoly. There are a number of overseas cases, particularly in the US and New Zealand where the matter of access to monopoly facilities has been raised.[4] These cases concern situations where refusals to allow access to 'essential facilities' on non-discriminatory terms have been held to contravene competition law.

In its submission to the Industry Commission inquiry into Energy Generation and Distribution, the TPC considered access issues in the context of section 46. It believed that when the owner of an essential facility is vertically integrated, unregulated and uses its power in the market (constituted by the essential facility) to eliminate or reduce competition in that or other markets, a contravention of section 46 is most likely to occur. However, as the section was not drafted specifically to deal with natural monopoly issues and there is a high burden of proof placed on potential plaintiffs because of the need to show anti-competitive purpose, the resulting uncertainty and time and cost involved in litigation raises considerable concerns about the application of section 46 to access questions.

The problem of access to natural monopolies raises two issues in relation to the appropriateness of the Act to regulate behaviour and promote efficient market outcomes:

- the Trade Practices Act is designed to address specific instances of anti-competitive conduct as they occur, but the problem of natural monopoly is a structural one, since the incentive for anti-competitive behaviour and high prices is a permanent feature of the market; and
- the Courts are not currently well-suited to the application of complex pricing determinations as a remedy for anti-competitive behaviour

The second issue extends beyond the natural monopoly problem. Access issues may arise in industries that are not natural monopolies, e.g., Queensland Wire Industries, which require some determination of price to establish an effective remedy. Securing access to an essential input helps the downstream competitor and may provide some benefit to consumers, but if the firm with market power retains the ability to determine the price of access, it will be able to retain most or all of the monopoly profits with detrimental consequences for resource allocation. Similarly, predatory pricing and price discrimination cases may require the adjudication of pricing issues.

Both issues suggest the need for a process of administrative review by an expert body, which could pre-empt the need for lengthy litigation of access and pricing issues for natural monopolies. The Prices Surveillance Authority (PSA) and Austel are administrative review bodies. Again, there are limitations to both of these.

The PSA deals exclusively with pricing issues. As previously noted, questions of access to natural monopolies are more complex than normal pricing questions. Access needs to be considered in a more general competition framework and may need to address other issues of market failure. Industry-specific regulation, such as that administered by Austel and by OFTEL, OFGAS and similar bodies in the UK, also has its weaknesses. In particular, it is more open to regulatory capture, it tends to duplicate efforts and as a result is more costly and it may lead to different and inconsistent approaches to the regulation of different industries. It can also suffer if it is isolated from a competition ethos.

These factors suggest that a more appropriate solution may be to modify the Act to provide for administrative review of certain types of conduct in 'declared' industries. This would allow a broad approach based on the achievement of economic efficiency to be applied. The problems of natural monopolies are different in degree rather than in kind to those in other markets. Economies of scale and market power arise to a lesser extent in other markets and similar competition problems arise. Moreover, natural monopolies may be eroded by technological change. It would be preferable to maintain the focus on promoting competition rather than the creation of specific regulatory regimes.

Divestiture

Deregulation and privatisation of natural monopolies also raise the more general question of structural versus conduct approaches to competition policy. The Industry Commission reports have put the question of divestiture on the public-policy agenda, at least for deregulated industries. In view of this, it is worth discussing some aspects of the case for and against divestiture, although no conclusions are drawn in this paper.

The Act for the most part seeks to curb the effects of a firm's market power through penalties such as fines, injunctions and ancillary orders for anti-competitive conduct rather than remove the source of market power to prevent the recurrence of the conduct. The notable exception to this is the merger provisions that provide for injunctions, fines and divestiture where a merger would be likely to result in a substantial lessening of competition.

The limited application of divestiture as a remedy under the Act is consistent with the approach taken in Europe, Canada and New Zealand, where divestiture is also restricted to merger-related conduct. This contrasts with the position in the US where divestiture is a more widely available remedy for anti-competitive conduct such as anti-competitive agreements and exclusion of competitors from an 'essential facility'.

Would a broader application of divestiture be appropriate under the Act as a remedy for offences under sections 45-6, particularly in the context of newly deregulated sectors? Divestiture represents a particularly severe incursion into private property rights and free markets. The costs and benefits of its extension need to be carefully considered.

The extension of divestiture powers would have several advantages. A primary argument advanced by some is that by influencing market structure it attacks the incentives for anti-competitive behaviour, preventing further abuse of market power and recurrent contraventions of the Act better than existing penalties which often seem to have little effect on firms behaviour. A counter argument is that an adequate level of fines will achieve the same outcome. The maximum fine has recently been increased from $250 000 to $10 million per offence.

The availability of divestiture as a remedy would not remove the need to bring about successful action in the courts. The TPC often faces considerable difficulties in successfully prosecuting offences due to problems of evidence and satisfying the courts' interpretation of the competition test(s). Furthermore, the courts would probably be reluctant to impose such a severe penalty except in extreme circumstances. It may be that its most potent effect would be to deter firms from engaging in anti-competitive conduct. This effect is likely to be substantial, given the serious commercial implications that would flow from a divestiture order.

There are also potential costs from the extension of the divestiture power. The most obvious is the potential loss of economies of scale, scope and transactions costs that could arise from divestiture. It would be left to the TPC and the court to consider the relative costs and benefits of such economies versus the improvement to competition.

One of the greatest difficulties with divestiture is in determining how far divestiture should go towards addressing the conduct in question. In the case of mergers, the shares or assets to be sold are those that have recently been acquired; they are easily identified and constitute a viable commercial entity. The same is not the case when addressing other types of anti-competitive conduct. The firm in question will be an established and fully integrated entity and it may not be at all obvious where to draw the line such that competition concerns are properly addressed, but the separate entities continue to be viable independent entities. Furthermore, the length of time taken to prove a breach of the Act in the courts may mean that market conditions have changed and the original divestiture sought is no longer appropriate. Posner's empirical work demonstrates a lengthy interval between instituting and implementing divestiture proposals.[5]

A further problem of divestiture is that it will almost certainly undermine the value of share holdings in the firm. Where ownership and control are separate, this may amount to punishing shareholders for conduct over which they had no control.

There could also be constitutional restrictions on divestiture. The Constitution has restrictions on the unjust appropriation of property and this could greatly limit the scope of divestiture. The decision of whether or not to adopt divestiture depends upon considerations of its benefits and costs. Legislators so far have presumably concluded that the costs outweigh the benefits or perhaps that the time has not been right. A possible change to this conclusion could occur in future at least in regard to deregulating industries where the Industry Commission — a notoriously dry institution — has called for extensive divestiture in electricity, gas and rail and may do so in other areas. The Industry Commission has implicitly left this matter to decisions by state governments. There is also the issue of whether the TAct should contain a divestiture power especially for deregulating industries. These questions are likely to receive attention as a public-policy matter in future.

Consumer protection

While much is said about fostering competition to promote the efficient use of resources, consumer-protection policy also promotes efficient markets and the personal welfare of consumers. This is achieved through the dissemination of information to consumers so that their purchasing decisions contribute to the functioning of competitive markets and through the protection of consumers where competition does not produce the best possible economic and social outcomes. Where tackling mergers and anti-competitive conduct affects the supply side of the market, consumer protection policy affects the demand side of the market. Both work towards overcoming market failure and making markets work more efficiently.

The two parts of the Act (part IV that deals with anti-competitive practices and part V with unfair trading practices) are complementary. Often consumers (be they individuals or business) will gain more real benefits from the control of monopoly power, price fixing and other anti-competitive practices than from the enforcement on a case by case basis of the consumer protection provisions of the Act. Hence, it is important to have consumer-protection policy at the national level linked with competition policy rather than have it follow a separate path. Consumer-protection policy is largely a matter of a market being made to work whether through competition, provision of clear, correct and sufficient information or reduced transaction costs. In this way, consumer-protection policy is likely to be more effective than if it is an isolated area of government intervention that does not comply with general competition policy.

Over the past year there has been an upsurge of consumer problems as a side effect of economic reform especially in banking, insurance, telecommunications and health-care services. Another area to come under the spotlight was the home-building industry. One of the strategies being adopted by the TPC has been to identify national problems as they emerge and seek broad solutions. The adequacy of remedies provided in the law is of concern to the TPC and for some time it has developed an 'integrated strategies' approach in which litigation, compliance and compensation arrangements can all be considered where parties are involved in breaches of the law. This means that all elements of the TPC's work are linked and support each other. In other words, instead of pursuing a particular complaint or inquiry that resolves just the problems of the individual, the integrated approach seeks to address the underlying market causes of the complaint.

The insurance cases in Aboriginal communities in Northern Australia and the subsequent study of the insurance and superannuation industry are examples of this approach. In an exhaustive eight-month investigation the TPC uncovered widespread exploitation of members of Aboriginal communities in Queensland. Language and education difficulties created severe information problems in this market, providing the opportunity for agents to divert efficient market outcomes. The TPC alleged that Colonial Mutual Life Assurance Society Ltd. (CML) and Norwich Union Life Australia Ltd., agents engaged in unconscionable conduct, misrepresented policy terms, and gave inadequate and misleading explanations to potential clients about insurance policies and savings plans. The TPC and the companies achieved court-noted settlements involving the refund of premiums, funding of consumer education programs for Aboriginal people and the upgrading of internal programs to ensure company compliance with the Act. The TPC realised that settlement in these cases provided the greatest number of advantages to all concerned; not only did it put in place a mechanism to ensure there was no recurrence of the conduct but it also eliminated the need for lengthy and costly legal proceedings.

Following on from these investigations and from consumer complaints about the practices of some agents and the high level of early termination of many insurance superannuation policies, in February 1992, the then Minister for Justice and Consumer Affairs, Senator Michael Tate directed the TPC to carry out a study of consumers' experiences with life insurance and superannuation agents. The study, which was completed in December 1992, recommended a two-stage strategy to address the competition and consumer problems that have been identified in the life-insurance market. Stage one requires the early implementation of measures directed at promoting more effective competition in the market to improving consumer information on life insurance and superannuation products, to improving the competence and conduct of agents and the availability of remedies for consumers. Stage two requires an assessment to be made after three years of the effectiveness of the measures addressing the marketing and consumer problems that have been identified in the report.

Economic rationalism and competition policy: two case studies

Merger policy

The merger provisions of the Act were recently amended. Section 50 previously prohibited only those mergers or acquisitions that created or substantially strengthened a position of dominance in a market, unless authorised by the TPC. Section 50, as now amended, prohibits mergers or acquisitions that are likely to substantially lessen competition and which have not been authorised by the TPC. Furthermore, section 50(3) requires regard for various 'merger factors' when assessing the likely impact of a merger on competition. These factors reflect the framework of modern industrial economics.

There was an inconsistency between the merger provisions and the remainder of the Act. Governments had accepted the principle that any competitive behaviour that substantially lessens competition should be prohibited unless authorised by the TPC for most of the restrictive trade practices provisions of the Act, but this principle had not been carried over into the field of merger policy. The TPC argued that in principle any merger that substantially lessens competition should be prohibited unless authorised — by definition a merger between two competitors that substantially lessens competition means almost certainly that they can raise prices significantly. Such mergers should be examinable.

'Dominance' normally refers to a situation in which one firm has a majority of the market, including imports and is free from effective competition. Other mergers (say they reduced the number of firms from four to two) could not normally be examined under this test. This is not a distinction that is rational. 'Dominance', it should also be noted, was interpreted more restrictively in Australia than in Europe. The dominance test meant that the ultimate restrictive trade practice — the merger of two rivals — may not be scrutinised whereas an anti-competitive arrangement between them as two separate entities (e.g., an agreement to fix prices) would contravene the Act unless authorised.

The TPC expressed concern that a substantial number of important mergers in recent years had not been properly examined by both the TPC or the courts despite concerns about their likely substantial effects on competition. The TPC's submission to the Cooney Inquiry cites a large number of examples, including News Ltd.-Herald and Weekly Times, Coles-Myer and Ansett-East West Airlines. The TPC conceded that because it did not challenge these individual cases in court there was insufficient information on which to test fully the validity of its concerns, but at a general level its contention appeared to be correct.

The need for mergers to achieve economies of scale and scope if Australian industry is to be internationally competitive was often cited as the reason for Australia's relatively weak merger test. In fact, the weak test had been used as a shield enabling anti-competitive mergers in those parts of the Australian economy not exposed to international competition. An uncompetitive domestic sector loads high costs onto sectors of the Australian economy involved in international trade and hinders international competitiveness. Furthermore, as Porter has demonstrated in his extensive empirical research, the key to international competitiveness is domestic rivalry. If firms cannot compete at home, they will not be able to withstand more vigorous competition overseas. Hence, a competition-based merger policy is critical both to minimise input prices and sharpen the competitive drive in output markets. The new 'substantial lessening of competition' test is compatible with mergers in the traded goods sector provided that the term 'competition' is properly interpreted by the courts to include international competition from imports. This has been reinforced by the inclusion of import competition as one of the statutory 'merger factors' to be considered in the assessment of 'substantial lessening of competition'.

In coming years, with the emphasis on the need for microeconomic reform and competition throughout the economy, including in the non-traded goods sector, the dominance test seemed inappropriate. One important lesson to be learnt from the experience of regulatory reform within OECD member countries is that merger activity becomes prominent in the period following deregulation. According to the OECD, 'competition authorities should be particularly vigilant in their implementation of merger policy' and these mergers, 'like mergers in any sector, will need strict scrutiny by competition authorities to ensure that they are not anti-competitive'.[6]

There is limited scope under the Act to do anything about a merger once it has taken place. This is because, as discussed earlier, there are limited divestiture provisions under the Act. Once a merger has taken place, it is difficult and often costly to unscramble. It is important that any mergers that are likely to lessen competition be subject to scrutiny, given their irreversible character.

A reduction of the competition test applied in the early years of the Act from 1974 to 1977 when policy-makers were on a learning curve. The test may have blocked some mergers that would otherwise have occurred, but nineteen years' experience later, these difficulties are not likely to recur. Furthermore, at that time the test applied to all markets, whereas the new test only applies to 'substantial' markets. The adequacy of the dominance test was the subject of extensive debate for many years. In May 1989 the Griffiths Committee decided by majority that there was not sufficient justification at that stage to return to a substantial lessening of competition test.[7] Just over two years later, the Cooney Committee reversed that recommendation, also by majority.[8] This did not end the debate since the Attorney-General's office and the Attorney General initially remained opposed to such a change.

Eventually, all those departments accused of being dominated by economic rationalists came to support the change, e.g., Prime Minister and Cabinet, Finance and Treasury; but those departments which are traditionally associated with interventionist policies and regulation continued to oppose it, e.g., Industry Technology and Commerce and Attorney-General's. This is not as paradoxical as might first appear. The new merger test fits within the overriding economic logic of the Act's underlying principles. It is directed at improving the way in which markets work to promote economic efficiency rather than overriding markets with regulatory economic engineering. That the new test involved a higher degree of government intervention was accepted on the grounds that the benefits of intervention were likely to exceed the inevitable costs. Eventually the government was also convinced by the rational-economic argument to change the test and make it consistent with the rest of the Act. The TPC has incorporated the statutory 'merger factors' in its draft merger guidelines which contain a five-stage evaluation process aimed at minimising the costs of enforcement and compliance.

Market definition is the first stage of the process, a necessary prerequisite for the calculation of market shares. Substitution possibilities are considered on both the demand and supply sides of the market and future market developments must also be considered, e.g., pay-TV decisions may need to give some consideration to the arrival of MDS, satellite and cable and possibly other modes of transmission in future.

At the second stage, market shares and concentration ratios are then calculated and compared to two threshold tests. The first test, whether the merged firm's market share exceeds 40 per cent, reflects concern about the potential exercise of unilateral market power; it is the merged firm's own market share which is the test. The second test, whether the four-firm concentration ratio will be over 75 per cent and the merged firm's share 15 per cent, reflects concern with the potential exercise of coordinated market power; it is the degree of market concentration which is of concern.

The next three stages involve the evaluation of import competition, barriers to entry and other factors. Data collection and analysis at these stages are progressively more complex. Only if the TPC is still concerned about the potential competitive impact of a merger after the evaluation of market shares and concentration will detailed evaluation of these subsequent stages be required.

The approach adopted by the TPC is similar to that used in the US and Canada where similar tests apply. The major difference is the greater importance attached to import competition. In a small open economy such as Australia, import competition is often a critical structural factor that provides the incentive for competitive conduct. In many markets all goods are imported. This is underlined in the list of merger factors in the Act and by the TPC's incorporation of it into the merger guidelines. Imports are fully incorporated in the calculation of market shares and the next stage is a full evaluation of the role played by imports in the market.

The significance attached to imports in the evaluation of the competitive impact of a merger is one way in which the government addressed continued concerns about scale economies and international competitiveness. If a merged firm faced significant international competition in the domestic market, the merger is not likely to lessen competition substantially and therefore, legal. This issue was also addressed through the authorisation process by specifying that the TPC must regard a significant increase in the real value of exports or a significant substitution of domestic products for imported goods as benefits to the public. The TPC must also take into account all other matters that relate to the international competitiveness of Australian industry.

Copyright

Competition policy is not a discrete set of policy instruments that uniquely affect the structure and conduct of market competition. As previously emphasised, the policy instruments that impact on competition are many and varied at all levels of government. This has been recognised in the recent debates about copyright protection in the markets for books, records and computer software. Intellectual property policy has rarely been looked at from the competition perspective. Although intellectual-property laws in Australia are fundamentally economic laws designed to overcome market failure caused by free-riding on creative activity, there has been little acknowledgement of the fact that intellectual property rights designed to overcome one type of market failure may create another in the form of insufficient competition. The administration of intellectual property rights has been hived off into different parts of the bureaucracy where the interests of rights owners rather than the efficient functioning of markets, often capture the agenda.

This approach was challenged by the PSA's reports into the prices of books, records and computer software. They looked at the total market picture in a competition framework. Prices in Australia were found to be significantly higher than overseas to an extent that could not be justified by the market's small scale and isolation. The PSA argued that the Australian market for these products was characterised by less competition than overseas markets. Suppliers, either individually and/or together, faced demand conditions that were less price elastic than in other markets. This made international price discrimination a profit-maximising strategy that could be sustained only if there was no arbitrage between markets. The importation provisions of the Copyright Act provided the necessary barrier, providing the copyright holder with a monopoly right to import.

Copyright protection is justified as a means of overcoming market failure caused by free riding on investment in intellectual property. If people can use an asset without paying for it, the market fails to transmit the demand to investors and there will be a sub-optimal level of investment; the market will fail to produce an efficient outcome. It is not justified simply to maximise the private (monopoly) returns of rights holders. The importation provisions were an example of the latter. There is no general market failure in the distribution of copyright products. Copyright rests on a general failure in the sphere of production, such that investors cannot exclude people from freely using their investment by copying, recording, performing and so on. This market failure does not justify a monopoly over importation.

Market failure may also arise in the sphere of distribution but this is not inherently related to the nature of the investment as intellectual property. Such failures arise in many markets independent of whether they are also characterised by intellectual property, e.g., motor vehicles and many large and complex consumer good items. Exclusive contractual arrangements are the usual solution to these problems and the Act provides a framework for considering the costs and benefits of these arrangements under the notification and authorisation provisions. This is the appropriate method for dealing with any market failure in the sphere of distribution, not through generalised legislation. In particular books, records and computer software markets, the PSA found that no market failures that could justify the monopoly over imports.

Opposition to the PSA came very much from those critical of the economic-rationalist approach to policy. The book and record industries in particular drew support from the more famous Australian authors and musicians who argued that their market viability depended on the existence of the import provisions. It was argued that Australian authors and musicians should be supported at the expense of market efficiency. The import provisions, with their widespread effects on prices and market efficiency seem a very blunt instrument for the task, even if they can be justified.

Donald Horne argued that 'books are different', that the PSA's economic-rationalist approach was too narrow and missed the value of culture and reading which cannot be expressed in financial terms. He argued that a 'market for ideas' was an essential part of a liberal-democratic society.[9] However, this argument was never linked to the need for a monopoly over imports. Rather, it seemed to reflect a prescriptive view of what that market should consist of, 'a wide variety of books written about Australia and/or by Australians'.[10] Australian culture was identified with books. The fact that the wider international literary world is priced out of reach of many Australians was not considered important.

The government's response to the reports on books and records is indicative of the gradual recognition of the fact that competition policy intrudes on many areas of policy making. Both responses involved political compromises but the second response to the records report is more accepting of the PSA's arguments and less of a compromise than that for books. In the case of records, protection will be retained only for recordings of Australian artists while in the case of books all authors and publishers could retain protection provided they released their books in Australia within thirty days of their release overseas.

The computer-software industry took a different approach to the book and records industries. The industry accepted that there were price differences but said that these reflected cost differences and argued that the import provisions were needed to correct for market failure, not that 'software is different'. The government has yet to respond to this.

The import provisions were criticised by the PSA on the basis that they are not justified on the grounds of market failure. However, even where there is a justification for intellectual-property rights on the grounds of market failure, there may also be costs in terms of anti-competitive detriment. There is a need to balance any potential conflicts within the framework of promoting efficient markets. Section 51(3) of the Act currently provides certain limited exemptions from the Act for licence conditions related to those rights. The question arises as to whether such a general exemption is warranted. Market circumstances vary considerably for different products involving intellectual property. It may be more appropriate to review potentially anti-competitive conduct in these markets within the overall public benefit framework of the authorisation process.

The Australian economic environment is changing. Not only is Australian business now exposed to far greater international competition than in the past — partly as a result of the government program of gradually reduced protection — but many other markets have been opened up to greater competition as a result of deregulation; for example, the airline, telecommunications and banking industries. Deregulation is likely to increase in coming years. Moreover, the commercialisation, corporatisation or privatisation of many public enterprises is likely to be accompanied by a much greater exposure of these sectors to competition than before.

Opinion about microeconomic policy has changed since the introduction of trade-practices legislation. The need for such legislation is generally accepted, even by the business community. There is a much stronger recognition now of the need for microeconomic reform. Such reform generally requires a reduced role of government intervention in order to allow markets to work more efficiently. Paradoxically, in the area of competition policy itself, there is need for greater government intervention in order to achieve improved efficiency.

As more Australian businesses become exposed to international competition it is vital that their suppliers be competitive and efficient. A strong, well-resourced and enlightened competition policy is needed to help achieve competitive outcomes and survival throughout the economy. Moreover, deregulation as well as commercialisation, corporatisation or privatisation of many public enterprises will only work well if accompanied by a much greater exposure of the affected sectors to the Act than in the past.

The lesson of overseas deregulatory experience is that deregulation must be accompanied by strong competition law if it is to work. For example, where deregulation has taken the form of structural break-up of existing enterprises, as has occurred in the energy industries, it has been necessary to have effective merger laws to prevent remerging of the broken up enterprises and anti-collusion laws to prevent agreements between the new enterprises, many of which have been managed by persons who have had close working relationships in the past.

Competition policy may at first sight seem to be a paradox for economic rationalism. Consider this scenario: free markets are regarded as the best means of promoting economic efficiency, and yet, competition policy involves the regulation of markets. The paradox is, however, imagined rather than real. Competition policy addresses market failure, and it is generally designed to make markets work better, not replace the market mechanism. Intervention is selective rather than general. Moreover, competition policy is not confined to the Act since it includes both the removal of barriers to competition and the promotion of competition through market intervention.

This discussion of competition policy is significant in the economic rationalism debate since it suggests that mainstream economists and dry economic departments are supportive of intervention in the form of competition policy.

It is interesting to consider what the response of anti-economic rationalists is to competition policy issues, particularly those likely to emerge in the remainder of the 1990s. They could be expected to be less concerned than very dry economists about the degree of government intervention involved in trade practices law. Some of the issues that may attract their interest are:

- How far should the principles of competition policy be extended beyond its traditional areas? Should it apply to health, education, pay TV, copyright, the practices (including the ethical codes) of the professions, public utilities, agriculture (including small farmers) and small business? Are these so different that, like books in Donald Horne's estimation, they should be immune from competition policy? Or, do anti economic rationalists see a more complex trade-off as being involved?

- If this extension is of concern, is the flexible character of the Trade Practices Act, with its authorisation procedures, adequate enough to enable their concerns about non-efficiency values to be satisfied?

- Is competition policy likely to be seen as highly desirable to help Australia progress or is it seen by anti economic rationalists as a policy, like lower protectionism, likely to destroy jobs and ultimately industry? Or, will it be seen as a means of enhancing employment, since competition typically lowers prices thereby boosting local demand and international competitiveness?

Notes

1 Malcolm Anderson and Richard Blandy, 'What Australian Economics Professors Think', *Australian Economic Review*, fourth quarter, 1992.

2 The only partial exception to this concerned BHP's takeover of NZ Steel. The TPC had previously opposed this takeover and had initiated some court orders limiting BHP's freedom to take over NZ Steel. When BHP approached the TPC about a full takeover, agreement was given on the basis that BHP and the TPC would gain the consent of the government (and ultimately Parliament) for an acceleration in the programme of planned tariff reductions regarding the steel industry.

3 Trade Practices Act Review Committee (Swanson Committee); Report to The Minister for Business and Consumer Affairs, August 1976.

4 U.S. v *Terminal Rail Road Association of St. Louis* 224 U.S. 383 (1912); *Otter Tail Power Co.* v U.S. 410 U.S. 366 (1973); U.S. v *American Telegraph and Telephone Co.* 524 F. Supp. 1336 (1981); *MCI Communications Corp.* v *American Telegraph and Telephone Co.* 708 F.2d 1081 (7th Cir. 1983); *Fishman* v *Wirtz* 807 F.2d 520 (7th Cir. 1986).

5 R. A. Posner, *Antitrust Law: An Economic Perspective*, University of Chicago Press, 1976 discusses this and gives empirical references.

6 OECD,1991, Synthesis Report on Competition Policy and Deregulation, Draft, Paris, 1991.

7 Report by the House of Representatives Standing Committee on Legal and Constitutional Affairs, *Mergers, Takeovers and Monopolies: Profiting from Competition?*, AGPS, May 1989.

8 Report by the Senate Standing Committee on Legal and Constitutional Affairs, *Mergers, Monopolies and Acquisitions: Adequacy of Existing Legislative Controls*, AGPS, December 1991.

9 *Australian*, 8 December 1989.

10 Ibid.

Peter L. Swan

Comments

The theme of Allan Fels' and Jill Walker's essay is that competition policy would seem to be a paradox in terms of rational non-interventionist economics: 'government intervention is needed to make markets work better'. They suggest that this paradox is more imagined than real and that 'competition policy addresses market failure, it is designed to make markets work better, not replace the market mechanism.' Fels and Walker looks towards authorities to provide the TPC and PSA with a positive report card, a fact I find worrying. These authorities include economics professors and central economics departments in Canberra. With friends such as these does one need enemies! I am much more convinced by Donald Horne's attack on the PSA that it is doing a good job. With enemies such as this one does not need friends.

Their discussion of recent changes to merger policy and the new section 50(3) reflects the likely impact of a merger on competition that are indicative of modern industrial economies. Their main focus is the the actual and potential level of import competition in the market. It is pleasing to see the TPC recognising contestability in the form of imports. However, their other points are a little strange: 'the degree of countervailing power' — it would seem that Kenneth Galbraith lives on! Their examination of the 'nature and extent of vertical integration in the market' doesn't take into account the fact that monopoly power arises from lack of competition at the horizontal level and is almost unrelated to vertical integration except insofar as it may impact on horizontal competition. It is not obvious, though, that vertical integration facilitates horizontal collusion.

In essence, Fels and Walker claim that competition law in Australia is not 'anti-rational' economics because it reflects modern industrial economics. Another way of viewing competition policy and its evolution in Australia is that it reflects with lags of 20 years or more the outcome of debates between the 'Chicago' or 'free-market' view of the competitive process and the older Harvard view that a highly interventionist anti-trust or trade-practices regime is necessary to combat entry barriers. This Harvard view is associated with economists such as Mason, Chamberlain and Bain. The older view argued that scale economies, capital costs of fixed investment and other outlays such as advertising gave rise to 'entry barriers' which in turn gave rise to monopoly and collusion and the need for a highly interventionist 'anti-monopoly' policy.

In contrast, the late George Stigler and others associated with Chicago rejected the Harvard view that just about any factor including incompetence that might frustrate the entry of a new firm, reflects entry barriers that may justify selective intervention. On the contrary, 'entry barriers' only arise if incumbents have cost advantages that are not in principle available to the new entrant and with the proviso that social welfare must improve if selective intervention is to be justified. Since technology, including scale economies, capital costs, advertising expenditure etc., does not differ between the incumbent and entrant, Stigler rejected the notion that the failure of firms to enter was necessarily evidence of market failure. He then went on to point out that entry barriers do arise when the incumbent has inherent cost advantages. The major source of these cost advantages — according to the Chicago view — is not the lack of intervention but 'the very presence of regulation promoting monopoly' rather than competition.

There is no shortage of examples of government ownership and regulation in Australia promoting monopoly exploitation of consumers and/or taxpayers. For example, within the transportation area the two-airline policy has now been removed with spectacular gains to consumers and considerable costs to the pilots who lost out as a result of the pilots' dispute. Coastal and trans-Tasman shipping is reserved for Australian ships and this adds considerably to the costs of doing business in both Australia and New Zealand. Each year there are effectively billions of dollars in subsidy to railways with the railways. There remain serious artificial restrictions on the numbers of taxis in most cities together with massive continuing subsidies to state-owned buses and limitations on intra- and interstate bus provision until recently.

Marketing boards with monopoly powers combined with import restrictions on rural products such as sugar artificially inflate the prices of many agricultural products. Moreover, centralised wage fixing and the rise in minimum wages for the relatively unskilled has added to unemployment. It is hard to imagine that an affluent country such as Australia could have over one million unemployed without the inhibiting effect on labour-market competition of centralised wage fixing.

Tariff barriers, particularly for automobiles, footwear, clothing and textiles have remained high and are only now declining. This decline has helped facilitate a major export boom to Southeast Asia in elaborately transformed manufactured goods. A very expensive monopolised telecommunications sector in the public sector is now subject to competition and reform. A high-cost, inefficient and monopolised electricity sector is now subject to major reform and productivity increase. Over the last decade, more so the last five years, electricity commissions have greatly lifted their game although there is still considerable scope for improvement. Unfortunately, virtually all of these monopolies were, and are, outside the control of the TPC. One of the few cases in which the TPC was effective in terms of removing monopoly privileges was the May 1984 deregulation of the stockmarket. Even the professionals have so far been unaffected by the efforts of the TPC to encourage competition. Fels and Walker refer to the Hilmer Inquiry and its concern with investigating the extension of the Act to cover Government Business Enterprises (GBEs). To date the TPC has been most active in areas in which private-sector competition operates but not where the true monopolies and inefficiencies lie.

Fels and the TPC argued before the Cooney Committee that section 50 on takeovers should be extended to mergers that 'substantially lessen competition'. It is suggested that major mergers such as the News Ltd.-Herald and Weekly Times takeover, Coles-Myer and Ansett-East West might not have gone ahead, at least in their present form, if a tougher test had been in place. It is not obvious to me if the outcomes of any of these would have changed in any major way with the more severe test in place.

Before the Print Media Inquiry the TPC argued in very simplistic terms about media monopolies along obsolete Harvard/Bain lines and emphasised entry barriers due to scale economies enjoyed by the incumbents. The House of Representatives Committee that conducted the inquiry had among its members a number of 'left-wingers' who were convinced that the so-called 'media magnates' strongly influenced the views of their newspapers. However, the Committee found no evidence of this actually happening. The Committee also found no evidence that the industry is any more concentrated here than in North America. Evidence was given to the Inquiry that costs fall by 23 per cent for each doubling of scale. Hence, had the TPC been successful in preventing print mergers, newspaper readers and advertisers would be denied the considerable benefits of large-scale and viable newspapers in Australia.

Fels and Walker are also critical of specialised regulators such as Austel in terms of potential capture although they agree that Austel can develop expertise which would not be possessed by the TPC. Do Fels and Walker want the TPC to monopolise the regulatory scene? Do we need another body to ensure competition between regulatory bodies? The TPC has also been very critical of the territorial licensing system for newspaper delivery. These are private monopolies that are promoted and organised not by the newsagents who have delivery monopolies thrust on them but by the newspaper proprietors themselves. Competition exists for these territorial monopolies insofar as more efficient new entrants can buy up an existing franchise. If such private territorial monopolies are anti-competitive and inefficient, why are they supported by newspapers? Newspapers, after all, are more interested in expanding their readership and efficient home delivery than in promoting high-cost distribution.

To end on a more complimentary note, Fels and Walker and the PSA are to be congratulated for having moved away from crude attempts to control prices in industries that are alleged to have excessive prices and, instead, address structural reasons for why prices may be excessive or competition lacking. For example, should copyright laws permit importers of books, music and software to price discriminate against consumers in Australia?

Ben Smith

Natural Resource Use and Environmental Policy

Economists typically see natural resource and environmental degradation problems as arising because people face prices that do not reflect accurately the full costs and benefits associated with their use. In some cases this may be the result of customary or institutionally determined property rights arrangements that are non-elusive or attenuated in a variety of ways. At least in principle, the establishment of full private property rights would resolve the problems in these instances. In other cases, though, the nature of the resources and the services they provide are such as to prohibit either the existence of fully specified private property rights or the development of complete and efficient private markets. Nevertheless, economists generally urge the use of market-based incentives in policies to control resource use. For them, it is the government's role to provide the institutional framework within which efficient private market outcomes can be either realised or simulated.

Direct management of resources by government agencies has increasingly been perceived to produce unsatisfactory results. This is partly because government agencies do not have the incentives or the information base necessary for efficient behaviour and partly because they are liable to be captured by 'client' groups and subject to political pressures. Perhaps the most notable change in economists' attitudes to resource and environmental issues, as in other areas of microeconomic policy, is the reduced willingness to conclude that the inadequacies of private-market outcomes automatically justify some form of government control. Rather, there is a growing tendency to emphasise the possibilities of improving market outcomes by extending and strengthening private property rights.

This essay will first discuss the objective of 'sustainable development' and the relationship between that objective and economic efficiency in the use of resources. The next section looks at property rights and incentive issues in the exploitation of Australia's natural resource stocks and this is followed by a discussion of conflicts between alternative types of land use. The following section examines the general issues of local and international pollution control, and this is followed by the briefest of conclusions.

Interest rates, evaluation of future benefits and sustainability

A particular concern of conservationists is the small weight that is placed on the future relative to the present; in either actual or simulated market outcomes. This is the result of discounting future costs and benefits in order to obtain comparable present values. Using a real interest rate of 4 per cent per annum, a real benefit of $1000 accrued in 50 years is the equivalent of a present real benefit of $140. If the $1000 benefit were to be realised in 100 years its present value would be only $20. When some significant immediate gain is being weighted against the preservation of an environmental asset that is capable of providing benefits forever, it can be seen that the process of exponential discounting can cut 'forever' down to size pretty quickly. This is an important effect: in the absence of such discounting a 'forever' stream of benefits would be of infinite value and any reduction in those benefits, no matter how small, would be infinitely costly and should never be contemplated. That is exactly the position that many environmental enthusiasts take, arguing that the discounting of future benefits using a positive real interest rate results in an excessively rapid depletion of natural resource stocks. The argument is over whether the market interest rate, or some lower discount rate, is appropriate for social decision-making.

The existence of a positive real interest rate in the market is the product of people's preference for current consumption and the availability of sufficiently productive investment opportunities that can generate that real rate of return while absorbing the supply of savings. An increase in the supply of savings would, *ceteris paribus*, require an expansion of investment into less productive areas, reducing the real interest rate that could be paid. The unwillingness of people to save an amount sufficient to drive the real interest rate to zero is not merely a matter of their impatience, it reflects also their views about the amount they need to save in order to achieve the desired future level of wellbeing.[1]

The argument that future events should be discounted at a lower rate than the market rate of interest, or not discounted at all depends either on the assertion that individual savings decisions are irrational, or on the presumption that society as a whole may take a different view of the importance of future events from individual members of society. Although this is an issue that has attracted much theoretical attention from economists, the conceptual arguments about the efficiency (or otherwise) of market-based outcomes in giving appropriate expression to the interests of future generations are not conclusive. A more practically useful approach is to base our view of the issue on what we believe will be the actual circumstances of those future generations. That is, do we believe that future generations will be unacceptably impoverished given decisions made about resource use that come out of market outcomes or reflect the same comparison of costs and benefits?

The concept of sustainable development, derived from the Brundtland Commission Report (WCED 1987) has provided a specification of what an 'acceptable' standard might be: that each successive generation should not be rendered worse-off than the one before. Most of the debate is about what sustainable development should in practice be taken to mean and what needs to be done to achieve it.

While the concept of economic sustainability has some operational significance, namely the ability to continue to deliver goods and services (including environmental amenities) that people value, allowing for substitution between different kinds of goods and services as technologies and resource availabilities change, the concept of ecological sustainability is more difficult to define. On one level it might simply require the degree of preservation of the natural resource stock necessary for economic sustainability. Alternately, and in the extreme case, it can be interpreted as requiring the maintenance of a more or less unchanged natural resource stock.

The simplest economics rule for sustainability, elaborated by Hartwick (1977), is that any depletion in the natural resource capital stock be accompanied by equivalent, equally productive, increases in the man-made capital stock, including improvements in technology as well as the creation of physical capital assets. With a growing population, man-made capital will need to expand sufficiently to maintain the per capita total capital stock in order to sustain a constant living standard.

The sustainability rule is the counterpart of the economists' prescription for optimal depletion/conservation of a natural resource stock: that investment in resource conservation, the cost of which is the forgone current benefit that could have been obtained from depleting the resource, should earn the same rate of return as is available from alternative investments. Assessment of the benefits flowing from resource conservation may often be a difficult and contentious issue. To remove that problem temporarily from consideration, suppose that the resource in question is a privately owned mineral deposit in an area of no conservation interest. The owner of this resource has strong incentives to obtain good information about the likely future course of minerals prices and mining costs. In deciding whether to extract more of the resource currently or to conserve it for later, the owner will want to compare the rent (net revenue) earned on marginal units today with the rent expected from postponing production of those units to a later date. The relevant yardstick of comparison is the rate of return the owner could obtain by investing the rents from current production in an alternative asset. That is, it will only be worthwhile to retain resources in the ground if their real value grows at a rate at least equal to the real rate of interest.

The efficient depletion/conservation rule and the sustainability rule are not identical. While both require that, at the margin, resource conservation and other capital investments earn the same real rate of return, the sustainability rule also requires that the total value of the stock of capital not decline. Thus, sustainability is, in principle, about both the efficient management of resource stocks and the overall level of saving that members of society undertake. In practice, it is unlikely that the second issue is actually a problem and it is appropriate to concentrate on the efficiency aspects of sustainability.

It is sometimes argued that the sustainability rule stated above is not in itself sufficient and that there is a further need for man-made capital to be a relatively close substitute for natural resource capital in production and consumption activities. In fact, the issue here is that of attaching appropriate values to natural resources, reflecting both the stream of benefits that can be derived from them and the ease with which such benefits might otherwise be derived. For resources such as oil, a properly functioning market could be expected to assign those values appropriately. That is, an expectation of future scarcity and the lack of ready substitutes would provide incentives for owners of such resources to reduce depletion, drive up current prices and rents to the point where the rate of return earned on marginal investments in resource conservation was again the same as that available from other investments. The relative ease with which man-made capital can be substituted for natural resources, and natural resources for one another, will be influential in determining how much and what types of both resource conservation and other investments is worthwhile to undertake.

It should be emphasised that the feasibility of sustaining a given living standard (or of sustaining a continued improvement in living standards) depends on getting the correct balance between different forms of investment. While it is possible that inadequate levels of investment in natural resource conservation may threaten sustainability, it is equally possible that sustainability may be threatened by excessive conservation investment at the expense of other forms of capital. It may be immediately argued that excessive natural resource depletion is the potentially more serious possibility because this may sometimes be irreversible over any reasonable time span. Inadequate investment in the man-made capital stock may cause a temporary reduction in living standards but that is capable of being reversed by subsequently higher levels of investment. The irreversibility problem does argue for some extra caution in depleting natural resources whose recovery powers are likely to be very limited and for which other capital assets are relatively poor substitutes. The essential issue, though, is still that of attaching the right values to natural resource assets and of providing people with the incentives to take account of those values in their decisions about resource use.

Ownership and incentives in the management of Australia's natural resource base

Australia has a high degree of public ownership of natural resource stocks. Practically all of the mineral resources *in situ* are owned by the Crown, with exploration and mining activity being conducted under conditional, fixed term, specific purpose leases. Approximately two-thirds of the continent's surface area is Crown land. Only about half of that is farmed, mostly as pastoral land occupied under fixed-term leases. More than 70 per cent of Australia's native forest is in public ownership and the exploitation of these forests is managed by state forest services. All of Australia's coastal fisheries resources are Crown owned, the traditional open access having been replaced with a steady increase in the degree of regulation. Control over the supply and use of water resources lies more or less exclusively in the hands of government agencies.

There has been a steady accumulation of evidence that policies pursued by government agencies, designed to promote social goals that have not been subject to careful scrutiny or analysis, have been directly or indirectly responsible for considerable inefficiencies in resource use. For example, while it is popular to imagine that land degradation is an environmental problem resulting from the unrestrained activities of farmers and that the intervention of government is required to ameliorate it, the evidence is that major causes of the problem have been government subsidisation both of land clearance and of the use of irrigation water and fertilisers (Dumsday and Chisholm 1991). The absence of secure tenure over leasehold land and restrictions on the aggregation of small blocks are also argued to have discouraged farming practices designed to maintain the productivity of the land (Kirby and Blyth 1987; Young 1987), while drought assistance policies and subsidies for soil-conservation investments are likely to have encouraged increased stocking rates and may have had little effect on the rate of land degradation (Chisholm 1987; Freebairn 1983).

Some land degradation may be socially appropriate since, up to a point, it may be desirable to 'mine' the natural productivity of the land. Thus, it is difficult to assess the extent to which the actual degree of land degradation constitutes a 'problem'. In particular, it is important to distinguish circumstances where an individual landholder's actions have spillover effects on others from those cases where the effects are purely 'on site'. The former are largely restricted to water quality and dryland salinity. Otherwise, if land is held with secure tenure (freehold or perpetual leasehold) and landholders are faced with unsubsidised prices for inputs it is reasonable to suppose that, within the limits of the information available, they will use the land in the manner that best maintains its value. The qualification is important. Much of Australia's policy-induced land degradation has occurred because of poor initial information on the consequences of particular management practices in the Australian environment. Such information is costly to obtain on an individual basis, so there remains an important role for government in coordinating the acquisition and transmission of that information. But that role is not open-ended: beyond a certain point it is optimal to act in some degree of ignorance and with appropriate caution. Government agencies also need to monitor and seek moderate spillover effects between landholders, particularly in relation to water-quality issues. But it does not seem unreasonable to imagine that they could do this in the Murray-Darling, for instance, by transferring the supply of irrigation water into private hands (giving clear incentives for water to be priced at its marginal costs of supply) and by imposing an additional government charge that reflected any off-site costs of water use that were not internalised in the private market.[2]

The management of Australia's forest resources has also been dominated historically by the pursuit of notional social goals rather than the maximisation of the value of the timber resources themselves. Forest services have pursued objectives of national self-sufficiency, assistance to the local timber processing industry, and conservation. Compared solely to what would maximise the economic value of the timber resource, it has been argued that a maximum sustainable harvest objective, with quota limitations on permissible cutting, has caused timber to be harvested later than is optimal (Industry Commission 1990). The consequent increased maturity of trees harvested has resulted in a greater long-term supply of timber for use as saw logs (rather than pulpwood) than is efficient. A number of studies and government inquiries (for example, ABARE 1991) have concluded that there is a substantial underpricing of hardwood resources, but most clearly for saw logs, in the royalty arrangements adopted by the various states.

So long as the quantity of timber cut and the timing of the harvest are regulated by forestry agencies, the underpricing of timber mainly has the effect of providing lump-sum transfers to the quota holders (capitalised in quota prices where these are tradeable) rather than influencing the level of activity in the industry. However, when forests also need to be managed for their recreational and conservation values, the fact that state forestry services have characteristically earned large losses does not inspire confidence that the efforts of harvesting are worthwhile. There is scope for greater use of market-based pricing of access to forest resources and for forestry management to focus more on maximising the value of the timber asset. That is what we should expect if ownership of forest resources were transferred to private hands. In the next section we take up the issue of the likely consequences of such a property rights transfer for recreational and conservation values of forest lands.

The problems created by open access to common property fishery resources are well known. Individual fishers have no incentive to forgo current harvest in order to conserve the stock and to maintain future harvesting levels. With increasing domestic demand and with changing technology allowing greater international marketing of products, pressures on Australia's fish stocks have steadily increased. The observable symptoms have been declines in both the total catch and the average age of the fish being caught. It is estimated (DPIE 1991) that most of Australia's fisheries are overexploited.

Regulation of fishing activity has suffered from a combination of government failure and political difficulty. The initial motivation for policy was more a response to declining profitability of fishing activity (industry assistance) than an interest in efficient management of the resources. Over time the management regime has gravitated towards specification of a total allowable catch (TAC) for each fishery, divided into individual transferable quotas (ITQs). This establishes a degree of property right over the resource for each fisher and provides incentives for efficient fishing activity. The transferability of quotas allows those who are less efficient to sell their quotas to those who, being more efficient, value them more highly. Given the limitations on current information about population dynamics and fishing costs, ITQs should best be specified as a share of a TAC that is variable both in light of new information and as the stock size adjusts. The government has a major, unavoidable role in establishing this regime. Having done so, it not clear that there remains a significant continuing management responsibility. If ITQs were permanently assigned, the holders would have incentives to set the TAC so as to maximise the value of their share in the fishery. Rather than worrying about the extent to which management costs incurred by government agencies should be passed on to the industry through licence fees (Industry Commission 1992a) it may be more appropriate to leave both the management responsibility and the cost with those who have the strongest incentive to get it right.

The Crown, in the form of state, territory, or Commonwealth governments has retained property rights over almost all mineral and energy resources up to the point at which they are removed from the ground. Access to areas for exploration is generally available on a first come first served basis but for a limited period of time during which bona fide exploration activity is required to take place. In the event that there is competition to acquire exploration rights over an area this may be resolved by ballot or by a process of work programme bidding in which the permit is awarded to the bidder submitting the 'best' (usually the largest and most costly) programme. When minerals are found, retention of the right to exploit them is only guaranteed by taking out a mining lease that normally requires mining to commence as soon as practicable.

The deficiencies of work programme bidding for exploration rights have been pointed out by a number of authors (for example, Willett 1985). Essentially, the point is familiar to economists, that the opportunity to gain valuable rights by expenditure of effort provides incentives to dissipate the value of those rights through wasteful activity. More contentiously, it has been argued that the potential for dissipation of mineral rents is endemic in the manner in which mineral rights generally are allocated and in the nature of those rights (Fane and Smith 1986; Industry Commission 1991). The essential point is that the regime operates on the basis of 'finders keepers', where people have incentives to find resources before others do. This encourages exploration to take place in an area as soon as it is expected to be marginally worthwhile, taking account of the uncertainties involved, and provides no incentive or opportunity for exploration to be delayed when this would be expected to yield a superior net present value outcome.[3] Offsetting this is the requirement that royalties (based on volume or value of output or, less frequently, on accounting profit) be paid on mining activity. Those royalties, while ensuring that rent values are not completely dissipated by premature and excessive exploration activity, generate their own inefficiencies in the pattern of mining activity.

The lack of incentive which mineral rights allocation arrangements currently provide for conservation would be overcome if perpetual, unconditional rights were auctioned, allowing the holders to decide for themselves when and if they wished to conduct exploration and mining activity (Smith 1992). In this particular instance, however, the assignment of effective private property rights has not found a great deal of favour. Both the mining industry and the state mines departments (but the former more definitely) are opposed to the notion that people should have the opportunity to sit on potentially valuable resources when there are others who (so long as they are allowed free access) would be prepared immediately to look for or mine those resources. Moran (1991) argues that potential, but undiscovered, resources do not have any value, so that there is nothing to dissipate in the process of looking for them, but that value is created by the process of successful search. The vesting of mineral rights in private hands would significantly increase the transaction costs faced by explorers and would impede the creation of value in which they seek to engage.

There is a division of opinion about what constitutes an appropriate property rights regime for minerals. Concern about the transaction costs of dealing with private mineral owners, and about the possibility that there may be eternal benefits flowing from exploration activity in one area to owners of mineral rights elsewhere, provides support for the continuation of the present arrangements. Concern about the potential for dissipation of the value of resources in the rush to discover and mine them and, as argued in the next section, about the prospects for achieving more sensible resolutions of disputes over land use leads one to the more normal economists' conclusion that clear and secure property rights are important for efficient outcomes.

Resolution of conflicts over land use

Most major disputes over land use have involved either mining or forestry, since these are both activities that often come into conflict with environmental interests. The mining industry points frequently to the area of land that is difficult to access or is closed to new exploration and mining activity. As at November 1992, the Australian

Mining Industry Council (AMIC 1992) indicated that 16.4 per cent of the continent was either Aboriginal land or land under claim, and 7.5 per cent was contained in national parks or nature reserves.

In general, exploration and mining activity are prohibited in national parks and reserves or are permitted only under conditions that are rarely likely to be satisfied. While it is appropriate for some areas of special significance to be set aside in this way, it does not seem sensible to adopt all or nothing approaches to the use of very large tracts of land. The Kakadu National Park, for example, is an area roughly defined to include the whole of the catchment for the relatively small wetlands area. While this definition of the boundaries may be appropriate for the exercise of careful control over the manner in which activity is conducted, it is difficult to see a compelling reason for precluding the conduct of exploration and mining over the whole area. Indeed, the Resource Assessment Commission inquiry on Coronation Hill (RAC 1991) concluded that there was no case for prohibiting the development of the mine on environmental grounds. The Conservation Zone area in question was not at that time formally part of the Park but, presumably, the conclusion of the RAC inquiry could equally have applied to other, similar areas within the Park boundary.

The issue, then, is that of arriving at the right trade-offs on a case by case basis. The mining industry clearly cannot expect that it should gain unrestrained access to areas of high conservation value or that any discovery of commercial minerals will necessarily be followed by permission to mine. But, rather than define cast-iron boundaries between areas where exploration and mining are permitted and those where they are prohibited, it seems more sensible to have gradations of sensitivity where the industry knows that its case needs to be stronger both in terms of the economics of the project and the degree of environmental protection offered.[4]

The Coronation Hill example is particularly illustrative of the cumbersomeness and unreliability of bureaucratic and political approvals processes in resolving these sorts of land-use conflicts, and the ultimate resolution of that issue left much to be desired. As noted above, the RAC did not believe that the project should be prohibited on environmental grounds, but it did indicate that the Jawoyn Aboriginal community that had laid claim to the area but did not yet have the title was opposed to the mining development. The Commonwealth's decision to include the area in the Kakadu National Park, and thereby preclude mining, was based on its desire to meet the wishes of this Aboriginal group.

The incentive structure facing the Jawoyn in the Coronation Hill case was an extreme version that characterises Aboriginal land holdings in general. In the Northern Territory Aboriginal landowners have the right to veto mining activity but do not have very strong incentives to allow exploration and mining to take place. They are granted inalienable titles so that they cannot sell mineral-bearing land and move elsewhere if they should wish to do so. Through the Lands Councils, Aborigines are able to gain royalty revenue from mining activity but only a small share of this accrues to the owners of the land. Thus, the incentive to for those landowners to permit mining activity is greatly attenuated. In the Coronation Hill case, the Jawoyn did not have formal title to the land and would not necessarily have gained any compensation for mining activity.

This is an area where, once again, the specification of property rights is critical. When Aboriginals are given title to land and the authority to determine the uses to which that land may be put, it is important that the nature of the property right they exercise provides them with full incentives for the land to be used efficiently and to their best advantage. In this particular instance, that would best be served by providing them with full mineral rights. Where the same person owns the mineral and surface rights, decisions about alternative land uses are internalised. This is not only important in relation to Aboriginal land. In a significant area of freehold land in the south-west of Western Australia landholders have the right of veto over mining activity but, apart from selling their property at inflated prices, do not have any means of extracting benefits from the mining activity that takes place. More generally, the ability to bid for combined surface and mineral rights would allow conservation groups to acquire areas of particular interest and to determine whether, and under what conditions, exploration and mining (or other development activities) should take place. The obligation to weigh benefits of conservation against potential revenues from development and the opportunities that these would provide for additional purchases of conservation areas would impose an important market discipline that is currently absent.

The ownership of areas by conservation organisations would permit them to raise funds through access fees, as well as through membership subscriptions and donations. While it is commonly accepted that the incentive to subscribe to such organisations is reduced by the possibility of freeriding on the contributions of others, that adverse effect is likely to be much larger in an environment where the expectation is that conservation services will be provided 'free' through government expenditure or regulation of land use and where donations to conservation groups can contribute only indirectly to the achievement of increased conservation through the lobbying and political activity which they support.

When people are not able to express their interest in conservation through market transactions there are substantial difficulties in determining what value they really place on it. Economists have developed techniques for eliciting these values by inference from observed behaviour and by hypothetical willingness-to-pay questioning. The problems of relying on these approaches were illustrated dramatically in the context of the Coronation Hill inquiry where a contingent valuation study revealed the apparent willingness of Australians to pay $650 million per annum for ten years to avoid mining in the Conservation Zone. Even if one thought that true valuations were only one-tenth of this figure that would easily have been sufficient to override the mining interest. The RAC concluded that mining should not be prohibited on environmental grounds.

In the case of forestry operations the major disputes have been over the logging of rainforest areas and over woodchip logging operations, particularly those around Eden in NSW. As indicated previously, the management and pricing practices of the state forestry services do not yield a high return on commercial exploitation of the timber resources. Equally though, the recreational and conservation benefits of the stock of hardwood forest are completely unpriced. Decisions about the use of these resources are swayed by the exercise of political pressure, the responses to which are inclined to be unstable and not independent of short-term electoral considerations. From the viewpoint of timber production alone, the incentives to efficient operation would be improved if forest resources were privately owned or available on a perpetual-lease basis with appropriate covenants which ensured that the nature of the land use was not substantially changed. The concern would be that this would not ensure that conservation and recreational values were protected. It is, however, an open question as to whether private forest owners would not find it advantageous in many areas to provide these benefits through market transactions involving, for example, entry fees for people who wanted to enjoy them. The Tasman Institute (1991) argues that the private provision of such benefits is currently rendered unprofitable by the free public supply and draws attention to US experience of private forests being managed for multiple purposes. Clearly, the operations of private forest owners (or of equivalently corporatised state forestry services) would not by themselves cater for wider conservation interests beyond those involved in recreational activity. But again, there would be nothing to prevent conservation groups themselves bidding for areas of forest land and managing it in a manner that was more consistent with their interest.

It is not sensible to suggest that the problems of land-use conflict would completely be removed if competing interests were free to obtain secure property rights over land and to determine the uses to which the land should be put. It does seem realistic, though, to argue that those conflicts would be less severe and less polarised if the market mechanism were allowed to play a greater mediating role. This would require governments to retreat from the high degree of concentration of ownership and control over land use planning which they currently retain and to allow decisions to be more freely made by people and groups with secure property rights. That does not mean that people should be completely unrestrained in their use of resources. For example, mining projects should continue to be subject to environmental impact assessment procedures and required to adhere to certain standards of operation, especially where the activity might impact adversely on other property owners. Similarly, the ownership of forest lands would presumably be subject to covenants that prevented substantial alteration in the use of the land and imposed certain environmental restraints (for example, relating to water quality in catchment areas). However, the issues involved would be considerably less complex than is the case where everything is public property and every one is deemed to have a legitimate interest in seeking to influence outcomes. Neither should it be supposed that movement towards marketable property rights would inevitably favour development rather than conservation interests. The essence of the market solution is that people get what they are actually prepared to pay for: while conservation interests would no longer be able to rely on assertions of immense environmental benefit, neither would developers be able to sway opinion by appealing to the considerable export revenues or employment opportunities that their activities would generate.

Pollution control

In the general area of controlling pollution, particularly of air and water resources, establishment of full property rights is not an option. Nevertheless, policies can be designed to generate market-based outcomes that involve the same incentives for people efficiently to trade-off different uses of the resources. The essential principle is that people using resources in ways which generate current or future costs for others should be required to pay prices that reflect the value of those costs.

The most direct application of such economic incentives would be the levying of taxes on the emissions of pollutants. Potential polluters would be given incentives to restrict emissions to the level at which it was more costly to avoid pollution than to pay the tax, so that if the charges accurately reflected the social costs of pollution an efficient level of emissions would be obtained. The main contribution of economists to the pollution debate has been the advocacy of such taxes.

The history of policy application, however, has been one of regulation by zoning, by requirements that particular production and pollution control technologies be applied, and by controlling levels of emissions on a source by source basis. Heavy dependence of environmental agencies on industry for information about feasible pollution control technology and its costs meant that attention tended to be directed to the 'affordability' of particular pollution control outcomes rather than to assessment of the social costs of pollution itself. This is exactly the opposite of the emission charges approach, where the job of the environmental protection agency is to attempt to determine the social cost of pollution at the margin and to set charges accordingly, leaving potential polluters to decide how much abatement to provide. A problem with the regulatory approach has been a lack of emphasis on balancing the costs and benefits of pollution control.

On the other hand, pollution taxes also have their disadvantages. First, they have the political drawback of redistributing income away from those who have customarily viewed the environment as a common property resource into which discharges of waste materials can be made freely Secondly, in cases where there is considerable uncertainty about the response of polluters to emission charges, but a fear that the social costs of pollution may be very high once some threshold level is passed, the setting of a total allowable quantity of emissions may provide a better solution than the application of emission charges. Thirdly, if the costs of any given level of pollution vary with weather conditions on a day by day basis, it will be much easier for environmental agencies to operate with variable mission permits than with variable charges. Finally, though probably not exhaustively, the use of mandatory technology standards has advantages in circumstances when the direct monitoring of discharges, required for either volume or price controls on emissions, is very costly to achieve.

The increasingly accepted compromise — the use of tradeable emission permits — meets most of the objections to pollution taxes but incorporates strong economic incentive effects. The permits can be allocated to people in proportion to their previous share of emissions; but they can then be exchanged in a way that allows those for whom emission reduction is relatively costly to acquire additional permits from those for whom emission control is relatively cheap. The existence of a market for the right to pollute reveals a value for those rights that can be placed alongside estimates of the social costs of pollution. If these appear to be far out of line, as for example would be the case if air pollution rights traded at almost zero prices when there was a perceived serious air pollution problem, then this would argue for adjustment of the permitted emission levels. Such adjustment might be built into the system by making entitlements a share of some variable total emission volume, or it might be achieved by the government purchasing existing entitlements.

The US is the only country to have taken the application of tradeable emission permits very far. There, the tradeable permits system was built directly onto an existing regulatory system, allowing trades within and across firms to reduce the costs of meeting existing standards. The system allows for the introduction of new emission sources through acquisition of credits from existing sources.[5] Although there is evidence that the costs of complying with established environmental standards have been considerably reduced, it is less clear that the market information such tradeability provides has been used to inform policy judgments about the appropriateness of the standards set.

The major air pollution concern in Australia is related to the use of motor vehicles which contribute about 70 per cent of air pollution in urban areas. The extent of the 'problem' varies considerably depending on traffic density, so that it is significantly greater in the major cities than elsewhere. On the other hand, direct measurement of emissions (and the locations at which they have taken place) is not a very feasible option, so that there are difficulties in imposing emissions charges which accurately reflect social costs. The regulatory solution that was adopted has required all new vehicles to operate on lead-free petrol and to employ specified pollution control technologies. In this approach Australia has followed the practice elsewhere, although the variation in levels of pollution damage between different areas of Australia is higher than in most countries.

Some commentators have suggested that this countrywide, mandatory standards approach was excessively costly, since the problem was largely confined to major cities with only about 30 per cent of the vehicle population. By raising the price of new vehicles, the incentive to replace older and more polluting vehicles was reduced. Grenning (1985) has suggested that charges based on emissions measured at annual vehicle tests and on distance travelled during the year, and which varied between metropolitan and country areas, would have provided a more direct and appropriate control mechanism. Whether or not that would have been a feasible initial control option, it now seems desirable to move in the direction of greater economic incentives. In particular, the application of charges based on emissions at annual testing and which varied according to location would have the advantage of driving older and more polluting vehicles out of metropolitan areas by reducing their resale value in those areas relative to their value in country areas.

The most recent pollution issues have been those that are international in their effects. Because of its comparative isolation from areas of industrial concentration and its large size relative to its polluting activity, Australia is neither a significant sufferer from, nor contributor to, the trans-frontier pollution problems (most notably acid rain) that have affected Europe and North America and which are starting to affect parts of East Asia. However, it is both a contributor to, and a potential victim (or beneficiary) of, the global effects of ozone depletion and increased concentration of greenhouse gases. In these areas, local pollution control is of no value unless it is matched by equivalent controls elsewhere. Although large relative to population and GDP, Australia's share of global greenhouse gas emissions is in the order of only 1 per cent. Thus, even a complete elimination of Australian emissions would not affect the global outcome.

The central problems for formulating policy responses in the greenhouse case arise from the major uncertainties about the consequences of global warming (and, indeed, about its very existence) and from the need to ensure a high level of international agreement in order to have any impact in avoiding or ameliorating its effects. In contrast to the international agreement on limiting the use of CFCs, international action on greenhouse gas emissions appears unlikely to be easy to achieve. This is because the existence of ozone depletion was relatively well established and its major causes and effects apparently reasonably well understood. The number of countries affected by agreement to control the use of CFCs was also relatively small and the technologies for substituting away from CFCs in major uses were available and not very costly to implement. None of these conditions characterise the greenhouse debate.

Whatever stance Australia should adopt on the necessity and extent of global action to control greenhouse gas emissions, it is important to emphasise the role of economic incentives as instruments of control rather than the arbitrary application of standards for technologies and emission levels applied on a country by country and activity by activity basis. For example, incentives need to be provided for patterns of activity to change, both within countries and between countries, in ways that minimise overall costs of achieving emissions reductions. One possibility would be agreement on an initial allocation of national emission quotas which would then be internationally tradeable. Within countries, achievement of the required reductions in emissions would ideally be achieved by pollution charges or tradeable permits wherever possible. The question whether to buy or sell emissions quotas internationally would then be determined by comparing the international quota price with the domestic prices needed to support compliance. In principle, an international quota system would need to give credit to countries which, through maintenance of forested areas for example, contributed to enhancing the absorption of greenhouse gases. An alternative and less comprehensive arrangement would concentrate on the major source of greenhouse gases, the combustion of fossil fuels. The suggestion for the application of a 'carbon tax' on consumption of coal, fuel oil, gas, and transport fuels at rates which reflect the volumes of carbon dioxide and other pollutants released in combustion of these materials. By itself, a carbon tax would not be entirely efficient because of its failure to penalise other sources of greenhouse gases and because of the absence of reward for investments in absorption of such gases. However, a concentration on fossil-fuel combustion has the advantage of providing a means of addressing the major issue.

In principle, carbon tax rates should be set equally in all countries since the damage costs are the same for emissions from all sources. Thus, rather than setting emission reduction targets separately for each country and having them apply the tax rates necessary to achieve those reductions, a global tax rate would be set to achieve the globally desired emission reduction. Whalley and Wigle (1990) have used an applied general equilibrium model to estimate the GDP effects of a 50 per cent reduction in carbon dioxide emissions under the alternatives of separate national carbon taxation and uniform global carbon taxation. For the world as a whole, the cost is slightly lower under uniform taxation, at 4.2 per cent of GDP compared to 4.4 per cent, but the major difference is the much larger share of costs borne by developed countries under a uniform taxation arrangement. This has important political implications since the developed countries are substantially more likely to be prepared to accept costs of adjustment than are the developing countries. The Industry Commission (1992b) has estimated as 1.5 per cent of GDP the costs to Australia of a 40 per cent global reduction in greenhouse gas emissions through uniform carbon taxation — this figure looks low compared to Whalley and Wigle's results for 'other OECD'. These sorts of estimates, though shrouded in considerable uncertainty, are important in providing a perspective of the dimension of the problem. Still, as Common (1992) observes, different people can look at the same numbers and arrive at quite different conclusions about whether the costs are 'large'. Roughly, the costs of uniform carbon taxation for Australia are in the ballpark of being equivalent to one year's GDP growth. Whether or not that is a 'large' cost depends on what one thinks one is getting in exchange. It also depends on the distributional implications of the change. Clearly, global carbon taxation (indeed any effective action to reduce carbon-dioxide emissions) will have adverse effects on coal production. It is important to Australia that international action does not sanction the application of discriminatory approaches that protect domestic coal-mining industries but this is a matter that, given past performance, one would not want to be too sanguine about.

Future environmental policy debate is likely to be dominated by global issues where the role of government and inter-government action (or inaction) will be critical. This would entail increased control of natural resource use in the hands of government agencies. In my view, such concentration of control has not hitherto been efficient, on the contrary, my argument has been for government to adopt a less directive role in a large number of areas of resource management through the wider and more secure establishment of private property rights and greater reliance on market-based economic incentives. It seems clear from the experience of other countries that we shall not 'plan' our way out of environmental and resource use problems. The challenge for government is to identify those areas where its direct involvement is genuinely necessary and seek to ensure that the framework within which decisions about resource use are made is sensible and balanced without incurring costly bureaucratic procedures.

Notes

1 In this discussion, the effects of the tax system have been ignored. The reliance is on income rather than expenditure since the tax base discourages saving by driving a wedge between the interest rates that savers receive and which investments are able to generate. The taxation of nominal interest receipts exacerbates this effect in inflationary periods. For a small country like Australia, domestic-policy discouragement of saving has no significant effect on (pre-tax) market interest rates that are determined on a global basis.

2 It should be noted that privatisation of the water supply would introduce incentives for much of the spillover effects to be internalised in market prices. That is, the adverse effects of run-off on the value of water supplied to downstream users (and, therefore, on the prices they would

be prepared to pay for water) would efficiently be reflected in the prices paid for water by upstream users.

3   The benefits of delay might, for example, flow from expected improvements in exploration technology, lowering the costs of this activity, or from expected higher future minerals prices.

4   This is especially the case when the boundaries of national parks are pretty arbitrarily defined in the first place. A look at the map will show that the larger inland parks have a remarkable propensity to be perfectly rectangular in shape. The Rudall River exploration site extended across such an arbitrary boundary. Eventually the boundary was moved to accommodate the minerals activity, but not without the generation of a good deal of unnecessary uncertainty.

5   The 'currency' of exchange in this system is credits which firms earn when their emission reductions are greater than the regulations require. See Tietenberg (1990) for a discussion of the existing application of economic incentives to pollution control.

References

ABARE 1991, Australian Bureau of Agricultural and Resource Economics, *Pricing and Allocation of Logs in Australia*, Discussion Paper 91.6, AGPS, Canberra

AMIC 1992, Australian Mining Industry Council, *The Mining Review*, November

Chisholm, A. H. 1987, 'Abatement of Land Degradation: Regulation vs Economic Incentives', in *Land Degradation: Problems and Policies*, eds Chisholm and Dumsday, Cambridge University Press

Common, M. 1992, 'The Sustainability Debate: Has It Affected Our Way of Thinking?', paper presented to an Australian Agricultural Society workshop, February

DPIE 1991, Department of Primary Industries and Energy, 'Submission to the Industry Commission Inquiry on Cost recovery for Fisheries Management', Canberra

Dumsday, R. G. and Chisholm, A. H. 1991, 'Land Degradation: Economic Causes and Cures', in *Reconciling Economics and the Environment*, eds J. Bennett and W. Block, Australian Institute for Public Policy, Perth

Fane, G. and Smith, B. 1986, 'Resource Rent Tax', in *Australian Energy Policies in the 1980s*, ed. C. Trengove, Allen & Unwin, Sydney

Freebairn, J. W. 1983, 'Drought Assistance Policy', *Australian Journal of Agricultural Economics*, vol. 27, no. 3

Grenning, M. 1985, 'Australian Motor Vehicle Emission Policy: A Costly Mistake', *CEDA Monograph*, no. 80, Melbourne

Hartwick, J. M. 1977, 'Intergenerational Equity and the Investing of Rents from Exhaustible Resources', *The American Economic Review*, vol. 67, no. 5, December

Industry Commission 1990, *Recycling*, Report no. 6, AGPS, Canberra

Industry Commission 1991, *Mining and Minerals Processing in Australia*, Report no. 7, AGPS, Canberra

Industry Commission 1992a, *Cost Recovery for Managing Fisheries*, Report no. 17, AGPS, Canberra

Industry Commission 1992b, *Costs and Benefits of Reducing Greenhouse Gas Emissions*, Report no. 15, AGPS, Canberra

Kirby, M. G. and Blyth, M. S. 1987, 'Economic Aspects of Land Degradation in Australia', *Australian Journal of Agricultural Economics*, vol. 31, no. 2

Moran, A. 1991, 'Property Rights and Efficiency Ownership of Innovations and Mineral Prospects', in Economic Planning Advisory Council, *Issues in the Pricing and Management of Natural Resources*, Background Paper no. 16, AGPS, Canberra

Smith, B. 1992, 'Microeconomic Reform and the Mining and Minerals Processing Sector', in *Microeconomic Reform in Australia*, ed. P. J. Forsyth , Allen & Unwin, Sydney

Tasman Institute 1991, *Markets, Resources and the Environment*, Allen & Unwin, Sydney

Tietenberg, T. H. 1990, 'Economic Instruments for Environmental Regulation', *Oxford Review of Economic Policy*, no. 6, Spring 1990

WCED 1987, World Commission on Environment and Development, *Our Common Future*, Oxford University Press, Oxford

Whalley J. and Wigle, R. 1990, 'The International Incidence of Carbon Taxes', mimeo, Department of Economics, University of Western Ontario

Willett, K 1985, 'Mining Taxation Issues in the Australian Federal System', in *Federalism and Resource Development*, ed. P. D. Drysdale and H. Shibata, Allen & Unwin, Sydney

Young, M. 1987, 'Land Tenure: Plaything of Governments or an Effective Instrument?',in *Land Degradation: Problems and Policies*, ed. A. H. Chisholm and R. G. Dumsday, Cambridge University Press

Comments

With environmental policy the solutions of economic rationalists are put to their most pressing test. Workable markets and exclusionary benefits are evident in almost all issues that confront policy makers. There are, however, other issues where the only question that policy makers can legitimately ask is whether they can comfortably allow people to make their own decisions on their working conditions, savings and expenditures, or whether a wise political system could do better.

Discounting

At the outset, Smith's essay disposes of the arguments against discounting future benefits on which much of the green case rests. In pointing out the triviality of the value of a dollar 100 years hence, Smith brings home the fact that environmental decisions reflect people's true valuations. Perhaps these are not the valuations that many policy makers wished people had, but they are nevertheless the valuations people hold and overriding them in favour of other preferences is against the democratic principles almost all of us subscribe to.

Smith dismisses as unhelpful the case that future generations should also have their interests taken into account by having those in the present make decisions for them. I might add that the system of passing on wealth to future generations has worked massively in their favour — and as the latest such 'future generation', this has operated particularly to our own advantage. Indeed, as a society we presently enjoy a state of affluence undreamed of by our forebears. That affluence comes from the previous generations' stinting on their current consumption. A dispassionate assessment of our own prosperity set against the poverty of our forebears would probably determine that intergenerational equity would have been better served had they been less generous.

In this respect, the Brundtland Report's concept of not rendering successive generations worse-off is likely to be easily met. This would not be the case if we seek to preserve present mineral deposits and environmental attributes. Nor, as Smith recognises, does Brundtland suggest they should be — though Brundtland does take the view that there are some limits to growth and that long before these are reached there needs to be an improvement in equity, by which he means equality.

Mineral extraction rates

If we are examining resources from the perspective of their valuation vis-à-vis other goods and services, the market's answer is that resources are getting more, and not less abundant. Paul Simon's celebrated bet with Paul Ehrlich was that commodity prices would fall over the decade to 1989. Ehrlich, fresh from winning one of the many prizes Scandinavian countries donate to doomsayers, had found that the price of every commodity he had designated fell contrary to what might have been expected if usage levels were promoting scarcity. The juxtaposition of demand, pricing action and the technology of retrieval of minerals meant they had become more abundant.

I am not very impressed by the Hartwick rule of sustainability in its application to actual mineral resource exploitation. It has always seemed more difficult for resource owners to pick future prices and use this information together with their costs to ration their output. Once a discovery is made a great deal of the expenditure has already been incurred, and it would take a very bullish view of future prices for the owner to reduce output that could be profitably produced in the expectation of higher prices in the future.

Smith argues that a major externality could conceivably occur where natural resources have few substitutes and when their recovery powers are very limited. The corollary is that it may be wise to intervene. Perhaps so, but this does beg questions of who is to make the judgements involved and why the market is not making them in the first place. Elsewhere, in the context of land degradation, he shows the answer to be secure tenure and removal of subsidies.

Smith and I have different views about the best system of tenure for prospective mining areas. My own view is to consider mineral wealth as being effectively unlimited, rather like potential new inventions. In that context, there should be no property right until something of value is discovered. By analogy, to do otherwise would be to allocate property rights to potential areas of new intellectual property development. In both cases, the correct allocation of rights to search could potentially mean major savings as prospectors and inventors channel themselves or were channelled into the areas where they might be most fruitfully employed. Yet, few would argue in favour of some form of exclusive franchise into yet undiscovered new technology. Most would maintain that to restrict search activity in the field of intellectual property rights would leave the community worse off. What needs to be examined is whether the analogy between intellectual and mineral discoveries is appropriate.

The approach taken by those in favour of no development when confronted with a discovery of value is to buy out the mining rights. It may be that some change is required in the legal arrangements to ensure that buy-out is permanent. In any case, it seems that those in favour of imposing a quarantine on an area would always prefer to hide behind a free-rider problem and use political muscle to ensure that their preferences are met.

Smith also suggests some form of gradation of land whereby miners are subject to different levels of risk. This is a policy approach worth further investigation. Appropriate action has to be taken if, for example, in uncovering mineral of value the miners also uncover other values that the government determines to be worth more than the mine output. The more refusals to allow mining occur, the higher the risk profile required and the lower the mining activity. Over the past fifteen years, governments have been taking actions that raise the cost of mining — through environmental impact statements and by overriding a previously anticipated automatic granting of a licence to mine. The upshot must be a reduction in search activity.

It certainly makes sense when refusal to mine stems from Aboriginal concerns. This however starts to give rise to a further agenda which Smith wisely steers away from, namely the security of any mining or pastoral rights across major stretches of Australia in light of the Mabo judgement.

Other externalities

On the more mainstream environmental issues I find myself in agreement with Smith's argument in favour of trying to vest rights to aspects of the environment. Because of free-riders and hold-outs, there will obviously be times when the profession sinks back into its second-best role of devising 'Let's pretend markets'. Under such markets, the economist assumes the role of the technocrat and seeks to determine the tax at which users will attenuate their usage of a public good, so that usage accords with society's view of its optimum. As the discussion of Coronation Hill has shown, the contingent valuation research into the price people would pay throws up some very high values — and even if these answers were credible, the fact that the people who value the pristine wilderness most highly don't actually pay for its preservation creates a distortion because they have more to spend on other goods and services.

Other solutions for other externalities — such as charging a premium for certain types of vehicle — also fail. It is a fact that vehicle emissions are largely a function of their servicing. Technology is coming to our assistance in the form of very accurate and very low-cost equipment to measure emissions from vehicles' exhausts.

This said, we will never devise taxes or tradable rights that will fully remove the distortions that give the polluters incentive to behave so that they compensate everyone for their actions. The chase for many of these externalities and the measures for their resolution is likely to continue to plague society and offer a growing source of job opportunities to economists and others who can turn their hands to things numerical.

R. G. Gregory and G. L. Woodbridge

Economic Rationalism and the Earnings Dispersion

There is a widely held belief that Australia has developed a range of institutions and policy attitudes that compress the distribution of earnings and that this is an attractive feature of the Australian labour market (Hughes 1973; Norris 1986). Over the last fifteen years, it has been increasingly suggested that the economy is producing greater income inequalities and the earnings dispersion is widening among the employed. There is also a feeling that economic-rationalist policies are changing the earnings distribution in ways that are unfair and inequitable. It is often alleged, for example, that adoption of a less regulated labour market will inevitably lead to the rich getting richer and the poor getting poorer. Australia will become a less attractive place to work and live.

This essay explores the empirical basis for some of these beliefs as they relate to earnings among men employed full-time. It begins by documenting changes in the dispersion of full-time earnings by men and shows that the earnings distribution has indeed become more unequal. It also discusses why this is happening and attempts to estimate the magnitude of change that might flow from labour market deregulation. This is done by a direct comparison of Australian and US labour-market outcomes. It appears that large changes in the earnings distribution are not a uniquely Australian phenomenon. Similar changes are occurring in labour markets with different degrees of regulation.

Background

Most Australians believe that by international standards they live in an egalitarian society and throughout Australian history, governments have adopted policies to narrow the income distribution and gradually widened the scope of welfare policies and increased the level of benefits. Australia is not unique in developing the welfare state to compress the distribution of income but it is more unusual in the extent to which institutions have been created to intervene in the wage-setting process. Since Federation the labour market has been heavily regulated by federal and state tribunals which enforce a system of award wages.[1] An important characteristic of this system is the relatively high level of the minimum wage. In the important Harvester judgement of 1907 Justice Higgins set an adult minimum wage at a relatively high level in order to meet 'the normal needs of the average employee, regarded as a human being living in a civilized community'. It was assumed that the 'average' employee supported a wife and three children. The contrast between this decision and the equity concepts underlying minimum wages in other countries is quite marked. In the US, for example, the minimum wage is around $4 per hour and no-one has suggested that this is a sufficiently high level to meet 'the normal needs of the average employee, regarded as a human being living in a civilized community'.

The ability of Australian labour-market interventions to compress earning relativities has been enhanced by a number of special features. First, trade unions tend to compress earning relativities and Australian trade-union membership is high, currently extending to about 45 per cent of all employees. Secondly, until quite recently, Australia pursued a policy of high tariffs to enable industries that compete with imports to pay relatively high wages. Even after reductions over the last few years the average 1990/91 nominal output tariffs on clothing and footwear, textiles and motor vehicles are 65, 21 and 28 per cent respectively. Thirdly, there was full employment throughout the 1950s and 1960s which was generally thought to narrow wage differentials. Finally, since 1975, there have been sustained periods of centralized wage-fixing — 1976-80 and 1983-1991 which should have led to further compression of earnings. The centralized wage-fixing system has sometimes emphasised across-the-board absolute wage increases and at other times delivered uniform percentage increases.

Each of these features of the labour market are either changing, or about to change in ways that suggest that earnings of the lowly paid will be less protected in the future. Both main political parties have announced substantial tariff reductions to take effect over the next decade. Trade-union membership is falling, for example, from 45.6 per cent of wage and salary earners in 1986 to 39.6 per cent in 1992. The award pay system is weakening at the state level, particularly in

Victoria, and, despite the 1993 Federal election outcome, may weaken a little at the national level with the inevitable fall in relative wages for those on the fringes of the Award wage system. In addition, union, government and business leadership seem to favour a move away from egalitarian centralized wage-setting towards individual enterprise bargaining, motivated in part to deliver wage increases to the most productive. Enterprise bargaining must widen the earnings dispersion as the stronger parts of the labour market are more successful at achieving wage increases. Finally, high levels of unemployment are likely to prevail throughout the next decade and will exert downward wage pressure on those receiving low pay. These changes inevitably lead to apprehension and concern among those who believe their relative earning position is protected by the current institutional framework and at risk if there is change.

Changes in the dispersion of earnings?

Despite the Australian interest in the dispersion of earnings and concern for relative earnings of the lowly paid, there is no accessible data series that extends for long periods of time (Hancock & Moore 1975). Since 1975 the ABS has conducted household surveys each August to collect the earnings of individuals on a consistent basis. We focus our analysis on gross earnings of adult men employed as full-time wage and salary earners. The data exclude the self-employed.

There are a number of ways the data can be presented and we have chosen to describe changes in the earnings dispersion as follows. For 1976 and 1992 individual earnings were ranked from low to high and earnings at each decile boundary is expressed as a ratio of the median.

Figure 1 plots the change in the earnings distribution over the 16-year period. From the figure, we can see that there has been a consistent widening in the earnings distribution. Earnings at the 10th-percentile have fallen about 12 per cent relative to the median, and earnings at the 90th-percentile increased about 8 per cent. These changes are all the more significant given that real median earnings have not grown but fallen by 2 per cent over the 16 years. Those in the bottom decile have sustained a real wage reduction of 9 per cent.[3] Even at the 90th-percentile real wages have only increased by 6 per cent.

This changing pattern is puzzling. Why have the earnings dispersion widened so much? It cannot be the result of labour-market changes associated with deregulation since most of these changes are yet to occur. Enterprise bargaining has only just begun. Furthermore, significant tariff reduction in low wage areas of manufacturing and large falls in the trade

Figure 1
Male full-time relative earnings Australia 1976 to 1992

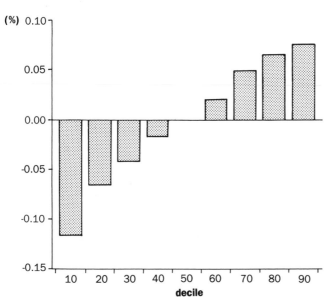

union numbers are also yet to occur.[4] There are two important reasons why we might have expected the dispersion to narrow. First, as suggested earlier decisions flowing from centralised wage-fixing over the last 16 years should have compressed the earnings dispersion. Secondly, the 20 per cent fall in the male employment-population ratio, and the large increase in unemployment since 1976 should have resulted in employment loss among lowly paid workers and, in the absence of any other adjustment, we would expect a further narrowing of the earnings dispersion of the employed.

Figure 1 inevitably brings into question the initial presumption that Australian labour-market institutions and policies have compressed the earnings dispersion relative to the operation of a less-regulated labour market. These results perhaps suggest that the potential for Australian institutions to compress the earnings dispersion has been exaggerated.

Australian and US labour-market comparisons

One way of answering this question is to compare the Australian wage dispersion with that of another, one with a less-regulated labour market that can be regarded as a counterpoint for Australia if the labour market here were to become less regulated. We would need to choose a country that has a labour market approximately similar in all respects to Australia's, except for special Australian institutions that are thought to compress wage relativities. The more comparable the labour markets the more confidence there will be in attributing different wage dispersions to different institutions.

The US is chosen for this purpose. There have been a number of Australian — US labour-market comparisons over the last few years and the operations of both markets are well understood (Gregory & Daly 1991). The labour forces of Australia and the US have a similar dispersion of education attainments and experience. The industry composition is comparable, as is the share of national expenditure on international trade. The largest differences seem to revolve around institutional structures. The US does not have wage-fixing tribunals that deliver similar occupational wages across the country, union membership is now quite low and trade tariffs are also small.

How does the Australian male earnings dispersion from full-time work compare with that of the US? The data used to answer this question are taken from household surveys collected in similar ways in each country. To avoid problems arising from the difficulties associated with comparisons of real earnings across countries, and to focus on the earnings *distribution*, earnings at each decile boundary are again divided by median earnings of full-time male workers.

The 1976 Comparison

The dispersion of earnings is much narrower in Australia. The employed adult male at the 10th percentile of the Australian earnings distribution earned 72.6 per cent of male median earnings; in the US the ratio was 52.7 per cent. At the 90th percentile US earnings were 172 per cent of median earnings and Australian earnings were 165 per cent. The comparison between the two countries is easier if we divide the Australian earnings at each decile by those of the US. Figure 2 presents the results for 1976.

At the 10th percentile Australian male earnings relative to the Australian median are approximately 40 per cent higher than those in the US. This is a considerable difference. The tenth-percentile Australian male wage in 1976 was $352 (measured in 1992 $A). The difference in earnings at this low level is $97. The relatively higher Australian wages are not confined to the bottom 10 per cent of the earnings distribution. At the upper end of the earnings distribution males do better in the US but the gaps are not as large as at the bottom. At the 90th percentile, for example, the Australian wage is 4 per cent less than in the US. In 1992 this was equivalent to $A35.

Figure 2
Adult male full-time earnings Australia relative to the US 1976

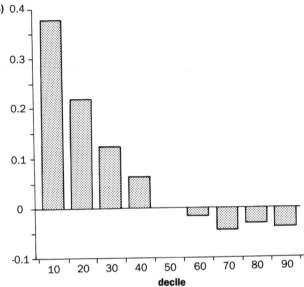

If the US labour market can be regarded as the counterfactual for a less-regulated Australian labour market then these results suggest that Australian institutions have had a large effect on the dispersion of earnings, particularly at the bottom of the earnings distribution. Further, if the differences between the two countries can be attributed to institutional differences then changes that might flow from institutional changes accompanying labour-market deregulation could be very large. As suggested above, Australia would become much less egalitarian.

If Australian institutions have compressed the earnings distribution and the institutions have not changed significantly since 1976, then what is the source of the widening of the Australian earnings dispersion? Perhaps an answer might be found by looking more closely at US experience since 1976.

Changes since 1976

Since 1976 there have been remarkable changes in the US. This is illustrated in Figure 3 where the ratio of the weekly earnings for males at the 10th and 90th percentile have been divided by median earnings for each year and expressed as an index number with the 1976 value set at unity.

R. G. Gregory and G. L. Woodbridge

Figure 3
Male full-time earnings dispersion Australia relative to the US

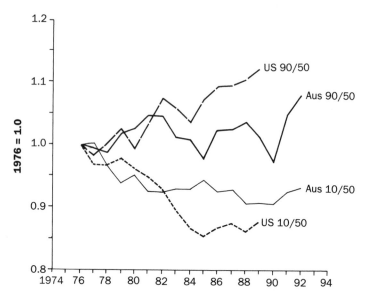

The lines fan outward with the passage of time, indicating that there is a substantial widening in the dispersion of male earnings. The position of the relatively better paid has improved as that of the poorly paid worsened. Between 1976 and 1989 the 10th percentile has experienced a 12 per cent reduction in earnings relative to the median, and the 90th percentile has experienced an increase of 13 per cent. The gap between earnings at the 10th and 90th percentile has opened a further 25 percentage points. The changes at the 90th percentile seem to be occurring at a fairly consistent pace through time but the fall in relative earnings at the 10th percentile seems to have stopped around 1985 after which relative earnings have increased marginally. Australia, therefore, has not been alone in experiencing a widening of the earnings dispersion.

Which country experienced the greater change? Figure 3 suggests that the relative fall in low earnings was proceeding at much the same pace in each country until 1982. The Accord which began in 1983 seems to have averted the sudden fall in Australian earnings for those at the bottom of the distribution. A considerable gap opened up between Australia and the US in the early 1980s but began to close in 1985 as low earnings in Australia continue to drift downwards and those of the US, slowly upwards.

The largest differences seem to be in the earnings of those above the median. Earnings at the 90th percentile have increased quite strongly in the US relative to the median but have not done so in Australia. It is as though the Australian institutions have their greatest effect on stopping top incomes from increasing. Although the dispersion has widened in Australia it is not converging towards that of the US; as the Australian dispersion has widened so too has that of the US. It remains a puzzle why centralised wage bargaining in Australia should prevent relativities from widening in one period, 1983-92, but fail to do so during another, 1976-80.

Why did the distribution of earnings widen in Australia and the US?

In the US there has been considerable research into the widening dispersion of earnings and there have been a number of theories conjectured to explain US outcomes (Levy & Murnane 1992). It has been suggested, for example, that the change might be related to the baby boom. The young are paid less than those of middle years and the large increase in young workers during the 1970s was expected to depress the earnings of the young and widen the earnings dispersion. The earnings of the young have fallen in the US, as it has in Australia (Borland 1992), but much of this fall occurred after the baby boomers passed through to the young age groups. It is now widely accepted that demographic changes have played some but not a significant part in the widening dispersion.

It has also been conjectured that the increased dispersion is related to the fall in the employment share of manufacturing (Harrison & Bluestone 1988). Manufacturing was seen in the US as an important sector for middle-level jobs at middle-level pay, the same applies to Australia which experienced a substantial decline in manufacturing employment. It is unlikely, however, that this is an important source of the change. The widening dispersion can be found in both manufacturing and non-manufacturing sectors. If labour markets worked perfectly, a change originating in one sector could produce the same relative pay change in the other as labour supplies moved quickly in response to relative wage changes in the declining sector. But labour markets do not work this quickly. The contemporaneous change in the earnings dispersion in manufacturing and non-manufacturing has to be explained by factors common to both.

It has also been suggested that the declining membership of US unions has played a part since unions tend to compress earning relativities.

Current research in the US, however, suggests that the effect of reduced union membership is likely to be small. A change in union membership is unlikely to have been a vital factor in Australia since most of the large changes in union membership happened only recently.

The most popular explanation in the US is that technical change is occuring in a way that is leading to reduced demands for low-skilled workers and increased demands for those with education (Katz et al. 1992). As the earnings distribution has widened so has the return to education in the US. This result presents another puzzle for us. The rate of return to education has not widened in Australia and has remained approximately constant throughout the 1980s (Maglen 1991).

There has been a substantial widening in the Australian dispersion of earnings among male wage and salary earners over the last fifteen years. Most of the changes have been associated with falling income of the lowest decile of wage earners and occurred between1976-82. Since the Accord came into being earnings at the bottom of the distribution have maintained their relativity with the median. There is an increase in relative earnings at the top of the earnings distribution but it does not seem as large as might be expected from the anecdotal evidence of the 1980s.[7]

The same broad phenomenon of a widening in the earnings distribution is occurring in the US. There, the change is larger and the fall in wages at the bottom of the earnings distribution have been quite substantial. Similar changes are also occurring in the UK (King et al. 1992). It is interesting that there have been similar changes across these three countries even though their macroeconomic performances have been very different. Real wages have increased in the UK since 1975 but not increased at all in Australia and the US. Australia and the UK have experienced large increases in unemployment and the US has not. The similarity these three countries experience with the earnings dispersion suggests a common cause even though the process is not yet fully understood. As is common with so many economic outcomes Australian experience reflects trends in our important trading partners.

The comparisons made with the less-regulated US labour market suggest that despite the large changes that are occurring in Australia, Australian institutions have compressed the earnings dispersion and that the operation of minimum award rates of pay are an important part of the Australian earnings compression. It is at the bottom of the earnings distribution that there are the greatest differences. The US results suggest that if Australia were to abandon fully its award pay system, its emphasis on a minimum wage set at a relatively high level, and adopt a deregulated approach to wages more akin to the US, low earnings could fall by substantial amounts. Males employed full-time at the 10th percentile in Australia earn about 40 per cent more than their US counterparts. Our focus has been confined to the dispersion of earnings among the employed. In Australia 11 per cent of the labour force is unemployed. In the US the current rate is 7 per cent. Is there a trade-off between a greater dispersion of earnings among the employed and a lower unemployment rate? Is it necessary for wages at the bottom of the distribution to fall relative to the median in order to create jobs for the unemployed? Many economists seem to think so. There seems to be some evidence that the aggregate level of unemployment is related to average real wage shocks (Gregory 1993) but whether changes in the dispersion of earnings play any part in this outcome is not clear. Women's pay increased 30 per cent in relative terms during the 1970s and since then the employment growth of women has far outstripped the men's. Lower minimum wages must increase employment to some degree. However it is likely that the increase will not be large so that the income share of the lowly paid group will fall. From an equity point of view perhaps the adverse effect on income distribution among the lowly paid may not be sufficiently offset by the positive effects of increased employment.

On the basis of US evidence it seems unlikely that economic rationalist policies have played a significant part in the widening of the dispersion of earnings to date. So much of the Australian change occurred during the late 1970s and early 1980s when economic-rationalist policies as they applied to labour markets had not yet been implemented. Our best guess, however, is that substantial labour-market deregulation would create a potential for a further widening of the earnings distribution, especially if the coverage of award wages is reduced and the community becomes less concerned about protecting the minimum wage. We have focused on the earnings of males employed full-time and stressed the changes in dispersion that are likely to occur in a less regulated labour market. But a widening of the earnings dispersion of those employed full-time is only one of many effects that may flow from labour market deregulation. Other important issues over the next decade will be whether deregulation will increase the rate of productivity change and whether a wider dispersion of earnings, and a fall in real wages for the lowly paid, are an essential part of the reduction in unemployment that we would all like to see.

Notes

1 A number of recent papers have begun to discuss this topic (Borland 1992; King et al. 1992; Gregory 1993).

2 Award rates of pay, which number many thousands, cover about 80 per cent of male and 90 per cent of female employees.

3 Real wages are calculated by dividing weekly earnings by the consumer price index. There has been no allowance for changing levels of taxation.

4 There have been substantial tariff reductions since 1973 but they have been concentrated on industries protected by low to medium tariffs. The highly protected areas of manufacturing have been able to maintain high tariffs.

5 The US data are available from the mid-1960s but the most recent data available at the ANU is for 1989. The Australian data began in 1976. There is another source of Australian data collected from firms that are not analysed here. They also show a widening of the earnings dispersion.

6 The relative earnings of individuals depend on a range of factors other than institutions. For example, those who are better educated earn more on average than those with little education and those of middle-age usually earn more than the young. Could it be that the differences in the earnings distribution across the two countries is not a response to institutional differences but that in the US there are relatively more young among the full-time employed and relatively more full-time workers are badly educated? Perhaps those who earn relatively low pay in the US are poorly endowed with human capital relative to Australian workers? A number of studies have investigated this question and they find that very little of the difference in the earnings dispersion across the countries can be explained by factors such as these (Gregory & Daly 1991). The best explanation for the differences is the dispersion of earnings in each country is the difference in institutions.

7 Data taken from business records (Distribution and Composition of Employee Earnings and Hours, ABS Catalogue no. 6306.0) suggest there are greater increases in earnings at the top of the distribution and that those on the bottom have continued to lose ground during the Accord period. The household data (Weekly Earnings of Employees (Distribution), Australia, ABS Catalogue no. 6310.0) are of better quality than the business data that has been subject to a large change in the sample in 1983 and seems not to be sufficiently representative in its coverage.

References

Borland, J. 1992, 'Wage inequality in Australia', April, Boston, Mass., National Bureau of Economic Research

Gregory, R. G. 1993, 'Aspects of Australian labour force living standards: The disappointing decades 1970-90', *Economic Record*, forthcoming

Gregory, R. G. and Daly, A. 1991, 'Who gets what? Institutions, human capital and black boxes as determinants of relative wages in Australia and the US', *Long-run Perspectives of the New Zealand Economy*, proceedings of the sesquicentennial conference of the New Zealand Association of Economics, vol. II, Auckland, pp. 477-503

Hancock, K. J. and Moore, K. 1975, 'The occupational wage structure in Australia since 1914', *Australian Labour Economics Readings* , eds J. Niland & J. Isaac, Sun Books, Melbourne, pp. 207-25

Harrison, R. and Bluestone, B. 1988, *The Great U-turn: Corporate Restructuring and the Polarizing of America*, Basic Books, New York

Hughes, B. 1973, 'The wages of the weak and the strong', *Journal of Industrial Relations*, vol. 15, pp. 1-24

Katz, L. F., Loveman, G. W. and Blanchflower, D. G. 1992, 'A comparison of changes in the structure of wages in four OECD countries', mimeo, July, National Bureau of Economic Research, Boston, Mass.

King, J.E., Rimmer, R. and Rimmer, S. 1992, 'The law of the shrinking middle: inequality of earnings in Australia 1975-1989', *Scottish Journal of Political Economy*, forthcoming

Levy F. and Murnane, R. J. 1992, 'US earnings levels and earnings inequalities: A review of recent trends and proposed explanations', *Journal of Economic Literature*, forthcoming

Maglen, L.R. 1991, 'The impact of education expansion on the distribution of earnings in Australia', *Australian Bulletin of Labour*, vol. 17, no. 2, pp. 132-59

Norris, K. 1986, 'The wages structure: Does arbitration make any difference?', *Wage Fixation in Australia*, ed. J. Niland, Allen & Unwin, Sydney, pp. 183-202

Comments

I would like to thank Robert Gregory and Graeme Woodbridge for a very interesting paper — albeit one with rather frightening implications for the future structure of Australian society. As Gregory and Woodbridge note, different sources often suggest different conclusions and the National Centre for Social and Economic Modelling will examine the income distribution surveys for the 1980s later this year to see if they generate the same results as the employment surveys they used.

I would like to examine the implications of these findings for current research about poverty and income distribution. When analysing income distribution, a number of different definitions of income and of the income unit can be used.

As Figure 1 indicates, some studies examine the distribution of market or private income before any redistributive intervention by government, while others look at the distribution of gross income that exists after the payment by government of cash transfers such as the age pension. Most of those researching poverty and income distribution, however, prefer to use disposable income as this shows the amount of money available to spend after the receipt of cash transfers and the payment of income taxes.

Some analysts add the value of indirect benefits received by households (from the use of government-provided or subsidised services such as health care and education) and subtract indirect taxes paid (ABS 1992). While many would see this as theoretically desirable,

Figure 1
The definition of income

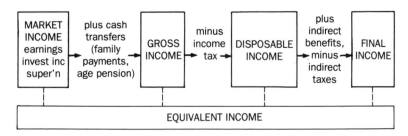

the complexities of simulating changing indirect benefits and taxes mean that many researchers simply use disposable-income measures. A separate issue is that, when comparison between income units of differing size and composition is required, an equivalence scale is often applied by analysts to any of these four income concepts, thereby generating equivalent income measures.

It is also important to appreciate that the income unit used in poverty and income distribution studies may vary greatly. Common income units include the individual, the family and the household. The critical decision here is the size of the unit within which income is assumed to be equally shared. If, for example, one assumes no sharing within married couples or families, and thus uses the individual as the income unit when measuring poverty, then measured poverty is very high. This is because there are large numbers of students or spouses without any personal income of their own (many of whom live in families where another member earns income).

Most analysts prefer to use a family income unit, deeming the individual income unit to be too narrow, but feeling uncomfortable with the assumption that all income is equally shared within households (such as group households consisting of unrelated single individuals). Even here there are traps for the unwary, as the apparent number of people in poverty may vary significantly with such apparently minor decisions as whether non-dependent children still living at home are counted as part of their parent's income unit or are counted as a separate income unit of their own.

The important point from this is that studies of income distribution and poverty may be — quite validly — using different definitions of income and different definitions of the income unit, resulting in at least 15 possible measurements of the 'income distribution' at any single point in time. Where do their research fit into this schema, and what are the implications for poverty and income distribution?

Gregory and Woodbridge's paper and a number of other recent studies (Borland, 1992; Rimmer et al. 1991) have focused on the increasing inequality apparent in the earnings of individuals. This research thus suggests increasing inequality of market income, when the income unit is the individual. However, such findings do not necessarily imply increasing poverty and growing inequity when the distribution of disposable income or final income among families is the measure used.

Whether growing inequality of market incomes translates into rising poverty and growing inequity depends in large part upon government responses via the tax-transfer system and social-service provision. For example, increasing market income inequality might be offset by a much higher tax threshold for low income earners, increases in marginal tax rates for high income earners or, alternatively, by higher cash transfers to lower income groups (such as increased family payments). Similarly, it might be offset by increasing provision of government health, education and welfare services or new or increased user-charges for higher income groups using such services.

What, then, happened to tax/transfer policy during the last decade while market income inequality has been increasing according to Gregory and Woodbridge's figures? Dealing with cash transfers first, since 1983 there have been very major increases in payment rates — 50 to 100 per cent for Family Allowance Supplement from March 1983 to September 1991, and 15 to 25 per cent for pensions and benefits during the same period (after allowing for inflation) (Harding and Landt, 1992). This suggests that cash transfers would have played an important role in offsetting increases in the inequality of market incomes.

On the income tax side the story is different. Changes in the tax thresholds and in the marginal income tax rates from March 1983 to September 1991 led to small tax cuts for those below average weekly earnings and larger tax cuts for those on about 300 per cent of AWE and above (Harding and Landt, 1992). This suggests that income tax changes would not have attenuated any increases in market income inequality (ignoring any possible behavioural responses to changes in marginal tax rates). It is difficult to be conclusive about the impact of social services during the 1980s, but a recent ABS study suggests that such services might have offset increased market income inequality (1992).

What about the overall effect? Recent evidence suggests that the distribution of gross and disposable income became less equal during the 1980s (Saunders, 1992). However, at the same time it appears that some measures suggest that poverty declined (Harding and Mitchell, 1992), although this is only a preliminary finding. While further research is needed, this suggests that tax transfer policy may have protected the very poorest, even in the face of growing inequality in both market and disposable income among families.

For the future, this suggests that if earnings inequality is going to keep growing, then unless the distribution of income among families is also to become much more unequal, tax transfer services policy is going to have to become more progressive. Experience in the 1980s suggests that increased progressivity in the marginal income tax rates is unlikely — unless the Clinton administration starts a global trend towards reversing the income tax cuts given to high income earners around the world during the 1980s.

If this does not occur, this suggests that the critically important area is the cash transfer system and social services. Perhaps we are looking at a society where transfers to the working poor become more common and the role of government becomes ever more critical in maintaining the kind of society that Australians want. Equally, perhaps pressures to target social services will increase — in the same way that targeting within the cash transfer system became more pronounced during the 1980s.

References

Australian Bureau of Statistics 1992, *The Effects of Government Benefits and Taxes on Household Income*, Catalogue No 6537.0

Borland, Jeff 1992, 'Wage inequality in Australia', paper presented at the International Conference on Income Distribution, Melbourne University, August

Harding, Ann and Landt, J. 1992, 'Poverty and policy: trends in disposable incomes, March 1983 to September 1991", *Australian Quarterly*, 64, 1, Autumn

Harding, Ann and Mitchell, Deborah 1992, 'The efficiency and effectiveness of the tax-transfer system in the 1980s', *Australian Tax Forum*, 9, 3

Rimmer, S J King and Rimmer, R. 1991, 'The law of the shrinking middle: inequality of earnings in Australia', Discussion Paper No 17/91, Department of Economics, La Trobe University

Saunders, Peter 1992, 'Longer run trends in the distribution of income in Australia', paper presented at the 21st Conference of Economists, University of Melbourne, July

Steve Dowrick

Australia's Long-run Macroeconomic Performance

An assessment of Australian living standards

I want to concentrate on the long-run real economy — looking at growth in real economic activity over the last few decades and looking ahead to the end of this decade. As the title suggests, I shall concentrate on productivity and the employment and investment dimensions of the growth process. I am not concerned with the prevailing definition of macroeconomics as the analysis of cyclical fluctuations in economic activity and, in particular, prices. Indeed I shall have next to nothing to say about current-account balances, inflation, interest rates, monetary policy or exchange rates.

I will start off with some comments on the ultimate benchmark of economic progress, the standard of living. A perennial question asked of and by economists concerns how well the economy is performing in relation to past performance and in relation to other countries. The motives behind such enquiries range from detached scientific curiosity to partisan concerns with either defending or attacking the institutional and policy status quo.

It certainly seems to be a particular Australian trait, though not, I suspect, a unique one, to bemoan both our sporting and economic performances — indeed I wonder whether the Hanrahan ('We'll all be rooned') economic and sporting attitudinal indices are not cointegrated series. More seriously, evidence that Australian living standards are falling below those of other countries is sometimes cited with scant attention to the broad picture and with an often transparent intention of arguing the need for some particular policy agenda.

The most scandalous example I have come across recently of selective Hanrahanism comes from the revered citadel of official economic rationality — the government's Industry Commission (IC).

In their annual submission to the Treasurer in September 1991, the IC argue for further deregulation of markets for the bulk of economic activities both within Australia and between Australia and other countries. In order to justify the need for further deregulation, the IC cite figures that purport to show that over the 1980s Australia's GNP per capita grew at an annual rate of some six percentage points below the performance of 'the dynamic Asian economies to our north [which] continue with reforms'. In particular, they suggest that the standard of living in Japan, measured in US dollars, was the same as Australia's in 1980 and was some 66 per cent higher by 1989. Their inference was crystal clear: if Australia is being outperformed so convincingly, the case for radical reform is overwhelming.

These IC comparisons perpetrate one of the most basic mistakes that can be made in the field of international economic comparisons, namely an assumption that exchange rates between currencies reflect purchasing-power parities. To even the most casual tourist or visiting government economist it is obvious that the basket of goods and services that can be purchased in Sydney for $A100 is hardly ever comparable with the basket purchased on arrival in Paris or Tokyo when the Australian dollar has been changed into francs or yen. Moreover, any repeat traveller can tell you that the purchasing-power discrepancies can vary substantially from year to year. There is substantial economics literature that explore and explain these discrepancies. Yet the figures quoted by the IC in support of their arguments for increasing the pace of deregulation are obtained using exchange-rate rather than purchasing-power conversions.

The purchasing power adjusted estimates of real economic growth suggest that a better estimate of the extent to which Japanese growth in the 1980s exceeded that of Australia is one and a half percentage points, not at all insignificant, but nowhere near the alarming 6-point gap suggested by the IC. Another key feature of any proper comparison of productivity levels or living standards between Japan and Australia is to take into account the hours of work. ILO estimates for 1990 suggest that average weekly working hours in Japan are one-third higher than in Australia — 46.9 hours compared to 34.6 hours. These estimates are supported by the government statistician Ian Castles in a recent book, *Australian Economy in the Japanese Mirror.*

While Japanese output per worker was marginally higher in 1990 than that in Australia, output per hour of work was substantially lower. In a series of papers John Quiggin and I wrote recently we demonstrate that once proper account is taken of purchasing power, and also of leisure, the average standard of living in Australia is probably higher than in Japan. We base this assessment on detailed OECD data supplied by the Australian Bureau of Statistics (ABS 1992) that gives a breakdown of 1990 GDP by prices and quantities for 40 categories of goods and services. These figures reveal that the average Australian eats four times as much meat, but only one-seventh the amount of fish as the average Japanese. Australians use more recreational and cultural services but invest much less, especially in production equipment.

Our judgement that Australians are, on average, better off is based on the revealed preference principle. Any Australian resident who was earning average Australian hourly wages could have afforded to buy the Japanese bundle of goods and services if they had worked Japanese hours. The fact that they actually chose the Australian bundle is taken as evidence of a higher standard of living, particularly since the average resident of Japan could not have afforded the Australian bundle of goods, services and leisure. An alternative explanation of observed differences in consumption and leisure is simply that Australians and Japanese might have fundamentally different tastes, but in general we find that international variations in consumption patterns can be explained as responses to the different price structures in each country. On this basis we make the judgement that Australia's average living standards rank somewhere in between tenth and twelfth in the OECD, putting us on par with Finland and Germany, and ahead of Japan.

These comments are not intended to suggest that all is rosy with the Australian economy and that the 'she'll be right, mate' attitude should be the cornerstone of economic policy. Certainly there are grounds for a negative report on the economy from the million-plus Australians who are currently unemployed — remembering that the official figures do not count those 'discouraged workers' who tell the interviewers from the Australian Bureau of Statistics that they have not actively looked for work in the last few weeks.

What I do want to suggest is that in respect of many of our economic problems, particularly faltering growth in productivity and living standards, Australia is very much part of the pack — these same problems have beset all of the OECD countries over the last two decades. While we should certainly be looking for ways to improve our performance, particularly in relation to unemployment and social justice, and in relation to efficiency and productivity, we should not be rushed into panic measures. This is not to argue, however, that gradual and piecemeal reforms are the only way forward. In particular I shall argue that, at least with labour market institutions, half-hearted or compromise policies are more likely to be harmful than beneficial.

In the second half of this essay I will discuss Australian productivity performance over the last few decades, suggesting that our rate of technical progress is not particularly bad. While reforms that raise labour productivity are generally welcomed, I suggest that the principal reason our labour productivity growth lags behind the OECD average lies more with the difficulty of investing in new capital equipment to adequately equip a rapidly growing labour force. We need to raise more finance for investment and not be afraid to raise it from overseas when necessary, and to change the financial incentives to direct more of our aggregate investment into modern machinery and equipment.

The next section is concerned with unemployment. A preliminary point I make is that this is an international as well as a domestic problem, one which appears to be getting more serious across the advanced industrialised economies. I discuss a body of theory and evidence that suggests that partial or ameliorating solutions may be found by promoting either highly decentralised labour markets or the opposite extreme of highly centralised, corporatist systems of industrial relations.

Finally I examine some policy prescriptions for reducing unemployment and raising productivity growth through labour-market reforms and suggest that current moves to partially decentralise wage settings are likely to lead us to the least successful of all possible systems of industrial relations.

Productivity and investment

The mainstream of the economics profession is at last beginning to move away from its macroeconomic preoccupation with short-term fluctuations in economic activity and prices to take a slightly longer perspective, measured out in decades rather than quarters, on economic growth. Part of this process has been the development of 'new growth theory' or theories of 'endogenous growth' that stem from a series of influential papers by Paul Romer, notably in the *Journal of Political Economy* in 1986 and 1990. As with most self-proclaimed innovations, the underlying ideas are not especially new. Any non-economist, indeed most non-neoclassical economists, would regard the central thesis as blindingly obvious, namely that continued investment, whether in physical or human capital, is capable of generating long-run economic growth. In one sense, what Romer has done is to provide neoclassical economists with the mathematical equipment with which to extricate themselves from a deep hole of their own making — the assumption built into most versions of the Solow-Swan growth model that marginal returns to investment diminish to zero, or at least to some point below the discount rate. Some of these tools were, however, available as early as 1960 when John Pitchford published a paper in *Economic Record* that demonstrated that long-run growth in per capita output was indeed possible within the model without resorting to manna from heaven (or exogenous technological progress).

The import of these developments within academic economics is that long-run growth is now back on the mainstream agenda. Neoclassical luminaries such as Robert Lucas and Robert Barro are recognising that industry policy, education policy and investment policy are actually capable of having some positive effects on economic development. With these professional developments in mind, I shall now turn to an examination of Australia's record over recent decades.

Figure 1 presents some clues to the state of Australia's productivity performance over the 1980s.[1] The vertical axis shows output per worker measured in 1985 $US at international prices (using Summers and Heston's 1991 estimates of purchasing power parities). This is our simplest measure of labour productivity which is related to average living standards. The horizontal axis measures the amount of capital stock — machinery, computers, buildings, etc. — available to the average worker. Other things being equal, we expect higher capital intensity to be associated with higher labour productivity.

Each country is represented by a circle for its position in 1979 and a square for its position in 1988, with an arrow representing its movement over the 1980s. One could superimpose some upward-sloping, concave frontier onto the diagram to represent the 'world production possibility frontier' and then measure each country's relative productive efficiency or technological advancement by its distance from the frontier. With any feasible frontier, the US is the world leader. Somewhat surprisingly, Australia appears nearer the technological frontier than most other OECD countries. After comparing the Summers and Heston estimates with the OECD figures cited in the previous section, I have some concern that they may have overstated the real value of Australian output (and capital) by perhaps some 10 per cent. If this is the case, then Australia should be repositioned to the southwest on the diagram, placing us somewhere in the region of Sweden and the UK.

Figure 1 suggests that although some of the leading European countries and Canada may have higher labour productivity than Australia, the differences are no more than 10 to 20 per cent. To the extent that Australia falls behind the leading group it is attributable not so

Figure 1
Growth in capital stock and output per worker 1979 to 1988

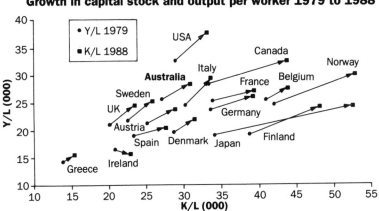

much to any technological or efficiency gap as to the much higher capital intensity found in these countries.

The importance of capital intensity is emphasised when we look at productivity growth, represented here by the length and direction of the arrows. Vertical growth represents pure technological progress or efficiency gain. Growth in the northeast direction, along, or parallel to the notional production frontier represents capital deepening. Growth that is steeper than the frontier represents some combination of capital deepening and technological progress. We can argue about the exact shape of the frontier, but I am prepared to make a judgement that Australia's rate of technological progress in the 1980s was quite reasonable by OECD standards; it was less than in the US, Sweden, the UK or Italy (all of which have steeper arrows) but better than most of the other countries. Australia's failure to increase labour productivity by as much as some other countries in the 1980s appears to have resulted from a relatively low rate of capital deepening, especially when compared to Canada, Norway or Japan.

To investigate Australian productivity growth in the 1960s and 1970s I have first calculated trend growth of total factor productivity (TFP) for each of the 18 OECD countries for each decade between 1960 and 1989. These results are plotted in Figure 2 against the productivity gap between each country and the US. The downward-sloping line indicates predicted technological catch-up. Measured against this line, Australian productivity performance is close to that predicted for each of the three decades, slightly below in the 1980s (by 0.1 annual percentage points) and 1960s (by 0.2 points), but slightly above in the 1970s (by 0.3 points).

Figure 2
Trend growth in total factor productivity vs productivity gap

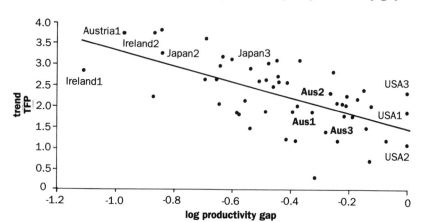

These estimates confirm Dowrick and Nguyen's findings (1989) that Australia's record on technological progress has been largely unexceptional. If there is a problem evident in our growth record over the last few decades, it appears to have more to do with investment- and capital-deepening than with technological efficiency and productivity. In particular, I suggest that our investment record, although high by OECD standards, is inadequate given a rapidly expanding labour force.

Table 1 shows the rate of growth of the labour force and the real (constant international price) share of investment in GDP for the 24 OECD countries over the period 1960 to 1988.

Australia's demographic structure, rising female participation (from a relatively low base) and immigration policy have combined to give us one of the fastest growing labour forces in the OECD. In most of the OECD population growth is stagnant and the labour force in many countries has barely risen throughout the 1980s due to ageing populations, early retirements and increasing tertiary-education rates. So Australia belongs to an exceptional group among the advanced industrialised countries in having to generate a substantial number of new jobs each year — an annual increase of over 2 per cent — simply to keep the unemployment level constant.

In order to keep labour productivity in line with other industrialised countries, Australia has to match their rate of growth of capital per worker. If Australia's labour force grows 1 percentage point above

Table 1 Growth of labour force and Investment rates In the OECD 1960 to 1988

country	labour force growth % p.a.	investment % GDP
Canada	2.44	22.9
Iceland	2.35	25.8
Australia	2.22	28.2
New Zealand	1.95	22.0
USA	1.78	17.2
Turkey	1.76	21.0
Norway	1.43	32.8
Netherlands	1.41	24.0
Portugal	1.14	23.7
Japan	1.13	31.0
Denmark	1.08	27.8
Sweden	0.97	22.7
Ireland	0.89	26.4
Switzerland	0.87	30.2
France	0.86	25.9
Finalnd	0.79	34.2
Spain	0.73	26.2
Belgium	0.58	23.0
Luxembourg	0.58	26.5
UK	0.46	18.1
Greece	0.44	25.4
Germany, west	0.41	26.9
Italy	0.39	27.9
Austria	0.16	27.5
average	1.12	25.7

Source: *Summers and Heston (1991)*

average then we need to devote an extra 4 to 5 per cent of GDP to investment. This calculation is based on an output-labour elasticity of 0.6 to 0.7 and a real rate of return to investment of 8 to 10 per cent as estimated by Dowrick and Nguyen (1989). While our investment rate is indeed above the OECD average, it is not sufficiently high to keep our capital labour ratio growing at the same rate as other countries. Australia's investment shortfall over the last few decades has been in the order of 2 to 3 percentage points of GDP, slowing our annual rate of growth down by around 0.2 to 0.3 percentage points.

The point here is that there appears to be a trade-off between population growth particularly in growth of employment and capital intensity. In principle, a country in Australia's position should be able to borrow to finance the additional capital investment required by an expanding labour force. But we observe that neither domestic commentators nor politicians are so sanguine about the long-term rationale of external debt financing against the promise of an expanding demographic and economic base. The problem of financing investment to equip a rapidly expanding labour force has been particularly acute for Australia in recent years because, as we shall see in the following section, our labour-force growth rate was accelerating and by the 1980s was the fastest growing within the OECD.

Aggregate investment rates in physical capital are only part of the story in overall economic growth. Another area of potential importance is education and training, but I have neither the space nor the expertise to deal with these issues here. I do want, however, to add some comments on the components of aggregate physical investment.

There is some evidence that the importance of investment in public infrastructure is downplayed in conventional measures. Aschauer (1989) presents evidence that public investment in core non-military infrastructure is highly productive. His 'core' of public investment includes streets and highways, airports, electrical and gas facilities, mass transit, water systems and sewers.

DeLong and Summers (1991) argue, however, that the key to growth is investment in equipment rather than investment in structures and transport. They find evidence from a cross-country study that the real rate of return on equipment may be as high as 30 per cent. They suggest that much of this return is in the form of external effects on productivity growth in related sectors, citing studies by Jorgenson as supporting evidence. Their evidence is impressive, involving tests for the influence of many other factors including reverse causation.

One plausible interpretation of the DeLong and Summers results is that equipment investment is the principle channel through which advances in technology are diffused both within a country but also, perhaps more importantly, across countries. This interpretation is strongly supported by their findings that among the high productivity group of 25 countries the impact of equipment investment is strongest in those countries lagging furthest behind the technological leaders. DeLong and Summers are, however, reluctant to come to such a conclusion because such a relationship does not appear to hold for their larger sample of 63 countries. But that failure to hold across a sample of high and low productivity countries is perfectly consistent with the findings of Dowrick and Gemmell (1991) that technological diffusion does not extend to the poorest economies that lack the physical and human capital infrastructure to exploit new techniques and new products. DeLong and Summers' conclusions are worth quoting:

> The social rate of return to equipment investment is 30 per cent per year, or higher. Much of this return is not captured by private investors. If these results stand up to scrutiny they have obvious implications. The gains from raising equipment investment through tax or other incentives dwarf losses from any non-neutralities that would result. A 20 per cent wedge between the social return to equipment and other investment has implications for all policies affecting saving and capital allocation.
>
> Our finding . . . suggests an explanation for the striking differences in economic performance realised by nations with 'interventionist' governments that have tried to jump start growth . . . We suggest that the poor performers have confused support for *industrialization* with support for *industrialists*. Policies that try to increase the health of the equipment sector by enriching producing industrialists end up raising prices and reducing quantities, and so are counterproductive — even though existing industrialists are happy with such policies. Frameworks that increase the quantity of equipment investment by encouraging purchases appear to have been more successful. the divergence between Latin American and east Asian outcomes and the divergence in their relative quantity and price structures carries an important insight into what a successful 'industrial policy' is, and how it should be implemented.

The price and quantity structures of east-Asian countries that they refer to are low relative prices for equipment and high levels of equipment investment. The ABS (1992) recently published OECD estimates of 1990 relative prices and per capita quantities for broad consumption and investment categories for some OECD countries. Some of the key figures are reproduced here in Table 2.

These estimates must be treated with some caution since they represent quantities for a single year that is not necessarily representative of recent trends. None the less a first glance does suggest that compared with the OECD as a whole, and with the US, Japan and Germany in particular, Australia invests too much in construction and too little in machinery and equipment. Australian 1990 relative prices were above OECD average levels for machinery and equipment, but construction was relatively cheap. If DeLong and Summers are correct in asserting that equipment investment has major beneficial spillover effects, then our relative prices for investment goods are clearly wrong.

Table 2 Investment quantities and prices

	per capita quality indices OECD = 100				price level indices domestic GDP = 100			
	Australia	Japan	USA	Germany	Australia	Japan	USA	Germany
Gross fixed capital	109	159	107	99	94	98	88	105
construction	121	142	101	101	86	109	90	104
residential buildings	130	116	118	87	79	112	90	121
non-residential bulidings	116	152	93	110	98	94	92	100
civil engineering	110	178	76	120	83	122	92	82
machinery and equipment	87	173	118	100	105	87	86	109
transport equipment	72	231	101	85	106	66	91	113
non-electrical equipment	103	127	138	96	106	106	82	107
electrical equipment	49	261	74	122	101	76	94	114

Source: ABS (1992)

Note: Prices are measured relative to the price of GDP, set out to 100

Unemployment

Table 3 compares our demographic and labour force experience over the last two decades with that of Japan and three other OECD countries that experience substantial immigration. Over the 1980s Australia experienced the fastest growth in the working-age population (due to our prolonged 'baby boom' which ended later than that in most other countries) — at nearly 2 per cent each year. The women's participation that started later here than in North America also buoyed the workforce. The result of these two trends generated a labour force that grew faster

Table 3 Demographic and labour force growth for five countires

		Australia	Canada	USA	NZ	Japan
growth of	1970-80 % p.a.	1.99	2.13	1.73	1.68	0.95
population	1980-90 % p.a.	1.80	1.03	0.91	1.18	0.90
15-64 years						
labour	1970-80 % p.a.	1.96	3.21	2.41	1.79	0.93
force	1980-90 % p.a.	2.31	1.68	1.53	2.05	1.23
growth						
employment	1970-80 % p.a.	1.53	3.06	2.36	1.61	0.84
growth	1980-90 % p.a.	2.22	1.62	1.73	1.54	1.22

Source: Labour force statistics 1970-90, *OECD, Paris 1992*

than any other OECD country. Australia also produced the highest rate of employment growth within the OECD, but it could not keep up with the labour force, causing a rise in unemployment.

These demographic trends suggest that Australia may find it particularly difficult to generate sufficient employment growth to keep up with the potential labour force, and make Australia particularly vulnerable to world economic recession.

Figure 3 tracks the unemployment rate in six OECD countries since 1961. Do not be fooled by the optimistic downturns predicted by the OECD for 1993 — these are figures fed to the OECD by Treasury Departments at the behest of their local politicians. Australia's official unemployment rate is given by the solid black line, and it certainly tells a sorry story in its own right.

The purpose of juxtaposing the unemployment series for the US, Japan, Germany, the UK and New Zealand is to compare our experience with that of the leading industrialised countries and of a near neighbour. Several features stand out. First and most worrying is unemployment, which has, on average, risen in each decade for each country (with the exception of the US where unemployment fell slightly in the 1980s). Associated with this rise is the observation that while unemployment rises rapidly in recessions, it is slow to decline in recovery periods and it usually ends up higher than when it started. (The speed of the apparently sharp fall in UK unemployment in the mid-1980s is probably more illusory than real, reflecting numerous redefinitions of unemployment, all but one of which had the effect of reducing the official figures.)

This phenomenon has been referred to as an example of hysteresis, whereby a system that is put out of equilibrium will find that its return path; but the new equilibrium position will be affected by the magnitude of the disturbance. In economic terms, people who are

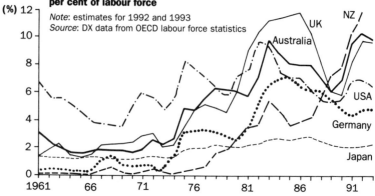

Figure 3
Unemployment rates for six countries 1961-93
per cent of labour force

Note: estimates for 1992 and 1993
Source: DX data from OECD labour force statistics

Correlation coefficients on annual unemployment rates 1961 to 1993

	USA	Japan	Germany	UK	NZ	Australia
USA	1.00					
Japan	0.66	1.00				
Germany	0.59	0.96	1.00			
UK	0.67	0.93	0.94	1.00		
NZ	0.33	0.63	0.69	0.71	1.00	
Australia	*0.66*	*0.91*	*0.91*	*0.92*	*0.84*	*1.00*

displaced from jobs for any length of time tend to lose relevant skills. In periods of rapid technological change, they may lose motivation, self-esteem and enthusiasm, and they lose their memberships in trade unions, and consequently, their chance to bargain over wages and jobs. All these factors combined imply that the sharper the increase in unemployment in a recession, the slower the recovery, and the new equilibrium or plateau will be higher.

A further feature of Figure 3 is that the peaks and troughs of the unemployment series for each country occur within one or two years of each other. The correlation coefficients given underneath the figure show that Australian unemployment most closely tracks the fluctuations of Japan, Germany and the UK. While correlation does not prove causation, there is suggestion here that when the industrialised world, especially Japan, sneezes, Australia catches cold.

Further information related to the comparative levels of unemployment can be gleaned from Figure 3. Why has Japan consistently kept a lower unemployment rate than any other country in the 1980s? Why have the UK and Australia for most of the three decades been at, or near, the top of the unemployment league? One possible answer is found in the work of Bruno and Sachs (1985) who have argued that a key feature of industrialised market economies is the extent to which labour market decisions in general, and wage-fixing in particular, is concentrated or centralised. Lars Calmfors and John Driffill (1986) have developed these arguments, following Olson (1982), to predict a non-monotonic, or hump-shaped, relationship between economic performance and the degree of centralisation of wage-setting institutions. The best economic performance — whether measured in terms of unemployment or inflation or productivity growth — comes from either the fully decentralised system or from the fully centralised system, with the halfway house of partial centralisation producing the worst results.

Calmfors and Driffill base their hypothesis on a model of the economy where wages and prices are determined by union-bargaining pressure. In their simplest model, unions can choose whatever wage they want. They are inhibited from pressing too hard by their concern over both employment and the effect of inflation on the real value of the wage. The first concern is with jobs: how many jobs will be lost if the wage is increased? The second concern is with prices: to what extent will a wage increase simply lead to an equal increase in price?

These two inhibiting forces on union wage pressure move in opposite directions when the level of wage-bargaining is changed. If we start with a decentralised system, say plant or enterprise level bargaining, any individual union will treat the rate of increase of wages and prices in the rest of the economy as given. Since an increase in nominal wages for just one plant or firm will have virtually no impact on the overall level of prices, the 'price effect' is negligible in restraining wages. On the other hand, the 'job effect' is strong in a decentralised system. If costs rise in a single firm, customers are likely to turn to other suppliers, causing that firm to lose its market share and shed its labour. In other words, the elasticity of labour demand is high at the level of the individual enterprise. Workers at one firm are in competition with workers at other firms for jobs within the industry. It is this indirect competition over employment (indirect in that it is mediated through firms competing in the product market) that restrains union wage pressure in a decentralised system.

When wage-bargaining is partially centralised, say through industry-level union-bargaining with industry-based associations of employers, this competition over jobs is attenuated. If all the firms within an industry grant the same wage rise, there is no reason that the workers in one firm should expect their share of total industry employment to fall. There will be some loss of overall industry employment as industry wages and prices rise and consumers substitute away from the products of that industry, but the proportional loss of employment may be relatively small since derived labour demand is less elastic at the level of the industry than at the level of the firm.

At the same time as the job effect is substantially weakened by the move of wage-setting from firm to industry level, the price effect is increased, but only slightly. Workers in the car industry, for example, may realise that a 10 per cent wage increase across the industry could raise car prices by, say, 4 or 5 per cent. But if cars comprise only 10 per cent of their consumption budget the impact on the real purchasing power of their pay-packet is still very small. The job effect dominates the price effect and the overall level of wage pressure is likely to increase when wage-setting is moved from firm to industry level. In the Calmfors and Driffill model, higher wages are associated with lower aggregate employment, hence unemployment increases when wage setting changes from firm to industry level.

Further centralisation, however, can have the opposite effect. If industry unions combine into one national body that sets or bargains over the national wage, the peak body will take account of the fact that any wage rise will be passed on almost completely into higher prices. Because the peak body internalises the negative price effects that are associated with decentralised wage-setting, it will reduce wage pressure and increase employment.

The Calmfors and Driffill analysis is mainly concerned with the centralisation of unions, though they do mention in passing the effects of concomitant centralisation of firms into employers' associations. If wages are bargained over rather than set unilaterally by the unions, the impact of a move from independent firms to an association of employers will increase wages. This is because any firm that concedes a wage rise to its own workers will face higher than average costs within its industry and consequently lose its market share and face a lower profit margin. On the other hand, an industry association that agrees to an industry-wide wage rise will be able to cushion the impact on profits by raising product prices. In other words, an association of employers is in a better position than an individual firm to pass the costs of wage increases on to the consumer. This phenomenon can be called the 'profit-margin' effect.

Horn and Wolinsky (1988) have also examined the impact of union structure on wages, but in their case they look at the structure of unionism across crafts rather than across firms. In a recent paper (Dowrick 1993a) I develop their argument within a more general context to show that wage pressure is likely to be higher under craft unionism than under general unionism if the different crafts are complementary in production — which is the situation we normally expect to find. This is because a wage-rise for, say, a group of electricians within a firm will tend to increase costs and reduce demand for the firm's products. Unless other groups of workers can be substituted for the electricians, and the historical basis of craft unionism is precisely resistance to such substitutions, then those other groups will tend to lose jobs too. It follows that a single enterprise union formed out of separate craft unions will internalise these negative job spillovers and exert less wage pressure.

Another important, but often neglected, dimension of the wage-bargaining problem is the degree of competitiveness in product markets. Where markets are dominated by monopolistic firms or by a small number of firms in an oligopoly, the firms will be able to price above competitive levels and earn monopoly rents. The existence of these rents encourages unions to bargain for higher wages, and monopoly-pricing power allows firms to pass on higher costs to consumers. It follows that monopolistic or non-competitive industry structures will generally produce higher wage pressure, at least under partially decentralised wage setting, than that experienced within competitive industries.

These arguments suggest that we should supplement the Calmfors and Driffill hypothesis of a hump-shaped relationship with additional curves representing outcomes under craft unionism and under competitive and non-competitive industry structures. In Figure 4 the horizontal axis displays the level of centralisation of wage setting in terms of its industrial dimension, distinguishing between enterprise, industry and national bargaining. Craft and general (combined) union organisations are represented by the upper- and lower-dashed lines respectively. The solid line represents the hypothesised relationship between macroeconomic outcomes and centralisation under a more competitive industrial structure.

Calmfors and Driffill claimed support in their 1988 paper for the hump-shaped hypothesis. Their evidence deals primarily with employment and unemployment over 1974-85, a period of considerable economic upheaval. They also consider indices of performance that include the effects of inflation and current-account deficits, and they consider not only the level of performance but also its change since the previous ten-year period (1963-73). Their evidence is summarised in Table 4.

Figure 4
The hypothesised effects of centralisation on economic performance with general or craft unionism

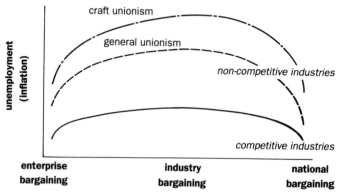

Table 4 Calmfors and Drifill's indicators of macroeconomic performance

	Unemployment Rate		Employment		Okun Index		Alternative Index	
	level	change	level	change	level	change	level	change
centralised economies	4.0	2.3	72.5	2.7	13.0	6.1	6.2	3.6
intermediate economies	6.1	4.8	60.9	-3.2	14.5	8.7	7.7	6.5
decentralised economics	5.8	2.9	65.8	-1.1	15.2	7.7	5.8	3.1

Notes: *Employment is expressed as a percentage of population aged between 15 and 64. The Okun 'misery index' is the rate of unemployment plus rate of inflation. The alternative index is the rate of unemployment plus the current-account deficit as a percentage of GDP. The countries are classified as follows — centralised economies: Austria, Norway, Sweden, Denmark, Finland; intermediate economies: Germany, Belgium, New Zealand, Australia; decentralised economies: France, UK, Italy, Japan, Switzerland, USA, Canada.*

These findings have been broadly confirmed by Bernhard Heitger (1987) and Bradford deLong and Lars Jonung (1988). I have attempted to test their findings by using more recent data to construct a panel of observations for eighteen countries over each of the last three decades. The test involves regressing the rate of growth of employment (as a ratio of total population) on an index that captures the degree of centralisation or coordination of wage determination. The index has been derived from Calmfors and Driffill (1988) and Soskice

Figure 5
Growth of the unemployment/population ration vs index of centralisation

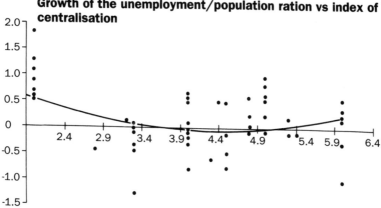

(1991) as described by Dowrick (1993b). Figure 5 displays the data and the OLS quadratic regression line.

The solid line is the predicted value from the following OLS regression (t-statistics in brackets).

$$g(E/P) = 1.9 \ (2.6) — 0.9 \ (-2.3) \ ^* \ I + 0.1 \ (2.1) \ ^* \ I^2; \ n=54, \ R^2=0.11$$

This regression has relatively small explanatory power and has not been subject to any diagnostic testing. It does, however, give some support for the hypothesis that the partially centralised economies perform worse than those at either end of the spectrum.

Economic prospects and policies for the 1990s

Any assessment of employment and productivity trends must rely heavily on prospects for world recovery, particularly in the US and Japan. I am not in the business of macroeconomic forecasting so I will restrict my comments to deal with the extent to which Australian domestic policy may be able to improve on, or slip behind, world trends. The evidence presented above suggests that domestic policies are unlikely to reverse world trends, but nevertheless they may have some significant ameliorative (or deleterious) effects.

The first area of policy on which I have commented in this essay concerns investment. I have argued that a combination of our immigration policy and demographics place Australia in the unenviable position of having the fastest growing labour force of all OECD countries. If we were to equip all the new workers adequately, we must devote a much larger share of national resources to investment than is required in other countries. It is not unreasonable to expect that some part of this additional investment should be financed from overseas.

I have gone on to highlight evidence that suggests that the structure of our investment is wrong; too much is going into construction, especially residential construction, and too little into machinery and equipment where we might expect to capture significant productivity spillovers.

The conclusions to be drawn here, that aggregate investment needs to be increased and that it should be directed more towards modern productive machinery and equipment, are hardly controversial. The means of achieving them are much less easy to prescribe. Tax policy is presumably one important area, though my ignorance in this field inhibits me from prescribing any detailed policy recommendation. I will, however, go on to make some comments on industrial relations.

The prevailing policy direction in the field of industrial relations is to relax the rigid central wage-fixing that prevailed during the first years of the Prices and Incomes Accord. The focus is now on 'enterprise bargaining', which allows unions and employers to trade-off enterprise-specific wage rises for productivity deals. The hope is that such flexibility will boost productivity and competitiveness.

Certainly in the short run I would expect pay flexibility to provide some stimulus to productivity, particularly through abandonment of unnecessarily restrictive working practices. There is anecdotal evidence to suggest that some such benefits have already been realised. However I am much less optimistic that there will be any sustained improvement to productivity performance, competitiveness or employment. Rather, my view is that the current policy direction in industrial relations is likely to lead to deteriorating economic performance over the next five to ten years.

The basis for this judgement is the observation that although the current IR catch-phrase is 'enterprise bargaining', the reality is that bargaining strategies are likely to be drawn up by the traditional partially centralised power blocs of craft-based trade unions and industry-based employer associations. If this is so, the abandonment of centralised wage setting will not lead to the extreme left hump in Figure 4, where the economies of North America can claim relatively good performance in terms of unemployment and also in terms of productivity (as can the UK in the 1980s with respect to productivity). Rather, we are likely to return to the intermediate position at the top of the hump with the worst outcomes associated with strong but partially decentralised parties.

With craft- and industry-based organisations dictating wage-bargaining strategies, it is likely that any short-term gains from pay flexibility will be swamped in the medium term by the inflationary consequences of wage rivalry. In particular, wage rises are likely to be financed not so much by productivity gains as by the ability of dominant firms in Australia's highly concentrated industries to pass on cost increases to consumers. In other words, we may revert to the inflationary and low productivity experience of the 1970s with any economic recovery stifled by the perceived need to cap inflationary pressure.

There are two alternatives to this scenario. One — let us label it the UK-US (Thatcher-Reagan) route — is to pursue decentralisation more thoroughly, to ensure that union and employer organisations have no say in bargaining over and above the enterprise level (or even the individual level), and at the same time promote more competition in product markets to prevent rent-seeking and cost-plus pricing.

The other alternative — the Scandinavian model — is to revert to the centralised wage-setting of the 1980s. While the Accord was relatively successful in the mid-1980s during a period of world economic expansion in promoting employment and keeping a firm lid on inflationary pressures, it might have to be supplemented in the recessionary 1990s with education, training and employment schemes. Such schemes would serve three purposes. First, to alleviate the debilitating effects of prolonged unemployment. Secondly, as investment in human knowledge and skills that should produce substantial social returns. Thirdly, to remove the fear of redundancy that motivates much of the opposition from both workers and management towards innovatory processes and methods of organisation.

The arguments of the 'hump hypothesis' would suggest that either of these alternatives should produce lower inflation, lower unemployment and higher productivity growth than the system towards which I fear we are currently reverting. A simple analysis of these macroeconomic aggregates suggests that there is little to choose between the extreme alternatives, except for maybe slightly better employment and productivity performance coming from the decentralised, competitive systems. On the other hand, those who believe that the Japanese system of employer coordinated wage-bargaining, the Shunto, is a veiled example of a highly centralised system, would suggest that centralisation can produce the most favourable results.

It would be a great mistake, however, to reduce the policy debate to an argument over the measurement of half a percentage point difference between the records of the centralised and decentralised systems with respect to productivity growth or unemployment rates. Many other issues are glossed over in the comparison of macroeconomic aggregates. In particular, there is a strong suspicion that decentralisation will increase inequality. Those groups of workers with weak union organisations, or those employed by firms in exposed and competitive sections of the economy, may lose out. This is certainly the case, according to Gillian Whitehouse's (1992) comparative study, with women's wages and women's employment opportunities. Any comparison of income distribution between North America and Scandinavia (for example, Mitchell 1991) will indicate that the decentralised industrial relations systems are indeed associated with far higher levels of both inequality and poverty. While it can be argued that the social-security system can redress some of these inequalities (although it patently fails to do so in the US), the choice between an individual-competitive or collectivist system of industrial relations also has far reaching implications for the values and ethos of the society in which we wish to live. A paper by Philip Pettit (1993) suggests that institutions that rely too heavily on individual incentives can cause people to switch from cooperative or normatively driven behaviour to the egocentric calculating mode that lies at the basis of the 'economic rationalist' view of the world.

Note

1   All of the discussion in this section will deal with averages — average output per head of population, average output per worker, average consumption per person, etc. I am well aware that such averages conceal a myriad of differences and inequalities. I am also aware that my treatment of output and consumption deals only with the national accounting measures, ignoring many important questions of environmental and social values. The picture I present here should be regarded as at best a partial indication of Australian economic performance.

References

ABS 1992, *Gross Domestic Product at Purchasing Power Parity in OECD Countries*, 1990, cat. no. 5226.0, plus supplementary tables, Australian Bureau of Statistics, Canberra

Bruno, M. and Sachs, J. 1985, *The Economics of Worldwide Stagflation*, Harvard University Press, Cambridge, Mass.

Calmfors, Lars and Driffill, John 1988, 'Centralization of wage bargaining', *Economic Policy*, April, pp. 13-61

Castles, I. 1992, 'Living standards in Sydney and Japanese cities — a comparison', in *The Australian Economy in the Japanese Mirror*, ed. Kyoko Sheridan, University of Queensland Press, Brisbane

DeLong, J. Bradford and Jonung, L.1988, 'Hysteresis, the corridor and the political economy of unemployment 1955-86'

DeLong, J. Bradford and Summers, Lawrence H. 1991, 'Equipment investment and economic growth', *Quarterly Journal of Economics*, vol.106, no. 2, pp. 445-502

Dowrick, Steve and Nguyen, D.T. 1989, 'OECD comparative economic growth 1950-85: catch-up and convergence', *American Economic Review*, vol. 79, no. 5, pp. 1010-30

Dowrick, Steve and Quiggin, John 1993a, 'International comparisons of living standards and tastes: a revealed preference analysis', *American Economic Review*, forthcoming

Dowrick, Steve and Quiggin, John 1993b, 'Comparing Australia: international GDP rankings and revealed preference', *Australian Economic Review*, forthcoming

Dowrick, Steve 1993, 'Enterprise bargaining, unions and wages', *Economic Record*, forthcoming

Dowrick, Steve and Gemmell, Norman 1991, 'Industrialisation, catching up and economic growth: a comparative study across the world's capitalist economies', *Economic Journal*,vol. 101, no. 405, pp.263-75

Heitger, B. 1987 'Corporatism, technological gaps and growth in OECD countries', *Weltwirtschaftliches Archiv*, vol. 123, pp. 463-73

Industry Commission 1991, Annual Report 1990-91, Australian Government Publishing Service, Canberra

ILO 1990, *Year Book of Labour Statistics, 1989-90*, International Labour Office, Geneva

Kendix, Michael and Olson, Mancur 1990, 'Changing unemployment rates in Europe and the USA: institutional structure and regional variation', in Brunetta, R. and Dell'aringa, C. (eds).

Layard, Richard, Stephen, Nickell and Jackman, Richard 1991, *Unemployment*, Oxford University Press, New York

Mitchell, Deborah 1991, *Income Transfers in Ten OECD Countries*, Gower

OECD 1992a, *National Accounts: detailed tables, volume II, 1978-1990*, Organisation for Economic Co-operation and Development, Paris

OECD 1992b, *Labour Force Statistics, 1970-1990*, Organisation for Economic Co-operation and Development, Paris

Olson, M. 1982, *Rise and Decline of Nations*, Yale University Press, New Haven

Pettit, Philip 1983, 'Institutional design and rational choice', in *Institutional Design*, eds H.G.Brennan and R.E.Goodin, forthcoming

Pitchford, J. 1960, 'Growth and the elasticity of factor substitution', *Economic Record*, vol. 36, pp. 491-504

Romer, Paul M. 1986, 'Increasing returns and long-run growth', *Journal of Political Economy*, vol. 94, pp. 1002-37

Romer, Paul M. 1990, 'Endogenous technological change', *Journal of Political Economy*, vol. 98, no. 2, S71-S102

Soskice, David 1991, 'Wage determination: the changing role of institutions in advanced industrialized countries', *Oxford Review of Economic Policy*, vol. 6, no. 4, pp. 36-61

Stewart, Mark 1990, 'Union wage differentials, product market influences and the division of rents', *Economic Journal*, vol. 100, pp. 1122-37

Summers, Robert and Heston, Alan 1991, 'The Penn World Table (Mark 5): an expanded set of international comparisons, 1950-88', *Quarterly Journal of Economics*, vol. 106, no. 2, pp. 327-68

Whitehouse, Gillian 1992, 'Legislation and labour market gender inequality: an analysis of OECD countries', *Work, employment and society*, vol. 6, no. 1, pp. 65-86

Comments

This essay limbers up by attacking the citadel of rational economics, the Industry Commission. In the context of this conference, it provides us with an excellent start by demonstrating the diversity of opinion within the economic family. In defence of the Commission, I should say that in the heat of the political debate, clear, simple, stripped-down arguments are often needed to win the day. The important thing is that these arguments should be well-founded and consistent. The general direction the Commission has taken on policy issues seems to have been the right one.

International comparisons of living standards are difficult. If Stephen Dowrick is right in highlighting the problems in the Commission's comparison, all comparisons have their problems. For my part I was convinced by Ian Castles' thesis (that Dowrick cites) that showed, on common-sense measures, Australia's living standards to be higher than Japan's; Dowrick-Quiggin (1993b) provide further evidence. At the same time, we should not puff out our chests and note that we are much better housed than the Japanese if, at the same time, we criticise the amount of investment that goes into housing in Australia.

I liked Dowrick's discussion on productivity. Every one acknowledges that productivity is important, but an understanding of what drives it may get lost in long-term averages. I suspect that the story on productivity is to be found in the shorter episodes where productivity moves well. An important issue of the moment is whether we are going through such a period, and if so, how this faster growth in productivity can be sustained, and how the benefits can be maximised by ensuring that there are jobs available for the workers who are on the receiving end of the labour-shedding productivity increases that have become common in recent years. These issues will only be understood by examining individual episodes. They can also get lost because the economist's tools — particularly econometrics — generally seeks out long-term stable relationships that either miss, or have less focus on, the sort of structural breaks that we may be seeing in productivity.

How productivity is measured can change the interpretation. OECD data, for instance, give quite a different story. According to the OECD, the absolute level of productivity in Australia, compared with that in the US, is still pretty poor (see figure from the 1992 OECD Survey on Australia). The following diagram shows our performance compared with the OECD average, using OECD data. It seems that in

Figure 1
Business Sector Labour Productivity
Average annual percentage change

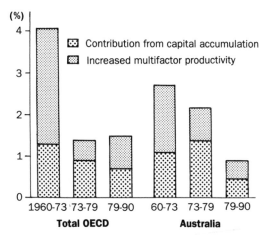

the most recent period, our problem is not just an absence of capital, but slow multifactor productivity growth as well. EPAC data (see chart 4 from EPAC Council Paper no. 43 'Australia's Capital Needs in the 1990s', October 1990) would suggest that we have a fair bit of capital per unit of output, indicating that our problem is not so much capital shortage, but the way we use the capital.

With such different results coming from the various sources, the question is which is more reliable. I am inclined to put more credence in the OECD data, partly because of the great resources that go into putting such data together, but also because the Summers and Heston data have some other anomalies, for instance, a capital-output ratio for Australia of only slightly over one, whereas the ABS data would suggest that our capital-output ratio is closer to three, which is more intuitively plausible.

Can we use our faster population growth as an excuse for poor productivity performance? As Dowrick says, countries that have faster population growth *do* need to have a higher ratio of investment to GDP, but my own calculations suggest that a couple of extra percentage points on the ratio is enough (and if the capital-output ratio was really as low as Summers and Heston suggest, we would not need a higher investment ratio). We do, in fact, have a higher ratio of investment to GDP than the OECD average.

Given that the required investment ratio for Australia is not *much* higher than other countries, and that we do in fact run a big current-account deficit such that foreigners are helping to fund the growth of our capital stock, I do not think that this aspect of population growth has been a serious problem for us. It may be, if there are difficulties with population, they are rather more subtle. I wonder, for instance, if the capital-output ratios of hospitals and education are higher than the general average and that a growing population might have to invest more in these capital-intensive industries. The same considerations may affect our productivity. But these issues seem to me to be marginal: there are plenty of opportunities for getting our productivity up through better management and use of our resources, without population growth becoming an important adverse factor.

To build on the point that important developments in productivity may be hidden within the short-term episodes, let me record — in a very tentative way — what seems to be an important fact about productivity in the current cycle. We might expect productivity to fall in the recession. During the 1990 recession productivity actually *rose*. Using the crudest figures, employment fell, peak to trough, by around 1 per cent more than the peak-to-trough fall in GDP. This is not unusual for Australia: in the previous recession (1982/83), we also had quite a good increase in productivity well before the trough of the cycle. We are also picking up the same sort of message in Jerome Fahrer and Alexandra Heath's work at the Reserve Bank (Research Discussion Paper 9215), that periods of recession are in fact periods of accelerated structural change. If that is true, the issue is how to make the best use of this. The UK went through a period of very fast productivity growth in the early 1980s and that largely seemed to result in unemployment shifting up a notch — a very substantial notch — and staying high for the rest of the decade. So, the trick is not just getting productivity up, but to make use of the people freed by that productivity improvement as well.

On wages, I thought Dowrick had a touch of the Hanrahan's himself. I do not see any compelling reason to get stuck on the high point of the hump-shaped Calmfours and Driffill curve. It seems inevitable that we will be moving in the direction of a more enterprise-based system and the debate is largely about the speed of the move — whether we go over the hump at full speed or whether we try to ease the economy over the hump. I do not know the answer to this, as arguments can be made on both sides.

Dowrick's essay is a good refutation of some of the criticism that is directed at economists. It addresses important issues, it uses a wide range of experience and common-sense in a non-doctrinaire way, and makes an excellent contribution to the debate.

Jonathon Pincus

Market Failure and Government Failure

The Rationalist holds that the only element of knowledge involved in any human activity is technical knowledge, and what I have called practical knowledge is really only a sort of nescience which would be negligible if it were not positively mischievous. The sovereignty of 'reason', for the Rationalist, means the sovereignty of technique.

Michael Oakeshott

The whole history of economic thought is stamped by the notion that by recourse to purely logical operations it is possible to construct on the basis of empirical observations the concept of a kind of 'value' which is somehow profounder than mere exchange value or price.

Gunnar Myrdal

Typically, the economic rationalist introduces the categories market failure and government failure by stating that markets are not perfect or, that decentralised decision-making alone cannot be relied upon to drive the economy to the highest possible levels of economic efficiency. Judged from a standard of perfection, markets mechanisms fall somewhat short. However, lest you walk into the trap of assuming that another decision mechanism can reliably be called upon to counteract market failures, the economic rationalist immediately warns that governments are not perfect: centralised decision mechanisms cannot be guaranteed to correct perfectly the imperfections of the market.

As an antidote against utopianism, the incantation market failure and government failure has been useful. If my remarks are sceptical and critical, they are not to be interpreted as support for the claim that government failure is a small problem in comparison with market failure. Rather, I believe that, although the categories market failure and government failure have served a useful function in Australian political economy, they have outlived their usefulness.

The terms market failure and government failure invite contemplation of a trade-off between two types of cost; one being the loss in economic efficiency due to the imperfect operations of the market, the other being the loss in economic efficiency due to the imperfect operation of the non-market, that is, of the government. How do we know the extent of these lapses? If there is no acceptable measuring rod of the two categories of failure, then the notion of a trade-off while useful as a textbook exposition is nonetheless impractical. My main argument is that some of the chief economic-theoretical underpinnings of the concept government failure can be used to throw doubt on the practicality or usefulness of the twin concepts, as contrasted with their undoubted rhetorical usefulness. In particular, I will draw upon ideas associated with Hayek, Coase, Buchanan and Brennan.

Microeconomic reform in Australia has represented a (partial) triumph of economic rationalism. Economic analysis and calculation have pointed to large losses imposed upon Australians generally from outdated or otherwise mistaken economic policy; losses, in short, from government failure. Somewhat paradoxically, however, the triumph I mentioned has not been one of economic liberalism, let alone of anarcho-capitalism (to borrow David Friedman's term). Rather, it has been the product of a rationalist mind-set only a few paces (to the right) of old-fashioned and now discredited central planning of the quantity-setting kind. In the place of production quotas is not exactly a price-signalling central planning, though it comes very close; the progeny of Oskar Langé are alive and thriving among the bureaucrats of Canberra and their mentors, calculating shadow prices.

The key notion, in its various forms, is the shadow price of an activity, meaning the change in aggregate or social economic wellbeing brought about by a unit increase in the level of the activity in question. If all shadow prices are correct and equal to actual prices, the economy achieves perfect economic efficiency. Calculation of one shadow price requires the calculation of all shadow prices, as though the economy in reality was fully computable. Once economic conditions change, shadow prices change: they are contingent upon policy settings, the weather, technology, and both consumer and producer confidence here and abroad. They embody what Hayek showed to be the impossible ideal, the gathering in one central location of all the relevant information inherent in the economy in operation. Although they can be written down in precise if general mathematical formulations, in economic practice brute force is used to 'simplify the model' to arrive at 'reasonable estimates'.

The advantage of a calculable shadow price is that it supports a possibility of infinite fiddling with the settings of microeconomic policy parameters. Every activity has its shadow price; it was previously called the 'just price'. In general, no shadow price, except through chance, is equal to the exchange price of an activity. And because divergences between the theoretically correct shadow price and the actual price signal a loss in economic efficiency, they therefore justify some kind of public-policy action. Thus, economic policy advisers have what all bureaucrats love, an in-tray that is never empty.

In recent years, there has been an addition to economic factors upon which decisions are modelled. The additional set of factors are the public-policy makers themselves. However, rather than including them formally into the shadow price calculations, the policy economist has tended to treat them informally. As a consequence, the *kind* of public policy receiving approval from policy economists has tended to change from regulation to deregulation; and this change has received great critical attention (e.g., from Pusey, Carroll and Manne). The policies prescribed have changed, but the underlying economic method — the policy-maker takes an estimate or guess at the difference between an unobservable shadow price and an observable market price and proposes a policy to reduce the difference — has not. The predominant practice of policy economist has been to support policy changes on the grounds that they improve economic efficiency. While there have been changes in the content of that policy advice — for example, from regulation to deregulation — the fundamental economic rationale has remained the same.

Some preliminaries before I go on. I will confine my attention to microeconomics — for me, macroeconomics is microeconomics with grosser aggregation errors. The criticisms I raise come from within the mainstream of economics and, in particular, I rely heavily on a notion explicitly rejected by the economic irrationalists, namely, that there are mutual gains to be had from voluntary exchange — I believe that gains from trade do exist. I also try to avoid the issues of how economists should or do conceive of individuals and their motivations, that is, I subscribe to methodological individualism but not necessarily to 'economic man'. I do not think it necessary for my argument to consider the alleged trade-off between equity and efficiency; instead, I want to consider the alleged trade-off between one source of inefficiency, the market, and another, the government.

Before I attempt the task of throwing doubt on the practicality of economic calculation, however, I first criticise any exclusive focus upon achieving improvements in economic efficiency. Is economic efficiency enough? I will argue that it is not economically rational to determine economic policy solely with reference to efficiency: to do so either assumes altruism on the part of ordinary Australians, or assumes implausibly, that Australians are not afraid of very large risks to their levels of economic wellbeing.

Is economic efficiency enough?

The main thrust of this essay is about the way in which the mainstream economist approaches the task of assisting policy makers to achieve economic efficiency. My objective here is to take some steps towards solving the puzzle of why rationalist economics is such an attractive target for criticism. The puzzle arises in part because most economists are economists because they believe (or believed) that economics can do good and make people's lives more fulfilling. Economics has also attracted and retained a following because of the intellectual challenges that it provides as a developing system of thought about how people interact through exchange. Economists generally believe that their ultimate allegiance is to service of the common good, not of particular or sectional interests.

How then is the common good to be interpreted? Almost by definition, the chief focus of economists as economists is the economic aspects of the good life; for the group called economic rationalists, concentration is upon how to improve *economic efficiency*. My contention is that an exclusive attention to economic efficiency offends many non-economists, and for good reasons.

Many economists also discuss issues like equity or fairness; however, these values usually are not integral to economic analysis proper, but an addition. There is a strong line in economics that goes something like this: tell me what the economic objectives are, and I will use my expert knowledge to devise ways in which those objectives can most efficiently be met. Even when acknowledging the existence of a goal like equity, the economist typically converts that goal into something else, say, the achievement of efficiency in the pursuit of equity. To be concerned with economic efficiency is a chief mark of the rationalist economist.

The basic concept of economic efficiency is simple enough: if things can be rearranged so that the collective benefits or advantages flowing from the rearrangement exceeds the collective disadvantages or costs (without regard to who gains and who loses), then economic efficiency has risen. The test is whether collective or aggregate benefits exceed collective or aggregate costs. When the allocation of economic resources is less than perfectly efficient, life is not a zero-sum but positive-sum game. Here then is a general rule of economic policy: implement policy changes whenever the benefits exceed the costs. To take a topical example: cut the tariff on imported motor vehicles if the economic benefits exceed the costs — if a tariff cut improves economic efficiency, then implement it. There are, however, difficulties in obtaining objective estimates of the size of the economic benefits and costs.

The criterion of economic efficiency raises some important questions such as 'Is it an attractive criterion?' and 'Is it an economically rational criterion?' Clearly, it is attractive to many people in the former USSR and allied countries that have had disastrous economic systems, ones incapable of moderate, let alone high, levels of economic output per head of population. In Australia we are not discussing central planning as an alternative to our largely free enterprise economic system. We are discussing what are, globally, rather minor variations in microeconomic policy; that is, is it an attractive economic policy strategy or policy rule in Australia that the *sole* guide to policy should be the pursuit of economic efficiency?

I want to give an economist's answer of 'no' to this question. There is more to economic goals than the single-minded pursuit of more economic efficiency, as economic efficiency is understood today by economic rationalists. The single-minded pursuit of collective gains in excess of collective costs can be very risky to individual Australians. The risks include the possibility of policy failure, that it would produce more collective costs than benefits. I do not want to pursue that pragmatic risk. Rather, I want to focus on the spirit of self-sacrifice that is implied in accepting that economic policy should always attempt to improve economic efficiency.

We economists are often criticised because our models assume that individuals are not altruistic, but selfish and not self-sacrificing. Yet, in proposing that the nation should pursue economic-rationalist efficiency, economists are calling on people to be willing to sacrifice something for the greater benefit of others. Measures of economic efficiency (or inefficiency) of the benefit-cost or shadow-price kind are utilitarian in that they offer a 'social' valuation formed by summing the values of all the affected individuals. Whenever the people who benefit from a policy change are judged by social commentators to have had a social or economic position superior to those who lose from the policy change, it is common for those social commentators to criticise the policy as inequitable. Maybe so. However, the criticism

I wish to make here does not depend on there being a systematic, *prior* difference between gainers and losers. My argument against the single-minded pursuit of economic efficiency begins with the assumption that we are discussing changes that are not biased towards rich or poor.

As an example, consider a policy change involving a set of individuals with identical levels of economic and social wellbeing. The policy will make some richer and others poorer. It is, none the less, an efficient policy in that the gains exceed the losses. Acting on behalf of this group of individuals, as their perfect agent, should the economist impose the policy change? If so, on whose warrant?

The test I wish to apply is one consonant with modern neoclassical economics. To pre-empt a later example (which is the exchange of a motor car for $30 000), when parties to an exchange agree to make the exchange, economics asserts that these parties expect to enjoy mutual gains, valued in their various and inscrutible ways. A voluntary exchange agreement thus increases the expected economic wellbeing of the agreeing parties. I ask whether or not a group of individuals would all agree in advance to a policy that states that whenever a particular policy change produces more by way of measured aggregate benefits than of measured aggregate costs, then the policy should be implemented.[1] The exchange here is of a right to veto or delay efficiency-improving policy changes and for the right to have all such changes implemented. Agreement is the economic test — there are mutual (expected) gains from previously agreed upon exchanges, even if the exchange is of one form of right for another form of right; one policy rule or regime for another rule or regime. Put simply, I am discarding the usual test of economic efficiency because the usual forms involve hypothetical values. Instead, I am adopting a test involving hypothetical agreement: would everyone agree to a policy rule that always strove for economic efficiency? To agree that economic rationality of this kind should be the only policy guide is for us to be willing to be altruistic, or to take a chance that it may work out well for everyone else but badly for us. When badly could mean losing your job or factory or prosperity even the most avid gambler will pause.

Many economists are somewhat familiar with the work of John Rawls who says 'no' to my earlier question. I do not want to defend Rawls' 'difference principle', but I do support a Rawls-like argument that depends on risk aversion. Individuals refuse the option to place bets, especially large ones, even when the bets are more than fair in that the prizes exceed the sum of the bets. A policy rule that always sacrifices your interests for the greater interest of others, and the obverse, however small the net advantage, would therefore be rejected in advance. Market processes have their economic justification in the claim that they, generally speaking, deliver net benefits, even though each market transaction hurts some interests and harms others. Policy processes have a similar justification in contemporary economics. Risk aversion, therefore, implies that the economist as the perfect agent of the anonymous principals we attempt to serve should support not only the social safety net, but also some forms of moderation of the efficiency drive inherent in markets, as well as in the policies of economic efficiency. That is, complete economic rationalism looks beyond economic efficiency as conventionally defined.[2]

At this point many economists will assert that if gains exceed losses then the losers could be compensated so that they can be gainers too. But the fact is that economic rationalism will only approve of the payment of compensation if such payment is not itself the cause of too great a loss of economic efficiency.[3]

It is also at this point that most economic rationalists claim that a series of improvements in economic efficiency is likely to satisfy the old goal: what you lose on the roundabouts you more than gain on the swings. A series of policy changes, all of which improve economic efficiency, is indeed more likely than is a single policy measure to create gains for all — more likely, but not guaranteed, just as with free enterprise. Therefore, rationalist economic policy towards economic efficiency carries the implication that individuals, groups and regions in Australia could become losers for the greater good of the rest. The single-minded pursuit of rationalist economic efficiency is not a good enough bargain — it is not economically rational.

Market failure and government failure on stage

I want to now consider how the notions market failure and government failure are used within a policy strategy aimed at improvements in economic efficiency.

According to analyses usual among economists, markets do not produce perfect results. For example, some forms of industrial activity produce not only marketable commodities or goods for sale but also some unmarketable by-products. One such by-product is a set of employees with enhanced skills or knowledge. With this greater 'human capital', these employees could command higher wages than usual from another employer. Employers who intentionally or reluctantly 'invest' in the formation of their employees' non-specific skills will not reap the full rewards. There

Jonathon Pincus

is a market for the labour of skilled employees; there is no market for the
sale or purchase of the skilled employees since voluntary slavery is illegal
and suppressed (for excellent reasons opaque to most economists); and
even if a voluntary slave market existed, there are good a priori reasons
in standard economic analysis to expect that it would not work 'perfectly
efficiently'. Thus, any employer other than an altruistic one would tend
to produce less of the industrial product concerned than would have been
the case if voluntary slavery did exist, because the industrial production
process is less rewarding to the employer than it otherwise would have
been. A plain case, then, for public or government intervention like the
Training Guarantee Levy; or subsidies to TAFE; or a production subsidy;
or even an import tariff (if all else fails)?

At this stage of the argument, government failure is introduced. Every
one knows that public policy is not guided by a benevolent, omniscient
super minister who aims to exactly offset market failures. Lobbyists
pervert well-intentioned policies programmes; well-intentioned policies
founder on incomplete and incorrect facts; public servants partly impose
their own idiosyncratic or paternalistic preferences on policy and its
implementation; politicians seek acclaim, re-election, and the exercise of
power, and not merely (or ever) to further economic efficiency; competition between politicians, public servants, lobbyists and others cannot be
relied upon to guarantee that policy can be rationalised after the event,
let alone before the event as a rational pursuit of efficient outcomes.[4]

'Public Choice' is the name adopted by a group of economists who
have insisted that lobbyists, public servants, and politicians are merely
people who, like all people, respond more or less strongly to the
incentive systems, be they external or internal, that reward and punish
them. The first key to the concept government failure, then, is the
notion that standard economic analysis can, and should, be applied
promiscuously to employers, employees, consumers, policy makers
and policy administrators. If it appears that an individual adopts a
'private' persona when making private decisions and a 'public'
persona when dealing with collective or public decisions, be warned
— public choice scholars deny that there is any good evidence of a
widespread epidemic of split personality. Instead, public choice
economists work on the simple assumption (using Occam's Razor)
that the differences apparent in 'public' and 'private' behaviour of an
individual are due to the different incentive systems provided for
'public' and 'private' choices. A person's motivations, knowledge and
so on remain the same, but the setting changes in important ways to
produce predictable qualitative variations in behavioural response;
only the constraints change.

For example, the owners of the industrial firm discussed earlier could support a public policy that forces them and all similar firms to spend more money on the training of workers; say, $500 more per year on each worker. and yet the owners could decide, individually and independently in the absence of such a public policy, not to spend the extra $500; or try to avoid paying the $500 after the legislation is introduced. Is it necessarily the case that we have to assume that they are being altruistic in supporting a public policy that requires more employer investment in on-the-job training, but being selfish in not going it alone and spending the extra $500 now, before even the public policy is legislated? The public-choice economist (along with many other commentators) has a simpler explanation to offer: the benefits in whatever form accruing to employers from lending support to the public policy proposal exceeds the subjective cost of lending that support; just as the cost from unilaterally spending an extra $5000 on each employee exceeds the benefits. In particular, it is possible that the employer hopes to gain more in money terms than lose if every employer spends an extra $500 per employee on training. If so, then simple profit-seeking itself could be part of the explanation of why they and other employers support legislation for a ($500) training guarantee. The public sector here brings benefits of coordination, benefits that often are not obtainable within market or voluntary institutions.[5]

Crowd scene: majority rules

The rules for public decisions rarely require unanimity. If all employers agreed that it was feasible to spend exactly $500 more on training per person per year and the law required it, then the existence of such a law certainly seems better than if there were none. Laws, however, rarely achieve unanimous support in parliament, let alone among employers. Some form of majority rule usually applies. In many instances, decisions made by majority rule favour those who occupy 'the middle ground'; majority rule produces unsatisfactory outcomes, and rarely results in economically efficient ones. For the sake of brevity, I will not explore further this source of 'government failure', except to note that like life itself, a majoritarian regime might be terrible, but it is better than the alternative.[6]

Enter public employees, stage left

A central idea behind the concept of government failure is that politicians and bureaucrats do not dance to a tune played by the economist. Even when we offer perfectly correct advice for an improvement in economic efficiency, the policy that emerges will not be perfect. If economic calculation shows that the level of investment in workers' skills through on-the-job training is inefficiently small and, as a consequence, a training guarantee levy is introduced, the policy is sure to offend the canons of economic efficiency. Politicians and bureaucrats will shape the policy to ends other than achieving a perfect match between the last dollar invested in training and the marginal dollar's worth of economic pay-off from the training. Among the bevy of attractive notions paraded by public choice, 'Capture Theory', an idea associated with Gabriel Kolko and George Stigler suggests that economic regulations tend to favour producer, rather than consumer interests. The producers have inside information about the industry and so are likely to supply not only the data that regulators rely upon, but also the very regulators themselves (or give lucrative employ-ment to ex-regulators). For example, subsidies for education go to the suppliers rather than the demanders; the suppliers have disproportionate influence on educational policy, they 'capture' the policy field.

More generally, there is the 'principal-and-agent' problem (it used to be called the master-and-servant problem). If the 'public' are the principals who need to employ public servants as agents to carry out efficiency-enhancing public policies, how can we devise a set of controls so that our agents serve us rather than their own interests? Much thought has been put into this problem by worried principals and harried agents as well as the exponents of public administration to produce piece rates of pay, deferred rewards like a trade certificate or an AO, eunuchs, high pay and prestige for judges, Yale, Oxford and Cambridge Universities, the ICAC, frequent and regular elections and so on. None pass the test of perfect solution to the 'principal-and-agent' problem facing the ultimate employers of public servants and politicians.

So beware when someone identifies one of the infinite ways in which a particular spontaneous, voluntary or 'market' arrangement fails to satisfy the test of perfect efficiency; that is, when someone identifies a 'market failure'. Beware, because the next sentence could well be a proposal for corrective public policy. Just as markets fail, so too do governments, and one needs to check that the corrective public policy does more good than harm. What is needed to carry out this sanitary check is a metric of economic efficiency to which I will return later.

The import tariff as example

Let me shift from the training levy to the import tariff, and give it a market failure-government failure interpretation. The alleged market failure was that the (white) Australian economy had too few people in the early decades of this century, voluntary migration had not produced the optimal population.[7] Two public sector means used to attract population were passage subsidies and import protection. The former reduced migration costs and was funded by taxation that included customs and excise duties, as well as land taxation and sales. Taxation has an efficiency cost, or an 'excess burden', but that cost was worth the economic advantage of attracting a larger population. The latter means to a larger population, the import tariff, to the extent that it was protective, acted to attract more people by raising real wages at the (greater) expense of land values; it was in effect another form of land taxation. Maybe a direct subsidy to employment would have been more economically efficient, but the protective tariff was superior to doing nothing. Maybe skilful lobbyists were able to shape the tariff for their own or their employers' interests, and the cost of protection did not produce the very maximum feasible by way of extra jobs: government failure was present, but in the first few decades of the century, the protected interests had not greatly captured the policy.[8]

Enter in the 1920s the Tariff Board, and later the Department of Trade. These bodies became captured by the protected interests, the Board less so than the department under John McEwen. Whatever economic-efficiency benefits a scientific tariff could be expected to deliver, the actual tariff delivered less.

By the 1960s, economists in Australia generally believed that the cost of government failure on the tariff exceeded the cost of market failure.[9] What to do? Standard theory had it that economic efficiency would be improved by a uniform across-the-board tariff cut, or by a tops-down strategy: the former was used by the Whitlam government. Although the latter has not been so popular, both the level and the dispersion of Australian rates of import protection (and industry assistance generally) have been reduced. The excessive costs of a government failure have been diminished.

Immanent criticism

What proof can be offered for the claim that a reduction in import protection of the motor vehicle industry will improve economic efficiency? My purpose is to argue the cases foreshadowed in the prefatory quotation from Myrdal and in my introduction, namely, that for the very reasons which induce economists to accept the existence of market failure and its twin, government failure, it is impossible to provide an accurate estimate of the extent of the failures.

There has always been a kind of utilitarianism behind the predominant thrust of Australian public economic policy advice (see Groenewegen and McFarlane (1990); for the earlier classic statement, Hancock (1930)). To become a practical guide to policy, utilitarianism needs two supports: a measure of the benefit or good enjoyed by the individuals concerned; and a method to aggregate those individual measures into collective or social measures. In modern Australian policy economics, the notion of a shadow price is involved in both steps.

Everything has its shadow price and every shadow price is subject to change when economic conditions change. The shadow price of an imported motor vehicle is the price that the collection of individuals ought to be willing to pay for one extra unit of import. The shadow price will exceed the actual price if the import brings with it net benefits not enjoyed by the person paying out the actual price in order to obtain the car. Alternatively, the shadow price falls short of the actual price if the import generates net costs not sheeted home to the person who pays the actual price. Motor vehicles cause air pollution. The shadow price of less-polluted air is the amount that all those who enjoy the cleaner air would pay for it if only the market that operated the industry elicited accurate public valuations. If the shadow price of a unit of clean air is less than the value of those things that have to be forgone in order to produce one more unit of cleaner air, then economic efficiency dictates that less-polluted air should be produced.[10] Thus the shadow price of the act of importing and selling for use one more motor vehicle includes (as a negative) the lost value of fresh air.

It is important to note that we are dealing with hypotheticals here and not actual exchange values. When a man refuses an offer of $25 000 for his motor car, we infer that retention of title to the motor car is worth at least $25 000 to him. When he accepts an offer of $30 000, we infer that the car is worth less than $30 000 to him, and $30 000 or more to the purchaser. These inferences, based on exchange values, seem generally rather secure; also, they do not necessarily point to any specific act of public policy. However, the purpose of shadow price calculations is to motivate policy. For example, if Australians really are willing to pay a sum many times annual GDP to preserve Kakadu Stage Three, then it should be preserved at the stroke of a pen.

Here, then, is the measuring rod that enables the economist to compare the costs of market failure and the costs of government failure. It is, in Myrdal's words, somehow more profound than mere prices at which real exchanges take place. It is a social valuation in the sense that it ignores from whom the valuation arises, and adds up the values of everyone who is affected. It uses a money metric.

The notion of a social valuation is very common in the writings of contemporary Australian economists; as an example, let me cite the monograph by Brooks and Heijdra (1991). They state that, by trading rights, two parties (a farmer and a grazier) have 'yielded a social optimum' (p. 25). The government, Brooks and Heijdra write, even if it had perfect information, may not have the incentive to provide the 'socially optimal policy' (p. 40). A random distribution of a scarce, valuable commodity leaves 'the collectivity' worse off than under an auction system (p. 53) — there is a loss of 'social value' to the 'collectivity' from a worker's decision to shift jobs. Again, unfettered competition among corruptible police results in too much corruption 'from a social point of view' (p. 87). These examples could be matched by countless more from other authors; they have been chosen because not only are Brooks and Heijdra fully aware of Hayek's damaging criticisms of the idea that an outsider can accurately assess another person's valuation of a commodity delivered in a specified manner in a specified time and place — Hayek's subjectivism — but they are also very alert to the argument that exchange values are contingent upon the institutional setting that shapes the exchange (for example, a change in the law concerning various property rights will generally change prices of seemingly unrelated commodities). None the less, Brooks and Heijdra's work nicely amplifies the thinking of many economists; that social valuations can be derived from hypothetical individual valuations to assist in guiding policy makers to encourage the economy toward a state of economic efficiency.

There is a crucial contradiction in the standard approach of contemporary economists. Included in the calculation of any shadow price are the exchange prices of various relevant commodities used as estimates of the social values shadow prices) of the latter set of commodities. What insight into individual valuations allows the policy economist to assert that a particular exchange value is equal to its shadow price?[11] What scientific observation permits the central bureaucrats in Canberra to accept confidently some valuations revealed by voluntary exchange, and to reject others? Who can be sure that the gains to Australian consumers of automobile services from a cut in the tariff and the gains to those Australians who now enjoy a greater demand for their productive services exceed the losses to those who become unemployed or accept a lower wage as a result of the tariff cut? Calculations requiring a detailed knowledge of the subjective valuations of everything (and their derivatives or the signs of their derivatives as circumstances change) seem a questionable basis for public policy.[12]

What has happened as result of the discovery of government failure is a shift in the onus of proof from the person opposing a policy intervention designed to correct a market failure to the person who is defending such policy interventions. The contemporary economist is involved when the grounds of attack and defence are those of alleged economic inefficiency. For victory, one side or the other has to show that the social benefits in terms of aggregate economic efficiency of the proposed policy change exceed the costs: retain the import tariff if a reduction would cause more damage than benefit; reduce the tariff if that action would bring net aggregate benefits. In these calculations, some valuation has to be placed upon the alleged benefits of a more diversified industrial structure, or a more decentralised location of employment; or a greater self-reliance in war; or the decline of confident and prosperous country towns; or the change in crime rates; and so on. To fight the battle on the turf of economic efficiency, both sides have to rely on the computation of shadow prices; or on assertions about their likely magnitudes.[13]

Various short cuts are used to indicate the likely sign or magnitude of the net aggregate economic benefits from a policy decision. The underlying economic rationale is the claim that the policy decision will generate aggregate benefits greater than costs, so that all those who lose by the policy could be fully compensated while leaving something yet for everyone else.

The term market failure indicates that measured against the standard of economic efficiency, spontaneous, voluntary market behaviour always falls short of perfection. The term government failure similarly indicates that measured against the same standard, planned, authoritative or coercive government actions likewise always fall short. Here, I have recapitulated the arguments of those economists who reject that standard as impractical and immeasurable. In addition, I have argued that even if the required measurement of social value or shadow price could be made, it would not be the complete guide to policy: economic efficiency in policy action is not the sole goal for the economist wishing to be a dutiful agent of the Commonwealth. Economists can more usefully offer advice on the choice between alternative sets of institutional arrangements or generalised policy frameworks, between alternative economic systems or economic constitutions, than on the choice between more or less of a detailed particularised policy action.

Notes

1 Brooks and Heijdra (1991) discuss this issue in terms of the possible payment of compensation to the losers. Strictly speaking, the payment of compensation is justifiable on the same benefit-cost criterion. However, economic analysis usually concludes that compensation is a negative-sum move: costs exceed benefits. My question in this section asks if a single policy rule, the rule of efficiency, is sufficient.

2 The argument should not be read to imply that a veto rule is desirable: anyone can at any time veto any action. In particular, it seems sensible for a community to adopt policy regimes in which the market has a fairly wide and fairly free scope — but not absolute *laissez-faire* (if such a concept has meaning); to confine centrally administered policy rules to general rules ('constitutions'); and to allow for a somewhat decentralised development of property right regimes (i.e., common law within the rule of law).

3 Ask a rationalist economist the following question: if compensation would eat up all the efficiency gains and more (because lump sum schemes are impossible), should a policy change go ahead without compensation?

4 See Brooks and Heijdra (1991).

5 I do not pretend to offer a complete explanation, but to illustrate how a single set of assumptions about what triggers action can be used to explain both changes in 'market' behaviour (as constraints change in the market) as well as differences between 'market' and 'non-market' behaviour (as constraints change when the decision setting shifts from the 'market' to 'non-market').

6 See Buchanan and Tullock (1962).

7 See, for example, Buchanan and Goetz (1982), or R. Boadway and F. Flatters (1982).

8 There are many economists, possibly some economic historians, who would reject the idea that import protection has ever been a good thing, producing more by way of economic benefit than it creates by way of the costs of an inefficient allocation of resources.

9 See in particular the Tariff Board and Industries Assistance Commission discussions of the case for a scientific tariff, that is, for a discriminatory tariff tailored to capture or offset various product-specific or sector-specific externalities.

10 For ease of argument, I have somewhat distorted the concept shadow price. Strictly, the shadow price of an extra unit of x is the benefit enjoyed by people from the extra unit of x itself, less the valuation of the minimum loss of benefits from those things needed to be forgone or sacrificed in order to obtain an extra unit of x. I have made a distinction between demand price and supply price.

11 The argument could be couched in terms of the calculation of the first-order conditions (F.O.C.) for a welfare maximum (in the jargon of welfare economists). But the terms included in the F.O.C. have to be observable to be of practical use. If no exchange values accurately reflect social values — and how could we know — the F.O.C. is practically useless. Peter Warr taught me this lesson long ago. This criticism is not

that of Lipsey and Lancaster in their theory of the second best, but is closely related to it.

12 There are alternatives relying upon the argument that voluntary exchange improves the wellbeing of parties to the exchange. Almost ignored by Australian economists — possibly because it suggests a more modest task than the achievement of Pareto efficiency — are the contractarianism and constitutionalism of the Virginia School.

13 Here I clearly run foul of Bhagwati's description of an unsophisticated, wrong-headed, careless economist who missed the central, overriding pro-free-trade message, which is always to recommend first-best policies i.e., to ignore the strictures of Lipsey and Lancaster; see also Kwang Ng on 'third best'.

References

Bhagwati, Jagdish 1989, 'Is Free Trade Passé After All?', *Weltwirtschaftliches Archiv*, vol. 125, no. 1, pp. 17-44

Boadway, R.W. & Flatters, F. 1982, 'Efficiency & Equalisation Payments in a Federal System of Government: A Synthesis & Extension of Recent Results', *Canadian Journal of Economics*, vol. 15

Brooks, M.A. & Heijdra, B.J. 1991, *Dividing the Spoils. Markets, Government & Corruption*, AIPP, West Perth

Buchanan, J.M. & Goetz, C.J. 1982, 'Efficiency Limits & Fiscal Mobility: An Assessment of the Tiebout Model', *ZJournal of Public Economics*, no. 1

Buchanan, J.M. & Tullock, G. 1962, *The Calculus of Consent. Logical Foundations of Constitutional Democracy*, Michigan

Groenewegen, Peter & McFarlane, Bruce 1990, *A History of Economic Thought*, Routledge, London & New York

Hancock, W.K. 1930, *Australia*, Ernest Benn, London

Myrdal, Gunnar 1953, *The Political Element in the Development of Economic Theory*, tr. Paul Streeten, Routledge & Kegan Paul Ltd., London

Oakeshott, Michael 1991, *Rationalism in Politics & Other Essays*, Liberty Press, Indianapolis

Comments

The term 'economic rationalism' has an interesting history. It first entered the Australian lexicon in the period of the Whitlam government (by its own leader's estimation, 'Australia's first free-enterprise government') and was used primarily in a positive sense by economic rationalists themselves. The connotation was that of policy formulation on the basis of rational analysis, as opposed to tradition, emotion and prejudice. With the exception of support for free trade, there was no presumption in favour of particular policy positions. Views were generally in the economic mainstream of the period — Keynesian in macroeconomic terms and support for the 'mixed economy' in microeconomic terms. In particular, most economic rationalists took an agnostic view about the desirable size of the public sector and tended in practice to support its continued expansion.

The term remained in use, though not so extensively, during the period of the Fraser and Hawke governments. During this time the term acquired its additional, primarily negative, connotations. First, there was the association of the word 'rationalisation' as a euphemism for 'cutback' in the public sector. Second, the methodological position dominant in policy circles came to be seen as 'rationalist' in a Cartesian sense. That is, economic analysis was seen as the result of a priori reasoning independent of, and indeed, contradicted by, real-world experience. This view was reinforced by the conjunction of very poor economic outcomes with regular claims from economic rationalists that economic policy in the 1980s was greatly superior to that of the 1950s and 1960s.

At the same time, the policy content of economic rationalism changed. A belief in the desirability of cutting back the public sector in particular became a core component of economic rationalist ideas. Also, where the economic rationalists of the Whitlam period strongly favoured progressive taxation, the economic rationalists of today are associated with support for income redistribution from the poor to the rich and from labour to capital.

In order to advance these policies, it was necessary to move away from the traditional forms of policy analyses that had been based on potential Pareto improvements. One problem with this form of policy analyses was that it left the door open to too many forms of government intervention based on efficiency arguments. Whenever there was a divergence from the conditions of the fundamental theorems of welfare economics (a 'market failure'), there was a potential Pareto improvement based on a corrective tax or public-expenditure programme.

The response here was the invention of the category of 'government failure' as a counterbalance to 'market failure'. This category was based on the valid observation that the existence of a potential Pareto improvement did not imply the existence of a feasible government programme to realise it. However, it was frequently used very loosely to cover any form of mistake or poor outcome from a government policy. Since mistakes made by market participants (the Leyland P76 and the PC Junior spring to mind) have not generally been regarded as furnishing a case for government intervention, this usage is unsound. What is required is an argument showing that government will systematically perform worse than is presumed in the standard forms of argument for intervention.

Public-choice theory furnished such an argument. The basic idea was that governments were responsive to the demands of interest groups rather than to some abstract 'public good' and hence would systematically choose inefficient policies. This argument, however, was undermined by its own inherent logic. There was no reason for interest groups to support inefficient policies if they could achieve a Pareto improvement through better policies. The presumption was, if a given set of policies were a stable outcome of the political process, they then represented the most efficient means of achieving the income distributional objectives of the interest groups that supported them. This is the core of John Pincus's argument.

The response of the economic rationalists at this conference has been to develop a rhetoric based on the notion of 'privilege'. In essence, 'privilege' consists of any income above that which would be earned in a free market. The *ex ante* distribution of endowments is unspecified, but is implicitly assumed to correspond to the existing distribution of private wealth. The rhetoric of privilege suggests that the loss of privileges should be regarded as a social benefit rather than a cost.

In addition to avoiding the apparent *reductio ad absurdum* generated by the traditional public-choice approach, the rhetoric of privilege yields a solution to a problem faced by economic rationalists working in the potential Pareto-improvement framework. Although economic theory suggests that a move towards free trade will normally generate a potential Pareto improvement, actual compensation of the losers proves impossible in almost any particular case. The absence of any form of lump-sum tax means that attempts to compensate the losers from the removal of one distortion inevitably creates another.

It might be supposed that on average, the losses and gains associated with market-oriented reforms would cancel out and that across-the-board reform without compensation would yield a Pareto improvement. However, the experience of the 1980s has been that the economic-rationalist programme as a whole is associated with a generally regressive redistribution of income. The rhetoric of 'privilege', as it turns out, runs in the opposite direction to the older notion of 'equity'. It allows economic rationalists to become explicit allies of those who benefit from their preferred policies (upper-income groups, business and the financial sector) and to dismiss the losers from the equation.

Pincus presents a final argument to suggest that, even in the absence of such biases, society might choose to forgo across-the-board reform because of risk-aversion. To end in the safe realms of pure theory, it should be noted that risk-aversion based on diminishing marginal utility of wealth, as in utilitarian theory, will not support this argument. Rather, it is necessary that risk-aversion be based on an overweighting of the probability of bad outcomes. This can be represented for individual and social choice by generalized expected utility models. For a further explication of this, see my *Rank-Dependent Expected Utility Model*.

Reference

Quiggin, J. 1993, *The Rank-Dependent Expected Utility Model*, Kluwer-Nijhoff, Amsterdam

Part III

A Politician's View

Peter Walsh

Economic Rationalism?: Economic Policies for the Nineties

A joke was published in the old *National Times* shortly after the 1974 federal election, at which I was elected to the Senate. You will probably remember that the Whitlam government had won the 1974 election by a small margin. It was widely and correctly believed at the time that the country was headed for a recession and had other economic problems. In an interview published in the *National Times* after the election, Gough Whitlam was asked, having won an election on the brink of a recession, did he see any ominous similarities between his own position as Prime Minister and that of James Scullin in 1929? Whitlam's reply was, 'No. Sixteen members of my Cabinet have university degrees; Scullin had only three.' The journalist's reply was, 'And Theodore was not one of them.'

I am not sure how many members of the various Labor governments throughout the 1980s had university degrees, but the majority certainly did. But I can tell you that the two who didn't: Paul Keating and I. And whether the country's current plight should be attributed to that or to different reasons is for others to judge.

The subject of today's conference is rationality. Steve Dowrick made the comment today that his daughter was terribly upset on Christmas morning because she did not get — I think he called it — a hairdo doll, which I assume is a doll with hair that could be coiffed. He mentioned that she had been manipulated by advertising and peer-group pressure, and that her response to the advertising and peer-group pressure was not entirely rational. Dowrick suggested that probably people other than children were at times similarly afflicted.

I think we could extend that point a little further. I believe that on the question of the importance of GDP, the last 5 or 10 per cent of Australian consumption is by affluent people — affluent but not terribly rational — and that that consumption has little utility.

However, if GDP were to fall by 5 or 10 per cent — apart from increasing the unemployment rate rather seriously — it is unlikely that the people who indulge in that not entirely rational consumption would reduce their consumption or that their purchasing power would fall. I believe it more likely that the burden would fall on the poor, almost all of whom are within the high marginal utility range.

I used to think some years ago — and I suppose I still half believe it — that one of the greatest prevailing irrationalities was the typical economist's belief in the ultimate rationality of mankind. But having said that, let me declare myself. I regard myself as an economic rationalist, defined as someone who has a general belief that the outcomes delivered by markets most of the time will be better than the outcomes ordained by governments, who also believes — as most rationalists do — in liberal democracy, an open society and a role for the state in income redistribution.

We have heard today, and before, assertions that economic rationalists believe that markets alone and market prices are always best; that markets and money can always do everything better than governments; that markets and prices are the only means of setting a value on anything. That is the belief allegedly held by anyone who regards themselves an economic rationalist. To my knowledge, no economist has ever been identified as having said those words, nor has any textbook that asserts them been produced either. It is, indeed, a bit of fiction.

I want to develop three points relevant to the subjects being discussed today. First, who or what caused the present recession; second, a fairly widespread and, it seems to me, naïve belief in the altruism of the public sector and the unions, and, finally, industry protection.

It has become popular to blame economic rationalists for the present recession. I do not think many people, economists or otherwise, will dispute that the present recession was precipitated by the policy response to the current-account deficit blowout of 1988 and 1989. I know that Pitchford from the ANU and some other academic economists have argued that, given that the blowout was in private rather than sovereign debt, no policy response was required from the government because it did not matter very much. I do not believe that, but I am not going to go into it now.

If you believe that some policy response was required, the present recession was precipitated by the policy response to that blowout in the current-account deficit. The option of tightening fiscal policy had been effectively closed off by a prior commitment to major tax cuts from July 1989 and the only avenue left was monetary policy. Hence we had interest rates running at around 20 per cent for twelve to eighteen months

I cannot speak with any certainty as to what the advice going to the government from Treasury was at that time, since I rarely spoke directly to Treasury officers, but I do know for certain that the view in the Department of Finance, put to me pretty forcefully on a number of occasions, was that too much emphasis was being placed on monetary policy and that fiscal policy should be tightened in order to take the weight off monetary policy.

That view, which I believe had a lot of merit, had been pre-empted by the prior commitment to major tax cuts in the middle of 1989. Those who believe that the push for small government, and low outlays and taxes was invented by the new right are quite wrong. The most effective resistance to higher taxation — at least when Labor is in government, comes not from the new right but from the ACTU.

Let me tell you some of the things that public-service economic rationalists did *not* do in the period preceding the present recession. They did not drive the demand for a big migration programme. That demand was driven by what we call today 'public interest advocacy groups' who are usually funded by the taxpayers.

Economic rationalists are not arguing that large portions of what is known or believed to be the most minerally prospective areas of Australia were quarantined from exploration. They are not arguing that the family home should remain a tax shelter. They are not arguing that widely held debentures should be exempted from interest-withholding tax or that the negative gearing of rental residential properties should be restored. Those moves are regarded by some in the private sector, those who ought to be in a position to make fairly well-informed judgments, as having been quite significant contributors to the late 1980s' asset-price inflation. Economic rationalists did not give the tick to nominal wage increases throughout most of the 1980s that had not been offset by productivity improvements, and hence, gave us a consistently and significantly higher inflation rate than most of our trading partners. The consequential inflation amplified whatever distortions remained in the taxation system. It has been argued — it could even be true — that the wage outcomes secured during the 1980s were the best available. No-one will ever know.

Economic rationalists did not launch repeated assaults on forestry operations or oppose resource security legislation, that is, any legislation that would decree 'These parts of Australian forests are available for economic use and the others are not'. Resource security is anathema to greenies who trenchantly oppose any portion of Australian forests being made available for economic exploitation. The greenies however prefer to keep all options open. They intend to discover some 'endangered' plant, bird or beetle in every potential timber production area as the prelude to a campaign — with the enthusiastic support of the media in general and the ABC in particular. The ultimate objective is to destroy the timber industry. All of these issues on which policy was made, *against* the advice of economic rationalists, helped precipitate, intensify and prolong the recession.

Economic rationalists in Australia or in the US, to the best of my knowledge, never gave the tick to Reaganomics or supply-side theory which said it was perfectly all right to run huge budget deficits so long as they were caused by tax cuts, because the supply-side response would be such that the budget deficit would get wiped out anyway.

There are some things that economic rationalists in the bureaucracy and elsewhere did. They argued for lower protection, with considerable success. Cuts in protection are not a major factor in the present recession or present unemployment. They also argued for deregulation of the financial system, starting with the floating of the Australian dollar in 1983 — a move that was opposed by then Treasury Secretary, John Stone. In a world of floating exchange rates, however, I do not believe that there was any realistic alternative for a small country such as Australia other than to float the dollar.

The subsequent deregulation of the financial system was probably qualitatively different. It is now history that the banks, not just some of the fringe financial institutions but mainstream Australian trading banks that have been around for longer than I have, behaved with almost unbelievable stupidity during the 1980s; lending hundreds of millions of dollars to paper entrepreneurs on no mortgage security whatsoever, on nothing other than a negative pledge, without even bothering to find out how many hundreds of millions the same paper entrepreneurs owed to other financial institutions. That certainly was not anticipated by the government, and I do not think it was anticipated by any of the economic rationalists in the bureaucracy. Maybe we are culpable for that.

However, speculative booms had happened before financial deregulation. Who remembers the Reid-Murray crash of the early 1960s and the Cambridge Credit crash of the early 1970s? True, what happened in the late 1980s was more spectacular. But the state banks, which pro rata at least sustained the most spectacular losses, were not subject to formal regulation by the Reserve Bank anyway.

My second point delves into what seems to me a naïve faith in the altruism, or perceived altruism, of the public sector. Public business enterprises, their unions and supporters claim that those sectors operate for the benefit of the deserving and the needy and of society in general, as distinct from the private sector, that thinks of nothing but exploitation. It is a bit hard to reconcile that claim with a number of known facts that have come into light recently.

The public-service salary increases of above 10 per cent in the last twelve months have been agreed on in a number of areas, in a period when general wage rises are very much lower and inflation is negligible. It has been reported that the communications union, within the year, will receive an average wage increase for communications workers of 5.6 per cent, well in excess of what the workforce in general will get and well in excess of inflation. Qantas, at the end of 1991, agreed to wage increases of 11.7 per cent, again in a period when the workforce in general was getting little if any wage increases and inflation was at a very low lever.

In the cases of Qantas and the communications union, staff-shedding was associated with those agreements. The staff who were retrenched received compensation but what is the justification for wage increases well in excess of the rate of inflation for the remaining employees of those public-sector organisations who did not lose their jobs? In other words, what really happened was that those public-sector enterprises had been carrying supernumeraries; they had been carrying surplus staff. When the surplus staff went, the benefits should have accrued to taxpayers or customers, but most of it accrued to the remaining employees.

I also remember, and was very annoyed back in 1983 when the newly elected Labor government moved to clean up some, or perhaps most, of the rorts that had been allowed to develop over a period of years in superannuation and introduced a lump-sum tax. I remember leaving Melbourne Airport. After the door to the plane shut, the TAA pilot decided he would give us a political lecture about the perfidy of the government that robbed hard-working pilots and others by imposing a tax on superannuation lump-sum payments. What annoyed me doubly so was that the Federal Government had just shovelled $100 million of taxpayers' money into that airline to keep it solvent and to enable these people to keep their jobs, even though they were only working an eight-hour week at the time.

When Labor first came into government there was, from the Budget, a total subsidy of close to $200 million going into the aviation industry. Apart from the objections that economic rationalists might have to the subsidy leading to underpriced aviation services and/or to featherbed inefficiency, who were the beneficiaries of that big subsidy? Certainly not the poor, the needy or the disadvantaged. The subsidy has now been eliminated.

Three years ago the trams in Melbourne were all parked along Bourke Street. In that case, the tramways union was fighting to retain conductors for whom there had been no functional need for many years. They may have unwittingly done the public of Melbourne and Australia in general a good turn. Members of the International Olympic Committee were in town the same time the trams were parked along Bourke Street — that scenario probably finished off whatever slim hopes Melbourne may have had of getting the 1996 Olympic Games. That, however, was not the intention.

In recent months a vigorous letter-writing campaign has been launched by people lobbying for a national accreditation system for childcare. Parents wanted to know that they were getting quality childcare, so the government had to have a national accreditation system. That may be a reasonable argument, but the sting came in the fine print that said you have to tie accreditation to fee-relief. In other words, if a centre is not accredited, the parents who use it will not be eligible for fee-relief. Though parents allegedly demand and value accreditation, just in case they happen to backslide, a huge financial penalty is imposed on them if they choose not to use a nationally accredited centre. In whose interest do you think that campaign was being driven and organised? Certainly not the parent or user's.

The public sector does not have a monopoly on feather-bedding, empire-building and rorting. In the private sector, there is generally the ultimate discipline that if the feather-bedding and the rorting goes too far, the firm will go broke and the employees will lose their jobs. That sort of discipline rarely, if ever, applies to the public sector.

Finally, the question of protection. It seems almost impossible to teach those who do not intuitively grasp it the concept of comparative advantage. Those who do not grasp the concept are led to these false conclusions: first, that because world trade is corrupted, that some foreigners dump their produce on us or somewhere else and sell it below cost price and so on, *ipso facto*, Australia must follow suit and indulge in similar practices. It fails to recognise — and there are a couple of complications I will come to later — the fact that the concept and potential benefits of comparative advantage are related to the varying degrees of international competitiveness of industry within Australia, regardless of what happens in the rest of the world.

The second false conclusion is that unless we join in this game of tariffs or export subsidies or something like that, or special tax breaks or whatever, no Australian industry will be able to compete with foreign industry. If an exchange rate was fixed that could conceivably be true. But when exchange rates are flexible, it isn't.

Now the complications. Say some foreigner is dumping a product under the common agricultural policy. If we believed that would continue in perpetuity, it should be regarded as a given. It does not provide any justification for Australia or any other government in any other country to do the same. But it is unpredictable. Sometimes that type of dumping occurs on a short-term basis, sometimes in the very long-term as with the agricultural products of the EEC. Something no government or economist can predict with certainty is how quickly or when those practices may be terminated by a foreign country.

The second complication related to the flexibility of an exchange rate is friction. There is friction in any economy, probably more so in the Australian economy. That is because we have become, for whatever reason, uncompetitive in a particular industry; we do not get a smooth transition of resources out of that industry or the new investment required in some other industry that is more competitive internationally. It may not happen for a long time, it may not happen ever. I think if people want to make criticisms, particularly of the Treasury of the J-curve days, it does seem to me that Treasury in particular failed to recognise how rheumatic the Australian economy was, or if you like, how much friction there was impeding the transfer of resources.

In more recent times tariffs seem to have gone out of fashion, but new protection or strategic trade theory or 'adding value' stunts are booming. A good friend of mine said that he thinks we should say 'adding costs' instead of 'adding value'. People might then get a more realistic appreciation of what the concept is really about. But these prescriptions are all variants on the theme of picking winners.

All this, in spite of Eastern Europe, in spite of the old Soviet Union, in spite of the VEDC, WA Inc., the State Bank of South Australia and the State Bank of Victoria. Lest anyone think that Labor governments pioneered these, Victorians should remember who was responsible for the Portland deal and some Western Australians certainly remember who was responsible for the take or pay contract with the north-west shelf. This way of picking winners was not invented by Labor. It probably developed into new heights of excess as so many other things did in the 1980s, but it was not invented by Labor, and the Labor Party certainly does not have a monopoly on it.

Indeed, in the recent election in WA, there was a proposal to build a privately owned coal-fired power station. One politician said something sensible about it. The deputy leader of the Liberal Party said if their party got into government they would look at the options to determine the best mode of action. He was put down smartly, rapped over the knuckles and told to shut up. Everyone else was saying that they were committed to building this power-station.

I will give you a few more details, because they are pretty important. The proposal was to build the station with private capital and electricity would be supplied into the SECWA grid at a lower cost than present average cost of generating electricity, but the first 600-megawatts of power generated at that station would be the first 600-megawatts of power used, leaving the rest of the SEC to carry the surplus capacity and peak-loading. The average cost of electricity would thus be pushed up, and not brought down. There was an alternative, a gas-fired power-station, for which WA through the SECWA had already purchased enough gas, *paid* for enough gas — thanks to the take or pay contract — to fire a 600-megawatt power station for five years.

The advantages of a gas-fired power-station are lower capital costs and almost constant per unit cost, whereas a thermal station has to operate around 500- or 600-million megawatts to obtain the economies of scale. Moreover, there was enough pre-paid gas for five years and since the 600 megawatts would not be used for quite a long time that probably meant free fuel for ten years, lower capital costs and negligible surplus capacity. But politics was driving the decision towards a coal-fired power-station. The National Party holds the coal seat of Collie and has always been very vigorous in defending its own territory. Some self-deluded members of the Labor Party thought that if we adopted the same policy we might win Collie back again.

That did not happen. We will have to see in the next few months whether the sole voice of sanity and reason, Colin Barnett, the Liberal Party deputy leader, or the pork-barrellers prevail in the new government.

This example among others demonstrates that even if bureaucrats and politicians are better-equipped to make judgments, the process still gets corrupted by politics. There has probably never been a dam built for irrigation in Australia that was a sound public investment. There are railway lines — many of them now closed — that were never sound public investments. There is a campaign going on right now to do that yet again between Darwin and Alice Springs. Don't we ever learn? Unless you believe that politicians will, for some reason that hasn't been explained, become more responsible public citizens, be willing to risk office, risk losing their seats in the public interest to a much greater degree than they have done in the past, why should anyone believe that politicians will put the public interest first in the future?

Michael Keating has referred to the propensity of politicians and of governments to pork barrel and fund untested schemes such as the Ord River scheme in WA. Keating's error is that the scheme was tested. More than two years before the political commitment to build the Ord River dam was announced in 1967, Bruce Davidson had published the *Northern Myth*. The proposed agricultural settlement had been tested, it had failed the test, but the dam was still built. There is still a small irrigation scheme operating in that area. At no stage has the amount of land under irrigation exceeded that which could have been watered from the diversion dam that had been built in the early 1960s.

Keating also mentions, as one of the more unfortunate examples of government intervention, the wool reserve-price scheme. The government intervened at the behest of the growers, certainly to the ultimate major disadvantage of the wool-growers and, to some extent — I fear, to a larger extent at some time in the future — to the taxpayers.

The wheat industry recently agreed on a tax of 2 per cent for adding-value purposes. If there was an opportunity to invest either at home or abroad in value-adding to the Australian wheat crop, the capital should be raised in the market, rather than by a de facto tax on wheat growers. But again, the wheat growers asked for it themselves.

We have had plenty of government intervention through the late 1980s, particularly in the mining and forestry industries, and usually at the behest of green groups that are themselves partially funded by the taxpayers. Rarely was there any valid environmental reasons — assuming that valid environmental issues are about such things as clean water, clean air, aesthetic beauty and so on, rather than secular religious zealotry.

The final point I want to make is somewhat critical of Richard Blandy. I do not think it is good enough to report, as Blandy did in the *Age* a couple of weeks ago, that 80 per cent of the academic economists in Australia hold these economic-rationalist views, unless there is also an explanation as to why they hold those views. The agnostics are not likely to be persuaded by the fact that 80 per cent of academic economists believe that something is so, unless they have at least been told why they believe it is so.

Notes on Contributors

Kym Anderson is Professor of Economics at the University of Adelaide.

Richard Blandy is Director of the Institute of Applied Economic and Social Economic Research at the University of Melbourne.

Geoff Brennan is Director of the Research School of Social Sciences at the Australian National University.

Kenneth Davidson is economics editor of the *Age*.

Steve Dowrick is Fellow in the Economics Programme of the Research School of Social Sciences at the Australian National University.

Henry Ergas is Counsellor for Structural Policy in the Organisation for Economic Co-operation and Development in Paris.

Allan Fels is Chairman of the Trade Practices Commission.

Vince FitzGerald is Executive Director of the Allen Consulting Group.

John Freebairn is Acting Dean and Professor of Economics in the Faculty of Economics, Commerce and Management at Monash University.

Stephen Grenville is Assistant Governor (Economic) of the Reserve Bank of Australia.

Bob Gregory is Professor in the Economics Programme and Executive Director of the Centre for Economic Policy Research of the Research School of Social Sciences at the Australian National University.

Ann Harding is Director of the National Centre for Social and Economic Modelling at the University of Canberra.

Ian Harper is Ian Potter Professor of International Finance in the Graduate School of Management at the University of Melbourne.

Joe Isaac is Professorial Associate in the Department of Management and Industrial Relations at the University of Melbourne and former member of the Arbitration Commission.

Michael Keating is Secretary of the Department of Prime Minister and Cabinet.

Stephen King is lecturer in the Department of Economics at the University of Melbourne.

Anne Krueger is Professor of Economics at Duke University and was Chair of the Commission on Graduate Education in Economics appointed by the President of the American Economic Association.

Phillip Leslie is a tutor in Economics at the University of Melbourne.

Peter Lloyd is Professor of Economics and Dean of the Faculty of Economics and Commerce at the University of Melbourne.

Robert Manne is Senior Lecturer in Politics at La Trobe University and a former editor of *Quadrant.*

Alan Moran is Research Director at the Tasman Institute.

Jonathon Pincus is Professor of Economics at the University of Adelaide.

Michael Pusey is Associate Professor of Sociology at the University of New South Wales.

John Quiggin is Fellow in the Economics Programme of the Research School of Social Sciences at the Australian National University.

Judith Sloan is Director of the National Institute of Labour Studies at Flinders University of South Australia.

Ben Smith is Head of the Department of Economics in the Faculty of Economics and Commerce at the Australian National University.

Peter Swan is Professor of Economics in the Australian Graduate School of Mangement.

Jill Walker is a staff member at the Trade Practices Commission.

Peter Walsh is a Senator from Western Australia and a former Minister for Finance in the Hawke Government.

Graeme Woodbridge is lecturer in the Department of Economics at the University of Melbourne.

Index